VAX DCL Programmer's
Reference

VMS 5

VAX DCL Programmer's Reference

VMS 5

K. M. Leisner and D. B. Cook

VNR VAN NOSTRAND REINHOLD
New York

Van Nostrand Reinhold

115 Fifth Avenue

New York, New York 10003

Van Nostrand

11 New Fetter Lane

London EC4P 4EE, England

Van Nostrand Reinhold

480 La Trobe Street

Melbourne, Victoria 3000, Australia

Nelson Canada

1120 Birchmount Road

Scarborough, Ontario M1K 5G4, Canada

16 15 14 13 12 11 10 9 8 7 6 5 4 3 2 1

Library of Congress Cataloging-in-Publication Data

Leisner, K. M.
    Vax DCL Programmer's Reference VMS 5|/ K. M. Leisner and D. B. Cook.
        p. cm.
    ISBN (invalid) 0443218340
        1. VAX/VMS (Computer operating system) I. Cook, D. B. (David B.)
II. Title.
    QA76.76.O63L45 1990
    005.4'44--dc20
                                                    89-16583
                                                       CIP

To

Garrison
George
Betty
Ginger
and Cindy

Contents

Illustrations

FIGURES

TABLES

Preface

This book is written to assist software professionals who want to make effective use of the rich command set in the VAX/VMS command language. As one of the most widely used and well developed command line oriented operating systems, VMS offers – through the Digital Command Language (DCL) – a means to rapidly automate various VAX operations. Programmers, engineers and scientists should find this book useful in the challenging task of software development. We have endeavored to produce a desk reference that can be used in conjunction with the manual set published by the Digital Equipment Corporation.

Enough background is given to provide you with a basic understanding of VAX systems, even if you have relatively modest prior experience with computing. The later chapters are divided along functional boundaries, with each class of features occupying a separate chapter. Finally, the Appendices include a comprehensive command reference summary.

TEXT AND GRAPHIC CONVENTIONS

Every attempt has been made to keep our examples consistent with the style of the DEC manuals and documentation. Specific formats have been adopted for representing what the VAX displays on a terminal, and what you, as the user, will type.

Terminal Display Typefaces

Examples are shown in a fixed-pitch font to differentiate them from the text used for this book. The initial DCL $ prompt is always included to help remind you that the example is seen on you screen, as in

```
$ DCL COMMANDS ARE SHOWN IN THIS TYPE STYLE
```

This is not an actual command, but illustrates how they are shown in print. Fonts (typefaces) used by actual terminals vary considerably, so your screen may or may not resemble the examples in this book. Example DCL commands may be followed by one or more lines of sample output from VMS; output lines do not begin with a $.

TRADEMARK ACKNOWLEDGEMENTS

The following are trademarks or registered trademarks of Digital Equipment Corporation: VAX, DEC, MicroVAX, DECnet, VT, VMS, DECUS, VAXcluster, VAXstation and PDP. All other trademarks mentioned in this book are the property of their respective owners. The use of these or other trademarks in this book is for illustrative purposes and is not intended to infringe upon the rights of trademark holders.

AUTHOR'S ACKNOWLEDGEMENTS

As with most serious projects, a great deal of effort from those close to the authors was required. We would like to thank those who contributed generously of their time without compensation to the direction and shaping of this book. Special thanks to Jay Wood and Bill Cooper from General Dynamics Data Systems Division, and Doug Palmer from Thermo Technologies Corporation. Their technical and editorial comments on the first draft of our manuscript helped greatly in shaping this book into its current form.

Thanks also to Tim Kraft of Science Applications International Corporation, and Martha Dennis of Pacific Communication Sciences, Incorporated. They are the author's direct supervisors, who have demostrated understanding and continuing support during the course of this project. Finally, thanks to Garrison Leisner, who tolerated having his mother's eyes glued to the computer screen at all hours, when he would much rather use the computer for video games.

VAX DCL Programmer's Reference

VMS 5

Part 1

Introduction

The three chapters in Part One will take you through the basic components and functions of the VAX computer, the VMS operating system, and the Digital Command Language (DCL). If you are an experienced user of computers from other manufacturers, you may wish to skip to Part Two.

Chapter 1, Introduction to the VAX, gives you some background about the hardware and software required for most computer operations and the development and use of the VAX computer system.

Chapter 2, Overview of VMS, sets the stage by giving you a top-level view of how the VMS operating system works in various VAX/VMS installations.

Chapter 3, Introduction to DCL, is the starting point for effective use of the Digital Command Language.

1

Introduction to the VAX

This reference, written for the novice VAX user, is geared toward those familiar with basic computer operations and editors from other systems. Elementary operations requiring only minimal effort with the DEC manuals, such as the EDT and TPU editors, have been omitted in favor of providing more examples and instruction about the topics found to be more difficult and time consuming to grasp without specific instruction.

The VAX/VMS operating system is widely regarded as a powerful, fast, mature, full featured and extremely user-friendly operating system with a well-developed programming environment and an excellent selection of software tools. For example, the extensive on-line HELP system provides enough information about most topics so you will rarely need to consult a manual.

When you reach the point at which you can cope effectively with the basics, you will find that the DEC manuals provide well-written and complete introductions to every conceivable topic. See Appendix A for an overview of the DEC documentation.

THE VAX COMPUTING SYSTEM

The acronym VAX is derived from Virtual Address eXtension. The VAX computer is designed to use memory addresses beyond the hardware's actual limits, enabling it to handle programs that are too large to fit into physical memory.

The VAX computer system is a member of the Digital Equipment Corporation (DEC) computer family. Currently the VAX series includes models spanning the desktop VAXstation to mainframe class multi-CPU VAX processors. These vary from the superminis, like the MicroVAX, to the older, moderate sized 11/7XX series, to the newer 6000 series. Figure 1-1 illustrates the commonality concept.

DEC's philosophy of upward compatibility over the years means that the same VMS you learn on the VAXstation or MicroVAX is used on the VAX 8800, and the converse. All VAX models are compatible with one another, and the VMS operating system, from Version 4.0 and beyond, is common among them all. From the user's viewpoint, the only significant difference among the various VAX models is speed — it simply takes longer to run the same program on a MicroVAX than it does on an 8000 series super-VAX. With limited exceptions, a program created, compiled, and linked on one VAX processor will run without modification on any other VAX processor.

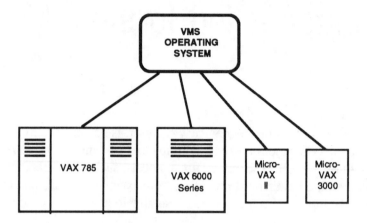

FIGURE 1-1.   *Various VAXes run the same VMS operating system.*

HARDWARE

A computing system of any sort consists of a central processing unit (CPU), devices for human interaction (keyboards), information storage (disk, tape, optical, or even video media), and a display (terminals and printers). Figure 1-2 shows a typical VAX configuration. Yours may differ from it.

CPU

The central processing unit of a computer system is the component that executes instructions for the computer. All information handled by the computer is processed by this unit, either by routing the task to another component or by completing the task requested by the user or another process.

All members of the VAX family of computers have 32-bit processors, often referred to as *superminicomputers*. This processor places the VAX in between minicomputers like the old PDP-11 series and large mainframes in power, size and performance. Performance improvements in the VAX processors are, however, bringing them out of this class now. Todays VAX family has representatives among the microcomputer class (e.g. the VAXstation) and full capability, superfast minicomputers (e.g. the VAX 6300).

The CPU is becoming a misnomer in the current days of clusters and networks, since it no longer handles all processing in the computer system it manages. All current computers, however, must have some component that makes the final decision of who does what in the circuitry.

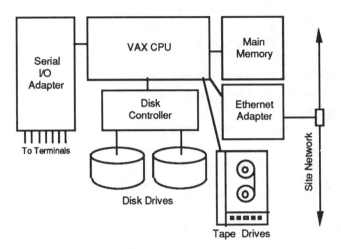

FIGURE 1-2.   A typical VAX hardware configuration.

The types and sizes of CPUs for the VAX vary greatly, from the smallest VAXstation to the MicroVAX family to the largest VAX-8XXX high-end computers.

Terminals and Keyboards

You may have noticed that a great variety of terminals exist and that each has some level of compatibility with the VAX. VMS supports terminals from the decade-old VT52 to the currently marketed VT3XX series. VMS is also compatible with graphics terminals capable of emulating the standard graphics terminal protocols such as the Tektronix 4XXX series and its clones.

The VT2XX series and clones seem to be the most widely used. The older models are dying out as repairs get more difficult and the price of newer models drops. The VT3XX terminal is very much like the VT2XX.

We have chosen to omit any detailed reference to the setup and use of the particular terminal and keyboard types. Much of the work involved in customizing your own terminal's operating characteristics can be accomplished using VMS commands. This topic is covered in Chapter 12, Terminal Characteristics. You will want to learn your own terminal's operating instructions, and this can best be done with your owner's manual. Figure 1-3 shows the layout of a very common keyboard configuration, the DEC VT220.

The QWERTY (name derived from the left side of the second row of keys) keyboard of the VT220 is essentially like that of any typewriter, with the addition of the <CTRL> and PF keys that offer many shorthand functions. These keys are also found on the earlier version terminals you may find floating around older computing facilities.

The special nontypewriter control keys expand the functionality of the keyboard. Among their functions, when used in combination with other keys, are the ability to pause or stop execution of an image file (or program) and to stop and restart screen scrolling.

The cursor keys and keypad add more functionality, as do the function keys (FKeys for short) across the top of the keyboard. Most of these keys have some default function assigned to them by VMS, which can usually be reassigned by the user or system manager. These and other functions will be explained further in the next chapters.

The VT240 and VT340 are DEC's foray into the graphics terminalbusiness. Essentially, they do the same thing as any other graphics terminal, while making use of the familiar DEC keyboard. The keyboards for the VT240, VT320, and VT340 are virtually identical to that of the VT220. Currently available DEC software will support any terminal capable of emulating the VT100, VT220, or a Tektronics 4XXX display, with just a little work with the terminal user's manual.

The VT320 terminal is definitely an example of computer technology becoming less and less expensive for the same or greater capability. This terminal and keyboard are currently about one-fourth the cost of the original VT100, with many times the capability and memory and a significant improvement in ease of use.

Disk and Tape Storage Media

You will need to store the data you generate on some medium, in the past limited to either a hard disk or a tape drive, or preferrably both. Recent developments have made new devices, such as video tape drives and optical disks available for backup storage media. Note this as the first mention of the fact that you should *always* make backups of your work. The usual configuration is to use a fixed disk for continual work and make periodic backups on tape. By far the least expensive and most popular method for the VAX minis and micros is the cartridge tape drive, with nine-track tapes, removable hard disks and new optical disks also vying for the hardware dollars.

Printers

The list of printers that will operate with the VAX is long. The basic categories of printers you will encounter are dot-matrix line printers, daisy-wheel or ball typewriter style printers, laser printers, and inkjet printers (either black and white or color). Each

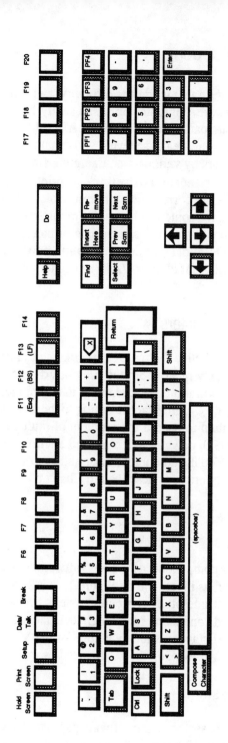

FIGURE 1-3. The VT220 Keyboard.

7

of these will produce text with little difficulty, and some will produce graphics with the appropriate software. Graphics printers usually have drivers supported by currently available software packages like DISSPLA™, PLOT10™, or GIGS™. Check out the graphics tools in your area to see what you can do with the system you have.

Several printers by various manufacturers are available; any one that understands ASCII format or standard Postscript®, a printing description language by Adobe Systems, and has the correct port for your cables will converse fluently with a VAX. Since you may have some trouble with graphics printers without specific VAX software, make sure you have the appropriate printer drivers to communicate with either the VAX or the terminal (for screen printing only). Otherwise you will not get any plotting or graphics out of your VAX, no matter what it looks like on a display terminal.

Networks and Clusters

The most distinctive feature of networks and clusters is the presence of multiple CPUs. As you may recall from the previous discussion, the CPU does the function handling and information processing for the computer system. Add more CPUs and you have added a lot of interface handling to the tasks you ask your system to do.

VMS is written to handle the problem of multiple CPUs quite well, and with the advent of VMS 5.0, network and clustered environments have become easier to manage than ever. You'll find enough information to whet your appetite for an expanded computing environment, as described in Chapter 15, Network Access.

SOFTWARE

The various components of system software in a VAX configuration are designed to work together, as illustrated by Figure 1-4. Although you are familiar with the operation of at least one other computer system, we will introduce the VAX software carefully to avoid confusion. Many high level language (HLL) compilers that adhere to the current ANSI standards are available for the VAX, meaning that code written for other platforms will work on the VAX with few modifications.

Operating Systems

The operating system is the software package that controls all of the operations of a computer. The VMS operating system is the system of choice for most VAX programmers today, but a large and increasing number of VAX installations are operating under UNIX. The UNIX installations are primarily in colleges and universities, because that is where UNIX development first began.

Editors

Editors are software tools that allow you to create text files that can be stored on a disk or tape and retrieved for future use or modification. Their features let you create and alter one or more files and insert characters in the file wherever needed. Editors also format information in a manner the computer can understand. Currently the two most used VMS-supported editors are EVE/EDT and TPU.

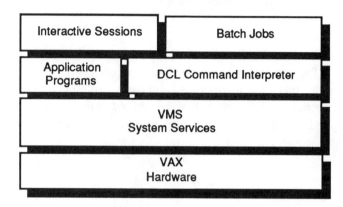

FIGURE 1-4.   The VMS software organization.

High- and Low-Level Languages

Computer languages come in handy when you are ready to do some application development of your own. A computer language is a highly structured syntax that creates an interface between human and computer instructions. You write your computation instructions in a particular language, and your compiler translates that into machine code.

A high-level language is one that uses a special syntax to relate English-like statements to computer functions. You must use a compiler to translate the high-level language into code your computer can understand and execute.

There are many high-level languages, but not all of them are VAX-compatible. Several high-level VAX-compatible languages are C, Pascal, FORTRAN, BLISS-32, Ada, BASIC, and LISP.

A low-level language is developed for individual processors only. The syntax of low-level languages consists of mnemonic operation codes that must be assembled on a line-for-line basis into a machine language for your particular processor. That is why they were named *assembly* language, or *assemblers*.

The low-level language for the VAX is MACRO-32. A program written in MACRO-32 is closer to machine language than a high-level language, meaning that it takes up less disk storage space and executes more rapidly. Some of the new optimizing HLL compilers can break this rule of thumb, however. Assembly language is more difficult to use and learn than the high-level languages, however, and certainly much less portable to other systems.

You will find that if you learn a low-level language and develop software using it, generally your code must be completely rewritten for another machine type. For the VAX, even the low-level MACRO tends to port from one VAX processor to the other, but this is not usually true for computers made by different manufacturers. This means that IBM assembly code will not work on a VAX, or vice versa.

Compilers

A compiler is the first real link between your system's hardware and your instructions. The compiler takes the instructions you have written (i.e., the program), and translates them, creating a relocatable machine-code *object file* that you can link to other separately compiled modules of the same program. In some cases the output of a compiler may be an assembly language program that is in turn fed to the MACRO-11 assembler.

Linkers and Debuggers

Linkers are software programs that join the separate chunks of object code created by various compilers and the assembler. They put the pieces of code together and give the computer a single starting point, or *address* that can be used when you execute the DCL RUN command. The linker resolves reference interfaces in a program and warns you of those it cannot resolve with DCL error or informational messages.

The VAX linker is not dedicated to any particular compiler but can link object modules of several VAX-supported languages together to produce workable executable code. The linker is not limited to compiled code; it can also link assembled code object modules. This feature takes a bit of practice, but you may have an occasion to use it if you are proficient in more than one language.

A debugger is a software tool that enables a programmer to look at memory in specific places in a program; it can show you where the program is producing incorrect values. VMS DEBUG is one of the most useful tools a programmer can learn and could be the topic of a book all by itself. With a good source-level debugger, you can trace the steps in your program until you see an event occur that is obviously an error in logic or calculation.

The VMS debugger is one of the best in the business. It is not really related to a specific compiler language, like most other debuggers on the market, but is linked to VMS. Therefore it works much the same no matter which VAX language compiler you use. You can learn it just once and use it in many different software development projects.

VIRTUAL MEMORY

One of the main claims to fame of the VAX is its ability to support programs that are larger than the machine's physical memory. This feature, referred to as *virtual memory,* works by keeping only a fraction of the program and data in physical memory at any one time and reading in (swapping) successive chunks of data and program as needed from the disk. The virtual address space of the VAX is more than 4 gigabytes (GB), or slightly less than 1 byte for every person on Earth.

Physical memory on a VAX is just like RAM on a regular personal computer. VAX memory is faster (and more expensive) but works just the same. A typical VAX will have anywhere from 8 to 128 MB of RAM, which must be shared among all users. The physical memory is divided into *pages*, which are swapped into and out of the hard disk as needed. When a page is needed that is not currently in memory, a *page fault* occurs and the desired page is read in from disk. At the same time, a not recently used page is copied out of RAM back to the disk. To make matters better, this whole process is completely invisible to the user and programmer writing an application. In most cases, you can simply program as if 4 GB were available.

You probably have been exposed a popular operating system that does *not* feature virtual memory – MS-DOS or PC-DOS, which runs on IBM PCs and compatibles. Its 640K physical memory limit is a well-known and sometimes crippling constraint on the development and use of large programs. Exceeding the 640K barrier in any way requires substantial effort on the part of the DOS programmer, who must either resort to *overlays* in which parts of the program explicitly remove themselves from memory or use a paged memory scheme such as the Lotus-Intel-Microsoft (LIM) expanded memory manager.

INTRODUCTION TO THE DEC MANUAL SET

As your skill in the use of VMS DCL grows, you will find DEC's manual set to be your most useful reference. You can also use additional books and periodicals available from other sources. A detailed listing of the help you can get in the DEC manual set is in Appendix A, DEC Manual Roadmap.

DEC's VAX/VMS document set is a comprehensive information set that can take you through your most complicated programming tasks with little pain and suffering. The various volumes contain a great deal of repetition and a lot of extraneous information that only the most sophisticated system managers and midnight hackers will ever use. Because of the abundant and repetitious data, care should be taken when you order your personal copies of the VAX/VMS documents, as well as those required for your companies' VAX installation reference set. Appendix A can help make wise and cost-effective purchasing decisions.

SUMMARY

This chapter is your first exposure to the following topics:

- Virtual Address eXtension – The operating system that maintains the VAX as one of the most programmer-friendly computers around.

- Hardware – An introduction to the components found in nearly any VAX installation.

- Software – A discussion of the types and features of some of the software available for the VAX operating under VMS.

- The DEC manual set – A preview of the usefulness of DEC's own very well done VMS reference manual set.

2

Overview of VMS

WHAT IS VMS?

VMS is an acronym for Virtual Memory System. It is an *operating system* developed specifically for the VAX computer. An operating system does the management functions of a computer. Because of the differences in hardware, even that developed by the same manufacturers, an operating system must be created specifically for each computer. In other words, even though the operating system you may be familiar with uses the same commands on many different computer systems, the software interfaces to each hardware configuration are unique.

Way back in the days of stand-alone computer systems, DEC had the germ of a great idea for streamlining the operation of their expanding family of computers for business and engineering. It conceived VMS as a way of allowing the basic computer management to be done by a user familiar with any of the multiple systems it made.

Computers for different applications have tended to have different hardware components that require specialized software for access. In the past, each operating system was not only created for a specific hardware configuration, but the behavior of the operating system language varied widely from computer to computer as well. User's are happier each time that operating systems like VMS become more widely used for a number of different platforms. It takes the drudgery out of learning an operating system, enabling them to get to the business of software use and development just that much quicker.

Carrying the portability of software still further, DEC and other industry leaders are introducing the concept of open system architecture. As the name implies, the trend is now toward interoperability and uniform interfaces across disparate hardware and software systems. Through new software products and common interface hardware, development of software applications will take place on one computer platform that will actually be used on others. VMS was developed at the beginning of this trend and continues to be upgraded to enhance its portability.

How Is VMS Controlled?

Virtual memory addressing, the interactive computing environment, and multiprocessing tasks are tied together through the use of the operating system. VMS is a group of software programs and utilities that run continuously. It is made up of the system executive, system services, schedulers, and device drivers. VMS must run continuously in the background of all computer operations without failing. It acts as the interface between you and other users and the computer, peripherals, and other resources.

You have control over many aspects of what VMS does with your software through the Digital Command Language (DCL). DCL is a series of commands in an English-like syntax that direct your VAX computer to perform requested tasks. These commands tell the VAX *what* to do but have little control over *how* everything happens internally – that was the job of the VMS developers.

VMS performs the tasks you request, ordering them according to priorities set by your system managers and the programmers at DEC. The VMS DCL command interpreter translates your command statements and then controls the system services and devices needed for their execution. The operating system and its file manager handle all of the work needed to carry out your commands; then, if you specify it, it will alert you to their completion status. VMS handles the overhead tasks for most simple operations automatically but will let you override the default behavior for most operations when you might desire a different result.

Commonality of VMS Among All VAX Processors

The VAX computer system you are working with is a part of the DEC family of computers. As such, it shares common features with all other computers in the DEC family through the VMS operating system. With the advent of VMS 5.0, all VAX/VMS systems – regardless of size – will share the same command language, DCL. The behavior of VMS has been fairly consistent from installation to installation and system to system for some time, but with the latest major upgrade, Version 5.0, VMS is now the *same* for every one of them.

The advent of a common VMS under Version 5.0 means that the commands and command files you learn in this book will work for any system running VMS, typically from Version 4.0 and up. It also means that any software you develop for any VAX computer system using VMS will run without modification on any other VAX, from the largest mainframes to the smallest MicroVAX.

VMS VERSION UPDATES

DEC supports VMS with an army of programmers who are continuously solving the hardware-to-software-to-user interface problems so you don't have to. System updates, or version releases, come out periodically, at approximately two year intervals. This book is current with VMS Version 5.0. Future updates are expected to add to current capabilities without destroying the old.

DEC's philosophy has been whenever possible not to remove a feature once it has been introduced into the operating system. Version releases with numbers in the tens position, like 4.X or 5.X tend to be small-scale updates that add or modify features, whereas version numbers in the hundreds position, like 4.7X or 5.0X, are bug fixes. Version releases that step a whole number like 5.0, have greater reaching effects and reflect more fundamental changes in the operating system's behavior. Because of the larger scale changes of the whole-number updates, some system managers are running very old versions of VMS in an attempt to avoid crashing other software on the system.

You may or may not be operating under the most recent operating system release. Some system managers worry about problems that may be created by frequent operating system upgrades. Talk to your system manager about his or her philosophy; to find out what your current version is and the estimated date of the next version update. If you are running an old version of VMS, some of the examples in this book may not produce the results you expect. Most of them, however, are at a pretty basic level of VMS and will work with older system versions without any problems.

What Makes a Command-Line Operating System So Useful?

Yes, command-line system languages are still useful and often preferred even in the current age of mice and windows. We are great fans of mice for many computer applications. Their usefulness goes without saying for graphics programs, where precise placement of lines and other screen objects is critical. They are also great if you cannot type well or like the format of menu-driven programming, which helps you with command formats and seldom lets you make a syntax mistake.

But the exclusive use of mice and window menu interfaces is not without its drawbacks. For the development of software applications, programmers with lightning fast fingers work well with command-line operating systems like VMS. Many who lack those impressive typing skills write command procedures to do the typing for them. You may be like many others who find that being *required* to use a menu interface and a mouse to do basic tasks actually slows you down a lot. VMS offers you a choice.

VMS is structured so that all of the things you want to do can be done on the DCL command line, in executable DCL command files, with software written either in the MACRO assembly or higher level language like C or FORTRAN. You never need to slow yourself down to reach for the mouse. Updates are also adding the windowing capabilities many of you like so well. You can have it any way you want and still enjoy the speed, efficiency, and accuracy of VMS.

Why VMS will persist in spite of UNIX

Many believe the specter of UNIX will drive VMS operations into oblivion. It will, however, take a while for that day to come, in part because of the millions of lines of code out there for those applications you never suspected were written in DCL. The current investment in VMS totals hundreds of thousands of man-years. Many factories are controlled by VMS software. Banking and financial software of many flavors is written entirely in the DCL, COBOL, and MACRO languages for VMS. Endless numbers of scientific and engineering applications are dependent on the behavior of the VMS command language and VAX/VMS FORTRAN to function correctly.

Historically, VMS has been a more secure operating system than UNIX; however, the security problems of all operating systems are continually being addressed to head off break-ins. The most likely occurrence is that VMS, UNIX and others will become more similar, and interfaces between each operating system will become commonplace.

Many just simply prefer VMS to UNIX because of its friendliness to programmers and software developers, its familiarity, and its continued *excellent* support from DEC. Add to that resistance the fact that almost no one wants to learn a new operating system every day and you have a pretty convincing case for retaining the VMS operating system even though it is definitely getting a run for the money from ULTRIX/UNIX and other competitors.

THE VAX HELP FACILITY

One of the great things about using a mature operating system like VMS is that the great array of programmers supported by DEC has had the resources to create one of the best HELP facilities ever. You can get information from the HELP utility that takes the place of making endless treks to the DEC manual bookshelf and will literally save you hours of work.

To use the HELP utility, just type HELP at any DCL command line, which in most cases is a dollar sign ($) prompt. You will be reminded of the topics available to you and provided with the first help level (Topic?) prompt for the next bit of information. Just enter a carriage return to get out of HELP, and you will be right back where you started. The display generated by typing HELP at a DCL prompt is shown in Figure 2-1.

The display continues when you press the <CR> key until all the information has been displayed. It then returns with another prompt.

```
$ Topic?
```

Note the capitalization of certain words in the text. All DCL commands in HELP are in all caps, whereas explanatory subject headings are in lowercase. When you type in the command or other topic name you get a display of text information and another prompt (Subtopic?). The HELP utility is set up in a tree structure, similar to many other VMS and DCL constructs. Figure 2-2 is a representation of this tree structure.

```
$ HELP

    The HELP command invokes the VAX-11 HELP Facility to display information
    about a VMS command or topic.  In response to the "Topic?" prompt, you can:

        Type the name of the copmmand or topic for which you need help.

        Type PROCEDURES for information on commonly performed tasks.

        Type HINTS if you are not sure of the name of the command or topic
        for which you need help.

        Type INSTRUCTIONS for more detailed instructions on how to use HELP.

        Type a question mark (?) to redisplay the most recently requested text.

        Press the RETURN key one or more times to exit from HELP.

    You can abbreviate any topic name, although ambiguous abbreviations result
    in all matches being displayed.

    Additional information available:

    ACCOUNTING ALLOCATE   ANALYZE   APPEND    Ascii      ASSIGN    ATTACH
    BACKUP     CALL       CANCEL    CLOSE     Command_procedure    CONNECT
    CONTINUE   CONVERT    COPY      CREATE    DEALLOCATE DEASSIGN  DEBUG
    DECK       DEFINE     DELETE    DEPOSIT   DIFFERENCES          DIRECTORY
    DISCONNECT DISMOUNT   DUMP      EDIT      EOD        EXAMINE   EXIT
    Expressions           File_spec FORTRAN   GOSUB      GOTO      HELP
    Hints      IF         INITIALIZE INQUIRE  Instructions         Lexicals
    LIBRARY    LINK       LOGOUT    MAIL      MERGE      MESSAGE   MOUNT
    New_Features_V50      Numbers   ON        OPEN       PRINT
    Privileges Procedures Protection PURGE    READ       RECALL    RENAME
    REPLY      REQUEST    RETURN    RUN       RUNOFF     SEARCH    SET
    SHOW       SORT       SPAWN     START     STOP       Strings   SUBMIT
    Symbol_assignment     SYNCHRONIZE         THEN       Time      TYPE
    UNLOCK     WAIT       WRITE
```

FIGURE 2-1.   *Terminal display of the HELP facility output.*

Try typing the topic SHOW. You will see the description of the SHOW command and the available subtopics. Now try getting information on the subtopic TIME. It is not necessary to type only one word at a time; you can type SHOW and TIME together.

```
$ Topic? SHOW TIME
SHOW

  TIME

    Displays the current date and time.
    Format
      SHOW [DAY]TIME
$ Subtopic?
```

When you have finished with your HELP subtopic, VMS asks you if additional information is required from HELP on another subtopic, then another topic, and then returns you to the DCL dollar sign ($) prompt.

```
$ Subtopic? <CR>
$ Topic? <CR>
$
```

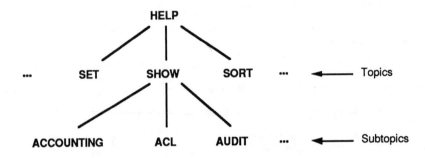

FIGURE 2-2.   The tree structure of the HELP facility.

HELP even works in the editors. Consult your manual or system manager for the keys that get you into the HELP library.

HELP has a facility for creating your own help libraries for use within software you develop. While we don't have the space to go into the specifics of how that is done, it will not be out of your reach once you have learned the basics contained in this reference.

MORE BUILT-IN COMMANDS AND UTILITY PROGRAMS

As you become proficient with VMS, you will find that there are many useful utility routines you may wish to learn. MAIL and PHONE will enable you to communicate with other users on the network. Many establishments customize these utilities and buy VAXes dedicated entirely to electronic mail. Several editors are available for use in software and command routine development. In addition, you may have the opportunity to use BACKUP if your system manager does not do routine file backups for you.

MAIL

MAIL is one of the nice features of the VAX for leaving written messages for members of your computer-user and software development team. To see how easy it is to use MAIL, just enter the MAIL command at any DCL dollar sign ($) prompt and MAIL will respond with its own prompt.

```
$ MAIL
MAIL>
```

Then type HELP to get the lowdown on the facility:

```
MAIL> HELP
```

You will be sending mail to everyone in no time. The HELP facility will respond with instructions on how to SEND and READ your mail. There are many other features for message filing and categorization, forwarding of messages, and so on.

PHONE

The PHONE utility works nearly the same way as MAIL. Just type PHONE at a DCL prompt, and you will see the PHONE facility's percent (%) prompt.

```
$ PHONE
%
```

To call another user, type his or her username at the switchhook (%) prompt. If the other user is at some other node than your own, type that node's name first, separated by a double colon (::) (there's more on node names and syntax later):

```
% CHOPIN::COOK
```

If you are both using the same node, all you need is the username:

```
% COOK
```

PHONE will now ring the other party. If the person answers, your screen will split into two sections, with you on the top and the person you are calling on the bottom. You can type in your message, and hang up when your're finished with a <CTRL/Z>.

EVE/EDT

EDT is the default editor under VMS. It is the editor you get when you type EDIT or EDIT/EDT. By default, you will begin in the EDT line mode. Type the word *change* (or simply a C) at the asterisk (*) prompt to get to the keypad mode. You will find the default editor a capable full-screen editor with some limitations you will not be annoyed with until you have gained some proficiency with it.

The detailed explanation of EDT or another editor is beyond the scope of this book, but it is not difficult to master the editor with a brief introduction. In any case, nothing beats trying it when it comes to learning a new editor, or any text processor for that matter.

To enter the editor, type EDIT with a file specification . Use JUNK.TXT as the file name for now. Since the file does not exist, DCL will tell that and then go ahead and create a blank file for you.

```
$ EDIT JUNK.TXT
[EOB]
Input File does not exist
```

The [EOB] represents the end of the file buffer. EDT will not allow you to type ahead of the start of the file buffer or beyond its end.

To get to the HELP facility for EDT, just press the PF2 key. You will get a display of the keypad editing keys. To get information about how a key is used, just press that key while you are still in the HELP facility.

Figure 2-3 shows a comparison of the normal keypad labeling and functions to those of the EDT editor keypad.

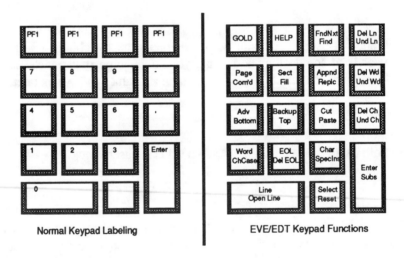

Normal Keypad Labeling   EVE/EDT Keypad Functions

FIGURE 2-3.   The EDT keypad.

To get back to the asterisk (*) prompt so you can enter line commands, type <CTRL/Z>.

When you are done editing your file, type EXIT, or EX, to save the file you have just edited. If you do not wish to save your file, type QUIT instead. QUIT is not something you should get used to, however, or you will be retyping your files a lot. When you EXIT, you will get a message telling you your file has been successfully saved and its size in lines.

```
* EXIT
  DUA0[200102.MYDIR]JUNK.TXT;1     4 lines
```

BACKUP

The BACKUP utility has an entire chapter devoted to it. After you've had a little more VMS and DCL exposure take a look at Chapter 11: Success with BACKUP, to see how BACKUP works .

SUMMARY

This chapter introduced the VMS operating system on a global level. It touched on the concept of an operating system and the nature of VMS updates.

The chapter also presented an example of the HELP facility and introduced these other VMS utilities you may find useful:

MAIL – To send filed messages to other people on your system.

PHONE – To send interactive messages to another person currently logged in to your system.

BACKUP – To create tape or disk backups of your files; this subject is covered in more depth later.

EVE/EDT – The default editor for VMS System 5.0.

3

Introduction to DCL

Digital Command Language DCL, the fundamental command language of VMS, is a set of commands used to issue instructions to the computer. DCL can be used at the command prompt line at any time or in command files. It has a very regular structure which lends itself to flexibility and easy understanding of command meanings.

WHAT ARE DCL COMMANDS?

DCL commands are simply English-like words, generally verbs, that describe the functions VMS performs when they are invoked at a system prompt or in a command file.

A simple example is the *command* SHOW, with the *object* TIME. When you type SHOW TIME the system will respond in the way you expect, by displaying the system clock's day and time. It will then return with a new DCL command prompt ($):

```
$ SHOW TIME <CR>
  17-MAY-1988 09:05:23
$
```

Commands can be typed in either uppercase or lowercase, since VMS converts them to uppercase internally at the time of execution.

Since DCL commands are part of the Digital Command Language, they have grammatical rules and a particular vocabulary, just like any other language. Its vocabulary is made up of *commands*, *parameters* and *qualifiers*.

THE DCL COMMAND LINE

DCL has a particular format for command lines, which can be easy to follow once you understand the command syntax. DCL is made up of more than 200 commands which DEC calls verbs. These command verbs are used much like those of the English language and are similar to those of other operating systems.

All functions found in the other major operating systems (UNIX, MS-DOS, etc.) can be duplicated by DCL. Taking a little time to learn the basics will pay off in the end by greatly increasing the speed with which you can do almost any programming task. The following illustrates the extended DCL command format.

```
$ LABEL: COMMAND-NAME PARAMETER(S) /QUALIFIER(S) !COMMENT
```

The optional *label* can be any name you choose, with a maximum length of 255 characters. It must precede the DCL command verb and be followed by the required colon (:) separator. Labels are usually used in command procedure files.

The COMMAND-NAME is the DCL command that VMS will execute, assuming the rest of the line is understood by the VMS interpreter. The DCL command itself may be comprised of more than one word, each separated by a space. A space must also separate the command verb from the rest of the command line and from the PARAMETER object.

The PARAMETER is the filename or other subject of the DCL command; in other words, the thing you want DCL to do something *to* . In some cases, a DCL command can operate on more than one parameter, usually in series. When this feature is used, each of the command objects must be separated by a comma. Spaces must not be used anywhere in the object list. In this PRINT command,

```
$ PRINT anyfile.txt
```

anyfile.txt is a parameter for the PRINT command, the input file specification. It indicates the name of the file to be printed.

Full commands are generally typed on a single line. Once the command name is typed, however, VMS will look for the parameter upon which it will operate. If that parameter is missing, VMS will prompt for it. An example of this is

```
$ COPY
$____FROM:          (Enter the name of the file to be copied)
$____TO: (Enter the name you are giving to the newly created
file)
```

In this case, if both the parameters are missing, VMS will prompt for both. If only the destination filename is missing, it will request only that filename.

The /QUALIFIER modifies or restricts the function of the DCL command line. Qualifiers always begin with a forward slash character (/). In the next example, you see how the /COPIES qualifier can be used to specify additional copies will be printed:

```
$ PRINT/COPIES=2 anyfile.txt <CR>
  Job ANYFILE (queue LA100, entry 188) started on SYS$PRINT
$
```

The !COMMENT is optional. But documentation about a command, such as information required for future reference, must be preceded by an exclamation point. All characters on a particular line to the right of the (!) are ignored. Comments are generally used only in command procedure files.

EDITING COMMAND LINES

Several keys and key combinations can be used to edit command lines. You'll generally use the following keys for command line editing:

DELETE – Moves the cursor back a single character at a time, and deletes that character. On some terminals, this key is labeled RUBOUT.

CTRL/A – A toggle key that changes command line editing mode to insert from overstrike and back again.

Arrow keys – Left and right arrow keys move the cursor left and right along a command line so you can insert or overstrike characters on the command line. The up and down arrow keys access the history buffer described later in this chapter.

Here is one note on the behavior of different terminals: On normal VTXXX series terminals in the alphanumeric mode, your keystrokes will erase the previous typed command. On some graphics terminals, most notably the Tektronix series, however, your keystrokes will overwrite without erasing. Don't let this obscured view fool you. The characters are recognized by the terminal as erased even though it is a mess on the display.

DCL is a complete command language, capable of doing virtually any task imaginable with the VAX. Because of space limitations, all commands will not be covered in the chapters that follow, but enough examples and detail will be provided to give you the tools to reach for the appropriate references for more details. For more details on particular commands, Appendix B, DCL Command Summary, will be invaluable. Of course, the DEC manual set provides the most complete information available on all DCL commands.

Reading a DCL Command Line

All of the punctuation in the examples of DCL command lines and in the references has specific meaning. This topic is covered in Chapter 4, but a short summary here is in order.

Figure 3-1 is a summary of the DCL command line format, illustrating the order of the command, command qualifiers, parameters, and positional qualifiers. The parameters can be an input file specification, an output file specification or the name of some other object.

Note that while spaces are allowed between commands, parameters, and qualifiers, no spaces are allowed within the parameters themselves.

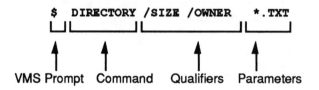

FIGURE 3-1.   The DCL command line format.

Command Line Format Specification

Gaining a little insight into the format of the DCL command line can make the language a bit more intuitive. All commands follow the same format, although most commands do not require the use of all of the specifiers listed below. Don't worry if it's confusing at first; things will clear up as you get additional exposure.

The DCL command line format allows the use of a command along with modifiers to each component of the command. The general format looks like this:

```
$ COMMAND/CMD_QUAL input-file-spec/POS_QUAL output-file-
spec/POS_QUAL
```

COMMAND – The command is entered on the line after the DCL prompt. The default prompt is the dollar sign ($), unless you or your system manager change it (you will learn to do this later). Any whitespace characters (e.g., spaces or tabs) after the prompt and before the command are ignored by DCL.

CMD_QUAL – Command qualifiers are parameters attached to the DCL command to modify its default behavior. They are preceded by a forward slash (/). The qualifier follows the command and can be used with other qualifiers. The order of the qualifiers is usually irrelevant.

Input-file-spec – The input file specification, if required, is usually in the first position after the command and any qualifiers to that command. This file is the one upon which the command acts.

POS_QUAL – Positional qualifiers are used like command qualifiers, modifying command behavior. The exact effect of the qualifier is determined by its position relative to the command, input-file-spec, and output-file-spec. Always be careful to note the position and use of these qualifiers to enable you to predict their results.

Output-file-spec – The output file specification, if required, is the destination of whatever result may come from executing a DCL command. An example of this is the COPY command. For COPY, the output-file-spec is the newly created copy of the input file.

Appendix B, DCL Command Summary is a summary of *all* DCL commands, including their use and qualifiers. It is current with Version 5.0 of VMS. The chapter summaries in this book contain information about the use of commands explained in that appendix. By using these resources and consulting with DEC's DCL dictionary and other manuals, you will be able to make expert use of all commands to which your system manager has granted you access.

Command Usage Specification

Often a command can be quite involved. Understanding its syntax is critical to reading the summaries in this book, as well as the references in the DEC manual set. The complexity is exemplified by the use of the punctuation characters required for multiple parameters, like a series of file specifications. DCL command specification syntax, when studied, provides a key for understanding the richness of information that can be conveyed in a single line of text. Here is the syntax for a more complex DCL command line:

```
$ COMMAND/QUAL=(parameter[,...]) input-file-spec[,...]
```

Parentheses – parentheses () are used to surround a list of parameters or options in a command. They must actually be included in the command line you type. If only one member of the list is given, the parentheses may be omitted.

Square brackets – The square brackets [] always denote an optional parameter. In the above example, only one input-file-spec is required, but several can be used if desired, separated by commas. Square brackets here are just a notational aid and are *not* actually typed in the command line.

Ellipsis – The ellipsis represents the usual, implying the same thing is repeated a number of times. Limits on the repetition are not usually noted in shorthand representations, but they are large enough that you are unlikely to be hampered by them.

Commas – When you see a comma listed, it is a required separator between the parameters that surround it. Do not use spaces and commas together in the DCL command line, as spaces are only legitimate separators between parameters.

Spaces – The spaces in a command line are critical. Any time you see white space in a shorthand representation, you may substitute at least one whitespace character for it without altering the behavior of the command. This is especially useful in creating readable DCL command files.

As you work your way through this book, be on the lookout for the command syntax notation. Further examples will reinforce your ability to understand this syntax and use the compact table references and will reduce your dependence on less convenient volumes like the weighty DCL dictionary.

It is worthwhile to stress that DCL is a very uniform command language. As you progress through the next chapters, you will notice that many commands share the same qualifiers and that a given qualifier almost always means the same thing each time it is used; for example "/OUTPUT=" specifies that output be sent to a specific place. This consistency results in a more intuitive approach to the use of DCL commands and qualifiers.

ERROR AND INFORMATIONAL MESSAGES

Face it, once in a while you're going to type a DCL command incorrectly. But when that happens, VMS will respond with a fairly informative error message. Fortunately for the survival of egos, VMS also provides success (or informational) messages as well as error messages. The general layout of such messages is shown in Figure 3-2.

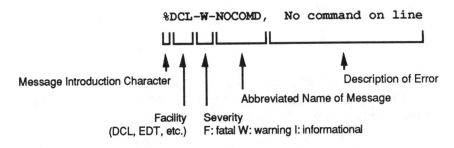

FIGURE 3-2.   VMS Message Format.

This message format actually applies to all VMS messages, not just DCL. All of them begin with a % character, which is then followed by three fields that identify the source, error severity, and an abbreviated name for the message. A slightly more verbose explanation of the message follows after the comma.

The severity codes are as follows:

I – Information message

W – Warning message (nonfatal)

F – Severe (fatal) error

E – Error (usually fatal)

S – Success!

LOGGING IN

Before using a time-sharing system, you have to alert the CPU that you want access. This is done by a process referred to as *logging in*. Here we will explain what happens during the VAX login procedure. The necessary specifics of logging in to your particular installation will be explained by your system manager, since we cannot assign you a user account or set your first password.

Getting the Terminal Ready

At the risk of sounding incredibly patronizing, we feel we must begin with the bare basics of VAX operation. Before you start using your terminal, check to see that the terminal is plugged in and the power is turned on. If your terminal has a LOCAL/REMOTE switch, the switch must be set to REMOTE.

Now the terminal should be ready to accept your login. If you have problems, check with your system administrator before getting too anxious. You may have a simple but stubborn problem that can be easily fixed, such as an improper connection with the computer or an incorrect baud rate setting. You might also be connected through a terminal server, which will demand a couple of extra steps on your part. In rare instances, you may have to reboot your VAX before continuing. But do that only if your system manager tells you to because it stops the computer entirely, interrupting others who may be using it.

Gaining Access to the System

Access is gained through the procedure commonly known as logging in. After getting your computer's attention by tapping on the <CR> key a few times, you will be prompted for your username and password. Your responses are checked for validity before VMS goes ahead with your login.

What Happens When You Log In

When you first log in to a VAX/VMS system by giving your username and password, VMS performs a number of operations and then you see the normal DCL $ prompt. Most of these operations are done through system-wide DCL command files rather than through any special programming of the operating system. The general sequence of processing during a login is as follows.

1. *Establish a Connection.* You begin by establishing a connection between your terminal and the VAX/VMS host on which you wish to log in. Details of this process vary depending on whether you are using a dedicated ASCII terminal such as a DEC VT220, using a terminal connected to a modem or terminal server, a terminal emulator program on a stand-alone workstation, and so on.

2. *Enter Username and Password.*   Once a connection is set up, pressing <CR> a couple of times at your terminal will alert the system that someone is trying to log in. At this point you may receive a brief introductory message (except at high security installations) and a prompt for Username:. After you type the username assigned to you by your system manager, you will normally receive another prompt, Password:.

The screen may look like this:

```
                     WELCOME
                     TO THE
            ROCKETSIM MICROVAX II SYSTEM
        Flight Simulator Development Environment
                   Number One
```

```
Username: COOK
Password:
```

Note that the characters that make up your password will not be echoed, or repeated, on the terminal screen as you type them; this prevents a casual observer from obtaining your password by looking over your shoulder.

3. *VMS Check of Username and Password.*   VMS checks your username and password against the list of authorized users and encrypted passwords contained in the User Authorization File (UAF). If they match, login processing proceeds. If not, a failure message is displayed on your terminal and you have a few more chances to log in.

Should you be unable to log in after a few tries, give up and contact your system manager for assistance. Repeated unsuccessful login attempts can trigger VMS system security responses such as disabling the terminal at which the failed logins are originating. This can be disconcerting to the person after you who sits down at the terminal, types an apparently valid login sequence, and is refused.

4. *Login Processing.*   When your name and password have been validated, the real login processing begins. VMS now creates or SPAWNs a *process* that will interpret your DCL commands and be the *parent* of all subprocesses you may later create. Your process is created with certain *attributes* such as privileges and memory quotas. Some of these attributes can be modified by you; some can only changed by the system manager or a user with similar privileges. One such attribute is the identity of your command processor, which is almost invariably DCL.

5. *Execute the System's SYLOGIN.COM.*   Once DCL is started, the system runs a special system-wide DCL command file called SYLOGIN.COM. This file contains DCL commands that the system manager wants all users on the system to execute when they log in. If you're curious, you can attempt to view this file by typing the following:

```
$ TYPE SYS$MANAGER:SYLOGIN.COM
```

You may not get anything but an error message if your system manager has protected the file from read access, however.

Running SYLOGIN.COM is initiated directly by VMS; you can neither prevent it from starting nor abort it while it's running.

6. *Execute Your Personal LOGIN.COM.*   When SYLOGIN.COM is finished, VMS looks for a file named LOGIN.COM in your *home directory*. We will explain directory structures in more detail in Chapter 4. You are not required to have a personal LOGIN.COM to operate under VMS, but most experienced users have them to run commands they wish to always have executed and to establish local symbols for their own use.

If you have a LOGIN.COM file in your home directory, it is processed automatically by DCL when you log in. LOGIN.COM is a file of DCL commands that you have control over. It contains commands that help set up the VMS environment to suit your preferences and work habits. Unlike SYLOGIN.COM, your can abort your personal LOGIN.COM before it finishes. It can even be disabled altogether by renaming or deleting it. Note that the system only recognizes files named LOGIN.COM during the login and that the file *must* be located in your home directory or it will be ignored.

7. *Appearance of the $ Prompt.* The login process is now complete. Assuming that the login command files did not alter it, the DCL $ prompt will now be visible on your terminal at the left edge of the screen. This indicates that VMS is now ready to process the DCL commands you type.

Logging Out

Logging out is as essential a step in the use of a time-sharing system as is logging in, although new users often forget to do it and just walk off after their session is over. The LOGOUT command does two essential things that you don't want to omit, so do remember to do it before you leave your terminal.

The first and probably most important thing it does is remove access to your files. If you were to just walk away from a terminal without logging out, your accounts would be exposed to anyone who just walks by.

The second thing that LOGOUT does is to release all system resources that were taken up by your session. If you allocate a tape drive to yourself and then fail to log out, the drive remains unavailable to other users.

To log out, simply type the command LOGOUT at the DCL prompt:

```
$ LOGOUT
```

DCL COMMANDS

Now that you can read the reference syntax for a command line and know how to log in and out of a terminal session, it's time to move forward.

Abbreviations

All DCL commands can be abbreviated to four or fewer characters. The only rule about this is that the command can only be truncated to its shortest unique length. The most common command users type is DIRECTORY. This command's shortest unique length is DIR.

When using DCL, any number of characters beyond the shortest unique length can be typed, with no effect on command performance. For example, the following three commands all have the same effect:

```
$ DIR
$ DIRECTORY
$ DIRECT
```

The result of a command reduced below its shortest unique length is an error message, as shown below:

```
$ DI
%DCL-W-AMBCOMD, ambiguous command verb - supply more characters
```

User-customized abbreviations can be created using DCL assignment commands. This will be covered in Chapter 5, Using Symbols.

DCL Command Defaults

Every DCL command has a default behavior assigned to it by VMS. You can generally override this by including the appropriate qualifiers with the command. A list of all the DCL commands, their qualifiers, and the defaults for each of these is in Appendix B, DCL Command Summary.

A more detailed description of each command, without specific examples, can be found in your installation's *VMS General User's Manual.* If you find that you really need it, exhaustive detail is contained in the DEC *DCL Dictionary.*

The *DCL Dictionary* is an optional purchase your system manager may have made for your installation. The DCL Dictionary manual also contains short code examples illustrating the correct use and expected outputs of some of the commands.

Using Command Qualifiers

The use of qualifiers is complex and therefore difficult to understand at the first reading. Essentially, a qualifier is a modifier to one of the components in the command line. It is used in any position in the line, and its performance is sometimes altered by that line position. To guarantee that the qualifier has the desired effect, it should be used directly following the part of the command line it is intended to modify. There will be more on this in later sections.

There are three types of qualifiers: command, positional and parameter. The qualifier must always be preceded by the slash (/) to be correctly interpreted by VMS, but it need not have a space preceding it. The qualifier is always present in the form of defaults assumed by VMS. Its real usefulness comes in when the user wants to override the default performance of a DCL command. Multiple qualifiers can be used when required. Just remember each qualifier in a command line must be preceded by an accompanying slash.

For example, suppose you would like a listing of all files you created since yesterday and the size of the files. You could type

```
$ DIRECTORY/SIZE/SINCE=YESTERDAY
```

The default behavior of DIRECTORY is to list all files in the current directory, but the qualifiers alter the behavior of the command to give you a list of only the files created since yesterday, along with the file storage space used in blocks. There will be more on the functions of the DIRECTORY command in the next chapter.

Aborting a Command in Progress

There are two ways in which you can safely abort a command or process in progress using control keys. These are by pressing <CTRL/Y> or <CTRL/C>. The behavior of each is a little different.

<CTRL/Y>

The <CTRL/Y> key combination is known as an interrupt. You can use it to stop a command in process, then continue again if you choose by typing CONTINUE. To stop the command process entirely, you must type STOP.

<CTRL/C>

The <CTRL/C> key combination issues the CANCEL command. The currently running program or command is aborted immediately and its context is destroyed. Command execution cannot be resumed by typing CONTINUE.

Multiline Commands

Continuation characters let you type in commands longer than the available space in one row of the terminal display. To continue a line further, type a hyphen (-) at the end of the line. When you do this, you can go ahead and press <CR>. VMS will be alerted to watch for additional text on the next line it sees. This also works for command files, as you'll see later.

USING THE HISTORY BUFFER AND RECALL

The history buffer is useful for displaying the last 20 commands you typed at the DCL prompt. To recall the last command you entered, type RECALL:

```
$ RECALL
 1 DIRECTORY/SIZE/SINCE=YESTERDAY
$
```

RECALL can usually be abbreviated to its first three letters, REC, without causing problems. To view all 20 commands in the buffer, type the command REC/ALL.

```
$ REC/ALL
 9 TYPE SYS$MANAGER:SYLOGIN.COM
 8 SHOW TIME
 7 PRINT anyfile.txt
 6 PRINT/COPIES=2 anyfile.txt
 5 DIRECTORY
 4 DIR
 3 DI
 2 DIRECTORY/SIZE/SINCE=YESTERDAY
 1 RECALL
$
```

When you determine which command you wish to execute without retyping, type REC [command-number].

```
$ REC [3]
$ DI
```

It's hard to imagine when the history buffer would get in the way, but if you want to clear it, type;

```
$ REC/ERASE
```

to clear all 20 slots in the buffer.

There is one more method for accessing the history buffer. You can press an up or down arrow to scroll through the last 20 commands in the buffer. When you see the command you wish to repeat press <CR>, and the DCL command will be executed just as if you had laboriously retyped it. This feature is worth its weight in gold when you are trying to get a long COPY command to work right.

THE TYPEAHEAD BUFFER AND HOW TO KILL IT

The typeahead buffer is the antithesis of the history buffer. While DCL commands are being executed, sometimes it gets a little boring just sitting there waiting. If you are confident in your spelling and typing skills and are doing something that will not cause any great problem if you make an error, you may want to take advantage of the typeahead buffer.

To use the typeahead buffer, you just continue typing as if the terminal were able to echo your keyboard entries. Nothing will appear on the terminal screen except the blinking cursor or the information messages from the last command you executed, but VMS will be keeping track of your every keystroke, just as if you waited until the screen display was alive. The characters you typed will be displayed the moment VMS is ready to accept them.

If you make typos, use the backspace key to clear characters on a single command. Once you have pressed a <CR>, though, you will have clear the buffer to avoid executing the command. To do this, press the <CTRL/X> key combination. This will erase the typeahead buffer without interrupting the command currently in process.

If any one of your DCL commands fails, the typeahead buffer is automatically cleared when the abort occurs and the error message is displayed at the terminal. The buffer gets cleared anytime an abort occurs, whether because of a DCL syntax or another error, or when you interrupt a command in process with <CTRL/Y> or cancel a command with <CTRL/C>. This gives you a measure of safety against executing unintended commands that assume the previous command completed successfully.

SUMMARY

This chapter introduced you to the ways that DCL works to interpret your commands and enables VMS to execute them. The chapters that follow will build on this information.

This chapter has covered the following topics:

- Text and graphic conventions – How to read the examples and reference material in this book and the DEC manual set.

- Logging in – How to log in and what happens when you do.

- The DCL command line – The parts of the command line and how to specify them, such as,

```
$ COMMAND/QUAL input-file-spec output-file-spec
```

- Editing command lines – <CTRL/A> inserts characters between existing ones or toggles back to overstrike mode if you press it again.

- What happens during command processing – Command translation by DCL and execution by VMS.

- Abbreviations – DCL commands can usually be shortened, at least to their first four characters.

- DCL command defaults – The behavior assumed by VMS if no command qualifiers are specified.

- Using command qualifiers – Altering the default behavior of DCL commands.

- Aborting or interrupting a command in progress – <CTRL/C> aborts the command and <CTRL/Y> interrupts the command; both of them clear the typeahead buffer.

- Multiline commands – Just type a hyphen (-) and a <CR> and continue typing on the next line.

- The history buffer and RECALL – Use RECALL to retrieve any one of the last 20 commands you typed and execute it again.

- The typeahead buffer – Continue typing during command execution to fill the typeahead buffer for execution after completion of the current command.

Part 2
Getting Started

The three chapters contained within Part Two present the basic concepts for getting started with VAX/VMS operations. The basic DCL commands are presented in greater detail because these are the essential skills you will need to learn and understand the more advanced topics in the chapters that follow.

Chapter 4, Directory Navigation and File Handling, explains the VAX/VMS directory and file structure as well as simple operations to create, modify, copy, rename and delete files.

Chapter 5, Using Symbols, develops DCL programming with the use of symbols. Symbols provide a shorthand way of invoking all or part of a command string.

Chapter 6, Command Files, is the beginning of the meat of DCL. With DCL command files, you can do anything off-line that you can do on-line. They let you automate your most frequently used command sequences, either during your current programming session or by using the VMS batch facility.

4

Directory Navigation and File Handling

THE VMS DIRECTORY TREE

The VMS directory tree is a construct that is used in most fully developed operating systems. The VMS directory tree system is not difficult to master, and navigation in the directories can be accomplished through the use of a few simple commands. An example of the directory tree structure is shown in Figure 4-1. The files and users mentioned in the figure will be used in other examples throughout this book. These examples illustrate the shared access of two users and a system administrator using a MicroVAX II for development of various software projects such as FLIGHTSIM.

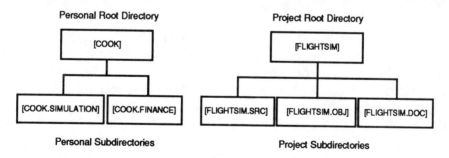

FIGURE 4-1.   VMS facilitates the sharing of a computer system between personal and project files.

The project directories and files and the COOK personal directories behave as though they are completely separate, even though their actual space in computer memory may be adjacent. File access is permitted only to the system manager or others with access privileges by using commands you will learn later in this chapter.

DIRECTORY SPECIFIERS

Directories and files are described through the use of hierarchical specifiers. The hierarchy begins with the root, or home, directory, continues with any subdirectories, and ends with the file name, extension and version number. The *full file specification* as it is defined in Figure 4-2 is rarely used in its entirety because of internal system defaults that are set as you operate the VAX for various tasks.

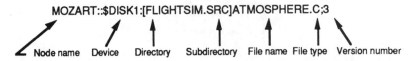

MOZART::$DISK1:[FLIGHTSIM.SRC]ATMOSPHERE.C;3

Node name   Device   Directory   Subdirectory   File name   File type   Version number

FIGURE 4-2.   *The components of a complete file and directory specification.*

The full file specification is essential for applications in which several projects and users share the same computer, especially when the VAX computers are networked or shared by a VAXcluster. Because the full file specification also describes the network node on which the file resides, a full file specification can be called a *network file specification*. Other operating systems will often call the full file specification the *pathname*.

A *directory specification* is a component of the full file specification illustrated in Figure 4-2. It includes the part of the specification beginning with the left square bracket and ending with the right square bracket:

```
[ROOTDIR.DIR.SUBDIRECTORY...]
```

You will see the node name as the identifier for the CPU your process is using or perhaps for another CPU on your network. Unless you are working in a network environment or in some cluster environments, however, the node name will often not be used. Since the node name never varies on a single CPU system, the default behavior is usually set by the system manager to eliminate its display in the file specification. When the node name does appear, it is separated from the remainder of the file specification by a double colon (::).

When you use the device name in the file specification, it will usually apply to a physical disk on which there are files of interest, but you will also use it to specify all of the devices in your operating group. Terminals each have unique device identifiers, as do the printers, plotters, and tape or disk drives. Device names are separated from the rest of the file specification by a single colon (:).

VMS devices consist of any peripheral that can be attached to the VAX. Devices are all identified in DCL commands by two-letter prefixes that indicate the type of the device.

Some common prefixes are as follows:

- DJ – Fixed disks

- DU – RA or RD series disks

- LP – Line printer on parallel interface

- MB – Mailbox device

- MU – Magtape, normally cartridge

- MS – Magtape, nine-track TS-series drive

- MT – Magtape, nine-track TU-series drive

- NL – Null device

- OP – Operator terminal

- RT – Remote (network) terminal

- TX – Terminal (physical)

- VT – Terminal (virtual)

- XQ – DEQNA Ethernet interface

Figure 4-3 illustrates some of the more common device types.

You can obtain information about devices known to the system by using the VMS SHOW DEVICE command. This command produces a listing of devices and their attributes; for disk devices, the current number of free blocks (1 block = 512 contiguous bytes on disk) is given. A sample listing of a SHOW DEVICE command is given in Figure 4-4.

Logical names resembling device names can also be assigned to a directory specification to reduce the number of keystrokes required to type the file specifications in that directory. This will be covered in Chapter 5, Symbols and Other Shorthand.

In the full file specification you saw in Figure 4-2, FLIGHTSIM is the name of the root directory in the directory tree of files. Your root directory specification will be preceded by the left square bracket ([), with no other punctuation. This directory specifier can be any collection of alphanumeric characters, but is commonly given a numerical value that represents the user's group and personal identification codes in timesharing systems.

The .DIR.SUBDIRECTORY... following the root directory specification takes the user further down the tree to where it begins to branch out more fully. All directory and subdirectory specifications must be preceded by a period (.). This will be explained in more detail later. A right square bracket (]) follows the last element in the directory tree specifier.

Following the right square bracket is the file specification, beginning with the word ATMOSPHERE. The *file name*, in this case ATMOSPHERE, is an alphanumeric name assigned to a particular file. It does not need to be unique, as long as the complete file and directory specification together defines a unique file.

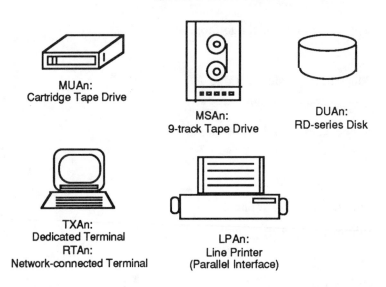

GUIDE TO VMS DEVICE NAMES
as seen in SHOW DEVICE

MUAn:
Cartridge Tape Drive

MSAn:
9-track Tape Drive

DUAn:
RD-series Disk

TXAn:
Dedicated Terminal
RTAn:
Network-connected Terminal

LPAn:
Line Printer
(Parallel Interface)

FIGURE 4-3.   Typical MicroVAX Device Names.

The *file type* is often used to give the file a name that the system will recognize by defaults and understand how to use. For example,

```
ROCKETSIM.FOR
```

implies that the file is a FORTRAN source file, while

```
ROCKETSIM.C, ROCKETSIM.OBJ and ROCKETSIM.EXE
```

imply that the files are a C language source file, a compiled object code file, and an executable image file, respectively. The type specifiers can be anything you choose, but to avoid excess typing, you may wish to name them so that the system will be able to understand them without you typing the extensions every time. More on this later, too.

The last element in the file specification is the file's *version number*, which is 3 in Figure 4-2. A version number is usually given to the file at its creation by VMS. For example, a version number 1 implies that the file is the first one created of its series. If another file is created with the same name, type, and directory specification, VMS will automatically give it the next higher version number, in this case 2, to maintain file name uniqueness.

Figure 4-5 is a more detailed example of a project directory tree. The directory and file specification syntax presented thus far is capable of reaching any point in this tree from any other point.

```
$ SHOW DEVICE
```

Device Name	Device Status	Error Count	Volume Label	Free Blocks	Trans Count	Mnt Cnt
DUA0:	Mounted	0	MICROVMS	27781	52	1
DUA1:	Mounted	0	UDATA	33584	48	1

Device Name	Device Status	Error Count	Volume Label	Free Blocks	Trans Count	Mnt Cnt
MUA0:	Online	0				

Device Name	Device Status	Error Count
OPA0:	Online	0
RTA0:	Offline	0
RTA1:	Mounted	0
RTB0:	Offline	0
TXA0:	Online	0
TXA1:	Online	0
TXA2:	Online	0
TXA3:	Online	0
TXA4:	Online	0
TXA5:	Online spooled alloc	0
TXA6:	Online	0
TXA7:	Online	0
XQA0:	Online	0
XQA1:	Online	0

FIGURE 4-4.   Sample SHOW DEVICE Listing.

Getting a Directory Listing

Directory listings can be made and sent to the screen or to a file to be printed. A general listing of file names within the default directory will be sent to the screen with no additional information if you simply type the command

```
$ DIRECTORY
```

or

```
$ DIR
```

DIR is enough for recognition, because as you may recall, DCL will execute any of its commands if you give it enough characters to recognize it as a command. The usual number of characters required for recognition is three to four.

Punctuation

VMS has special requirements for file and directory punctuation. Any deviation, unless covered by a VMS default, will cause an error message to appear. Table 4-1 shows the components of the full file specification and the required punctuation separators

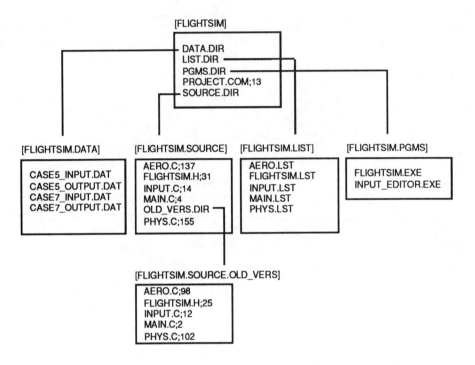

FIGURE 4-5.   *A more detailed project directory tree.;*

Maximum Name Lengths

As you would probably expect, there are system specified maximum lengths for all parts of the file and directory specification. The VMS maximums are shown in Table 4-2.

The characters for all components, except the version number, can be any combination of alphanumeric characters or the symbols underscore (_), hyphen (-), or dollar sign ($). No blank spaces are allowed anywhere in the file or directory specification.

TABLE 4-1. *Punctuation used in directory specification.*

NODE NAME	double colon	(::)
DEVICE NAME	single colon	(:)
DIRECTORY NAME	brackets	([...])
FILE NAME	lleading period	(.)
FILE TYPE	semicolon	(;)

TABLE 4-2. Maximum length for filenames under VMS.

NODE NAME 6 characters	
DEVICE NAME	4 characters
DIRECTORY NAME	39 characters
SUBDIRECTORY NAME	39 characters
FILE NAME 39 characters	
FILE TYPE 39 characters	
VERSION NUMBER	5 decimal digits between 1 and 32,767

DIRECTORY SPECIFICATION DEFAULTS

When using a file specification, VMS provides defaults that enable you to omit most of the components of a file specification, depending on what you want. The defaults for your file specification are your

• Presently active default directory

• Current device name

• Current login process node name

These defaults are sufficient if you work with files within your currently connected directory. Pay attention to your system default hierarchy if you need to access a file in some directory outside of your currently active default directory. Just specify as much of the file specification as is different from your default.

Accessing Parents and Children of a Directory

The directory tree would be cumbersome to navigate without some shorthand ways to refer to the parent or children of a particular directory. If you are currently connected to [ROCKETSIM.SRC.VER1] and want to look at [ROCKETSIM.SRC] to see what other versions of the source code there might be, you can use

```
$ DIR [-]
```

The hyphen always refers to the parent of the current default directory. If you then discovered that there was also a VER2 subdirectory under [ROCKETSIM.SRC], you could obtain a directory of it using

```
$ DIR [-.VER2]
```

A different syntax lets you refer to child subdirectories of the current default directory.

If you were connected to [ROCKETSIM.SRC] and wanted to get a directory of [ROCKETSIM.SRC.VER2], you could merely type

```
$ DIR [.VER2]
```

In this case, the initial period in the directory specifier tells DCL to begin following the path from the current default directory.

WILDCARD FILE SPECIFICATIONS

A wildcard is a special character that can be used in any part of a file or directory specification to specify multiple files or directories. Wildcards are very handy when you want to apply the same operation, e.g. deletion, to a group of files. The DCL wildcard characters are the asterisk (*), the percent symbol (%), and the ellipsis (...).

The Asterisk Wildcard

The asterisk (*) is the wildcard you will use most often. Sometimes called the splat operator, it can be used as a substitute for all or part of the filespec – specifically the file name, type specifier, or version number. Asterisks are not permitted in node, device, or directory specifications. An command showing a use of the asterisk wildcard is

```
$ DELETE *.*;*
```

In this example, the wilcdard will result in all of the files in your default directory being deleted.

Wildcards are useful when you are preparing to delete a useless or redundant directory. A special note concerning the DELETE command is that file version numbers *must* be explicitly specified with a wildcard, a number, or a bare semicolon. DELETE is the only DCL command with this unusual requirement. Its purpose is to force the user actually think about whether or not to delete a file. Exercise care with wildcards and the DELETE command, since you can erase a large number of files with a single command.

To ensure that only the desired versions are deleted, you can force yourself to confirm all deletes by typing a few more characters:

```
$ DELETE/CONFIRM *.*;*
```

In response to this command, VMS will display the filespec for each candidate file and will require you to confirm (Y) or deny (N) each file for deletion. It is usually unnecessary to do this, however, since most users have the intelligence to delete only those files they wish to have disappear. But it is not a bad idea for the novice VMS user!

Another example using the * wildcard is

```
$ PRINT *.FOR
```

It will print the latest version of all files of type .FOR. To print all versions, type an asterisk in the version number portion of the filespec:

```
$ PRINT *.FOR;*
```

The previous example is also equivalent to the following command without the last asterisk:

```
$ PRINT *.FOR;
```

You can reference a group of files with names that begin or end with the same group of characters using the asterisk as a positional wildcard. For example,

```
$ PRINT BODY*.DAT
```

will cause the data files BODYTUBE.DAT, BODYTRANSITION.DAT and BODYMASS.DAT to be printed.

The Percent (%) Wildcard

The percent (%) wildcard is even more selective than the * one. Use % when you wish to specify files with different characters in a single position. Multiple % wildcards can be used when specifying more than one character. Using the PRINT example above with four % wildcards gives

```
$ PRINT BODY%%%%.DAT
```

In this case you will be printing the files BODYTUBE.DAT and BODYMASS.DAT, since both of them have exactly four characters following BODY in the file name. When you use the % wildcard, only files having names that exactly match both the placement and number of % symbols will be printed.

The % wildcard, like the * wildcard, can only be used with file specifications and is not permitted in node, device, and directory specifications.

The Ellipsis Wildcard

The ellipsis [...] wildcard is used in a similar manner to other wildcards, but it applies only to the directory specification in the filespec and is not permitted in the node, device or file name fields. The ellipsis refers to the entire tree of subdirectories lying beneath the directory otherwise indicated in the command. For example, if you wish to print a complete listing of all .FOR source code files in the ROCKETSIM group directory, you would set your default directory to the root directory for the project and type

```
$ PRINT [...]*.FOR
```

The ellipsis wildcard is also useful for search operations using the SEARCH facility. Say, for example, you wish to find all instances in your FORTRAN source code of a call to the subroutine MOMENTS. You would set your default to the root directory and type

```
$ SEARCH [...]*.FOR "CALL MOMENTS"
```

VMS will respond with a complete listing of all string matches in each file found throughout all your source files.

CUSTOMIZING THE DIRECTORY COMMAND

The behavior of the DIRECTORY command can be customized to your needs. If you don't funish any command qualifiers, it produces a very plain display of the filenames found in your current directory. One way to alter the default behavior of the command is to specify some other directory you wish to list. For example,

```
$ DIR [ROOTDIR.DIR.SUBDIR]
```

will cause VMS to list the contents of the named directory, formatted exactly as if you had set your default as that directory. Your default directory setting will not be altered by this command.

Directory Command Qualifiers

Command qualifiers modify the behavior of DIRECTORY in other ways. For example, if you would like to see additional information about the files you are listing (sometimes the names don't tell you enough), add one or more qualifiers to the command to allow the display of more data.

The command

```
$ DIR/SIZE/DATE/OWNER/PROTECTION
```

will list the files in your default directory and tell you the size of the file in blocks, the date of creation, the owner or creator's name, and the file access protection restrictions on that file's use.

The information displayed with this command can get a bit overwhelming, so if the file names begin to spill over and cause the display to wrap around and become unreadable, add the /WIDTH qualifier like this:

```
$ DIR/SIZE/DATE/OWNER/PROTECTION/WIDTH=(FILENAME=15)
```

Now you've limited those overgrown file names to 15 characters of display space. Any file names that exceed that limit will be truncated on the display from the right end of the file specification. This does not affect the actual file names, only the way they are displayed by VMS.

Finally, if you want a copy of the listing to print or view at some later date, add another qualifier to the list as follows:

```
$ DIR/SIZ/DAT/OWN/PRO/OUTPUT=MYFILE.TXT
```

The /OUTPUT qualifier will send the output from the DIRECTORY command to the file MYFILE.TXT. Now you can look at the file listing anytime you want by using the TYPE or PRINT command.

Incidentally, you may have noticed the use of abbreviations on the qualifiers in the examples you've seen. Remember that VMS usually knows what you want from just the first three letters of a DCL command. The same rule applies to qualifiers. If your qualifier is an exception to the rule, DCL will inform you with one of those frustrating little error messages. No matter what, it never hurts to try to get away with less typing.

Other qualifiers to the DIRECTORY command are in the summary at the end of this chapter and in the DCL reference in Appendix B.

FILE NAMES

File names have the same limitations as directory names in terms of length and keyboard characters allowed. The file name can be anywhere from 0 to 39 characters in length and can be comprised of any of the alphabetic characters, numbers from 0 to 9, and the dollar sign ($), underscore (_), and hyphen (-) characters. Don't use the hyphen as the first or last character in the file name, though. File names containing other characters will produce an error message.

Uniqueness Requirements

All file names in VMS must be unique. Two files in your default directory with the same file name and type specifiers can, for example, have different version numbers in order to maintain this uniqueness.

You will be reminded of this by VMS if you try to get the uniqueness requirement. VMS issues a warning message when you attempt to create a file with the same name as another file in your current default directory.

FILE TYPES

The file type is an optional parameter. It can serve one or both of the following purposes:

- as a code to identify the contents of a file, often differentiating the file from other related files with the same file names

- as a way to identify the file type for DCL or VMS operations, such as identifying source code files used by a particular language compiler.

As an example of the first purpose, you may be running a series of test cases for a program you are developing. You might want to name your files something that will be meaningful to you and remind you what the particular case is that you are testing.

The second use, to identify file types, provides an additional level of organization in the VMS file management scheme – which may not be fully appreciated until you've had to work on a system without this feature!

A first case file name for your input values might be CASE1.INPUT. You might name your outputs according to what you wish to do with them next..

One technique for using this feature is to use descriptive types such as these:

- CASE1.TABLE

- CASE1.PLOT

- CASE1.DUMP

These file types might represent a line printer table output, a plot file for a laser printer, and a dump of intermediate values to use for debugging the program, respectively. Your names, of course, will depend on your particular application.

Default File Types

With many DCL commands you can omit the file type specifier if you use DCL's default values for the file type. Defaults are available for certain DCL command inputs and outputs, such as .COM for a DCL executable command procedure file, .DAT for a data file, .EDT for an EDT editor command file, and .EXE representing an executable image file.

A complete table of default file types is given in the summary at the end of this chapter.

BASIC FILE MANIPULATION COMMANDS

You're now ready for some of the basics in file manipulation. The default behavior of several commands is mentioned below, along with some of the modifications to the default behavior that can be accomplished through the use of qualifiers.

For further information on the range and behavior of the file manipulation commands, consult the summary at the end of this chapter, Appendix B of this book, and DEC's documentation. Excellent command summaries can be found in the *DCL Dictionary* (best), the *General User's Manual* (almost as good) and the *Mini-Reference* (brief).

Creating Files

Files can be created using any of the VMS text editors. Beginners usually start with EDT, since it's the one you get when you type EDIT. The text file is created when you end the edit session by typing the EXIT command. Files are also created through the use of the COPY or BACKUP commands. There are other ways to create files as well, such as by writing to them with an executable program. These methods are beyond the scope of this book.

Modifying Files

Files are usually modified using the same procedure with the editor as that used for creating the file. When EXITing the editor, a new file is created with the same name and a version number one larger than the version being modified.

Copying Files

Creating duplicates of a file is generally accomplished with either the COPY command or the BACKUP facility. BACKUP is covered in some detail in Chapter 11.

The use of COPY is fairly straightforward. The command

```
$ COPY source-filespec destination-filespec
```

creates a duplicate of the file named by the first argument and names it as specified by the second argument.

As mentioned in Chapter 3, VMS will prompt for required arguments that are omitted as follows:

```
$ COPY
$    FROM:        (Name of the source file)
$    TO:          (Name of the destination file)
```

In this case, if both the parameters are missing, VMS will prompt for both. If only the destination file name is missing, it will request only that file name.

If you COPY a file TO a file name that is already in use, VMS will use that name, giving the new file a higher version number, provided that you have the requisite WRITE privileges in the destination directory. For example, suppose that a file SIM_INPUT.DAT;278 already exists and you issue the command

```
$ COPY AEROBEE_350.DAT SIM_INPUT.DAT
```

The result will be a new version – SIM_INPUT.DAT;279. The old SIM_INPUT.DAT;278 will be kept if the version retention count for the directory is greater than 1.

In all cases, COPY requires you to specify the full file name plus the file type or an appropriate wildcard. The default for COPY is to refer the file matching your specified file name with the highest version number. If you wish to copy an older file, you must specify not only the file name and file type but the version number as well.

COPY works within a single directory without using any special directory specifications, across different directories if the full directory/file specification is used, from one disk to another, and even from one node to another across networks. All you have to do is to specify the destination file completely with its node and device names as well as the directory and file name specifications normally required.

Renaming Files

The RENAME command works in a similar fashion to the COPY command. The command

```
$ RENAME source-filename destination-filename
```

works by assigning a different file specification to the named file. It does not create a copy of the file.

As with COPY, RENAME causes VMS to prompt for missing information. Wildcards for RENAME also work the same way as with COPY.

To RENAME from one directory to another, you must fully specify the directories you are naming FROM and TO. If either of the directories you specify doesn't exist,

RENAME will generate an error message. RENAME will not create a directory for the destination file; you must use CREATE for that.

RENAME works within your default directory and across directories on a single device, but it does not work from one device to another, since that would require copying the file to another device rather than just changing a name in the directory tree. To rename across devices, you must use COPY or BACKUP to cause the file to be written to the new device and delete your original file if it is no longer wanted. COPY works best for device-to-device renaming of files that require ready access. BACKUP works best for writing to magnetic or other archival storage media since it creates files that require less storage space.

Deleting Files

The normal way of deleting files is through the aptly named DELETE command. You've seen some instructions about DELETE in the section about wildcards. Here you will learn more about its use and operation.

To delete a particular file, you simply type

```
$ DELETE filespec
```

where filespec is any valid DCL file identifier that includes the file version number. Unlike other commands such as COPY and RENAME, DELETE *requires* the version number (or wildcard in its place) and will not perform its operation unless the version number is furnished. The following command is okay and will be accepted by DCL (note that you don't have to type semicolons in the filespec before the version number; periods will also work):

```
$ DELETE integrator.for.*
```

but DCL will refuse the following:

```
$ DELETE integrator.for
```

The purpose of this seemingly strange restriction is to avoid accidental deletion of file versions that you'd really rather keep. Nonetheless, the DELETE command is very powerful and can get you into hot soup if you're not careful. For example, the following will delete *all* files in a given directory:

```
$ DELETE [VAXPROJ]*.*.*
```

On a VAX, unlike on some other machines, once a file is deleted it's almost always absolutely gone. Only in very special circumstances is it possible for your local

VAX/VMS wizard to recover a deleted file. If your system administrator has erase-on-delete set as a security option, not even a wizard can restore a deleted file. Be careful when deleting. When in doubt, make sure that a backup copy of the file exists some-where.

You can selectively delete only the latest version of a file by using a semicolon in place of the file extension.

```
$DELETE database.c;
```

This command will delete the most recent version of the file and leave any previous generations intact. For instance, if you had the files

```
DATABASE.C;3
DATABASE.C;2
DATABASE.C;1
```

and issued the above DELETE command, DATABASE.C;3 would be deleted and you would have these files remaining:

```
DATABASE.C;2
DATABASE.C;1
```

Displaying File Contents

To display the contents of a file, your choices are to use an editor, to send the file to an available printer, or to use the TYPE command to display the file on the terminal screen. In fact, if you are feeling like being perversely difficult, you can even COPY the file to your terminal screen.

The syntax of the TYPE command is

```
$ TYPE filename.type
```

Wildcards work on the TYPE command, but you probably don't want to use them here since you could inadvertently direct lots of output to your screen. TYPE only scans files in one direction; you can't back up once something has gone by. An editor will be much more convenient for viewing a lot of files. If you get a near-endless TYPE going, you can abort it by typing CTRL/C.

TYPE causes the file's contents to scroll by very rapidly on the screen. Since you probably can't read quite that fast, you can use the CTRL/S key combination to freeze the scrolling and the CTRL/Q key combination to resume scrolling. On many terminal keyboards, like the VT220, you can use the HOLD SCREEN button. This button acts like a *toggle* – press it to stop the scrolling, and press it again to start it.

In the same manner as with other DCL commands, the default behavior for TYPE is to display the latest version of the specified file from your default directory on your terminal. To modify this behavior, add the appropriate parameters to the file specification as follows:

```
$ TYPE [.ANOTHER_DIR]filename.type;3
```

This command will type version 3 of the specified file from the ANOTHER_DIR subdirectory.

Printing Files

For those occasions when nothing but a printed copy of your file will do, you will need to use the PRINT command to send your output to some hardcopy device. Printing is easy if your system manager has set up the appropriate defaults; it's still not bad if your system manager leaves everything to you to figure out.

The general command syntax for PRINT is

```
$ PRINT filespec
```

This command will send your file to the print queue specified by your setting for the SYS$PRINT queue. Usually, this is a line or laser printer.

If the bare-bones PRINT command does not produce any output on a device near you, there's probably no default set, and you will need to specify the print queue the system should use as follows:

```
$ PRINT/QUEUE=LA100 file-specification
```

where LA100 is the usual specifier for a line printer.
If you do not know what the printer queues are, type

```
$ SHOW QUEUE
```

The SHOW QUEUE command will display all printer and batch queues available, their names, and any PRINT or BATCH jobs in process.

To see what the default is for the SYS$PRINT queue, type

```
$ SHOW TRANSLATION SYS$PRINT
```

This will give you the translation of the logical name SYS$PRINT. To learn more about this command, see Chapter 7, Logical Names.

You can omit the file type specifier if it is the default .LIS (this also works for the TYPE command). Only the latest version will be printed unless you specify otherwise by indicating either the specific version number or use a wildcard to print all files with the same name or type.

You can get fancy with the PRINT command, just like with any of the other DCL commands, through the use of qualifiers. For example, the command

```
$ PRINT/HEADER filespec
```

will add a header made up of the full file specification, creation date, and page number to the printed listing.

```
$ PRINT/AFTER=time filespec
```

will hold the print job until whatever time you specify. Be careful that you don't delete the file between the time you issue the command and the time you specify for printing or you will have a disappointing result – your file will not be printed. Lastly, the command

```
$ PRINT/COPIES=number file-specification
```

will produce any number of copies of the file that you specify. The default is one copy.

At most installations, you will find that there's a variety of different printers in use. System managers will normally set up some system-wide symbols or .COM files that are tailored to the specific printing environment. Actually using the DCL PRINT command may therefore be something of a rarity for you. For example, PRLASER can be defined to print in a standard 80-column format on a system laser printer and PRWIDE can be defined to print in 132-column wide format on the same printer.

Purging Files

After a while, you will find you have large numbers of out-of-date or otherwise unnecessary files. To get rid of them, you need some familiarity with the PURGE command. PURGE eliminates all but the latest version or versions of a file. To purge your default directory, the standard syntax is simply

```
$ PURGE
```

This command will delete all files with the same file specification except those with the highest version number. In other words, the default filespec for the PURGE command is *.*.

The command

```
$ PURGE/BEFORE=time
```

will delete all files with the same file specification created before a time you specify, saving only the most recent version(s) or the highest version number.

By using a couple of extra qualifiers, the command

```
$ PURGE/KEEP=number/EXCLUDE=file-specification
```

will keep the specified number of generations of files and exclude (i.e., skip the purging of) all files matching the file specification. Wildcards are allowed in the exclude file specification.

The command

```
$ PURGE/LOG
```

will behave in the same manner as the default, as well as display an informational message containing the complete file specification for each file deleted by this command, and the total number of blocks of disk space cleared by the purge.

Your system manager will usually define some default behavior for PURGE, such as a limit on the number of files you will keep. Barring that, the default behavior is to keep only the highest version number.

Editing Files

The use of the VMS editors is beyond the scope of this book. You will find useful information about the available editors in DEC's documentation set, specifically the VMS *General User's Manual* and the TPU and EVE *User's Manuals*.

The long-standing full-screen editor EDT is no longer supported by DEC. Moreover, with EDT you have display access to only one edit buffer at a time. Replacing the old EDT is a TPU emulation of EDT, accessible when you type EDIT/EDT or just EDIT.

The EDT emulation is a pretty good beginner's editor, supporting the usual terminal screen capability. For full-screen editing with multiple file and file buffer display capability, take the time to learn the TPU and the new (Version 5.0) EVE editor by going through your base documentation set.

Default File Types

Some of the most common default file types are shown in Table 4.3.

TABLE 4-3. Default File Types.

File Type	Description
.ADA	Ada compiler source file
.BAS	BASIC compiler source file
.B32	BLISS-32 compiler source file
.C	C compiler source file
.CLD	DCL command description file
.COB	COBOL compiler source file
.COM	User-written command procedure file
.DAT	User- or system- generated data file
.DIS	User- or system- generated distribution list file for the MAIL command
.DIR	Directory file
.EDT	Command file for the EDT editor
.EXE	Executable image file created by the VMS linker
.FOR	FORTRAN compiler source file
.HLP	Source file for HELP libraries
.JOU	Journal file created by the EDT editor upon an unnatural EDT session termination
.LIS	System listing file created by a VMS language compiler or assembler; also default file type used for the PRINT and TYPE commands
.LOG	Batch job output log file
.MAI	MAIL message file
.MAR	MACRO compiler source file
.MEM	Digital Standard Runoff (DSR) output file
.OBJ	Object code file created by a VMS language compiler or assembler
.RNO	Source file for DSR
.PAS	Pascal compiler source file
.PLI	PL/I compiler source file
.SIXEL	Sixel graphic file
.SYS	System image file
.TJL	Journal file created by the VAXTPU and ACL editors upon an unnatural edit session termination
.TMP	System-created temporary file
.TPU	VAXTPU editor command file
.TXT	Text library input file or MAIL command output file

THE BASICS OF DIRECTORY AND FILE PROTECTION

Traditionally, DCL file protection has been described via the System, Owner, Group, World scheme, which establishes four categories for access to a particular file. Each category of user can be assigned Read, Write, Execute, and/or Delete (RWED) access separately. This is useful for simple security functions such as giving members of a project group read-only access to a set of project files while denying any access to unaffiliated users. But it doesn't provide the flexibility of access control demanded by sensitive financial and government applications.

The second form of DCL protection and access control is called the Access Control List, or ACL. ACLs are more cumbersome to use than the traditional system, but they allow the granting or denial of specific access on a per-user basis. Fortunately, DEC has provided a utility called the ACL Editor that simplifies the job of creating and maintaining ACLs.

To view any ACLs on your files or directories, use the DIRECTORY/ACL switch. Enabling the use of ACLs adds considerable system overhead and is therefore disabled at many installations. The use of ACLs is an advanced topic and is treated later on in this book.

The ordinary protection attributes of a file or directory are controlled via the SET PROTECTION command and can be examined through the DIREC-TORY/PROTECTION command. For example, if you want to provide members of your group with read-only access to a certain file in your personal directory, you might type something resembling

```
$ SET PROTECTION=(GROUP:R) [MYDIR]INERTIA.C
```

Of course, some combinations of protection codes don't make much sense. One example would be giving (WORLD:D) access to some file – it's kind of silly to let people delete files they can't even read first. But this would support the famous spy spoof Destroy Before Reading messages.

A sometimes overlooked fact is that in order for someone else to read your file, both the file and the directory containing the file must be set to permit that person access. If the protection codes for MYDIR.DIR permit no GROUP access, the above command typed by you will not work.

It's also important to know that if an ACL exists for a given entity (file, directory, etc.) the ACL overrides all traditional file protection/access specifiers. The easy way to find out if an ACL exists for a given file is to use the DIRECTORY /SECURITY command; for example, type

```
$ DIR/SECURITY [ROCKETSIM]*.FOR
```

This will show both the ordinary protection attributes plus any ACLs for the specified files.

Be aware of the fact that DIR/PROTECTION does *not* display ACLs. If you're having unwarranted trouble deleting a file, check to see whether an ACL has been attached. Methods for doing this are covered in the advanced chapters toward the end of this book.

CREATING AND DELETING DIRECTORIES

You've read a lot about navigating through the VMS directory trees. Now it's time to learn how to create and delete directories at will.

Creating Directories

Creating a directory is really no problem. In order to do it, set your default directory to the level above the desired new directory location, then type

```
$ CREATE/DIRECTORY [.DIRECTORY_NAME]
```

To see if the command worked, list the directory. Once you know it exists, you can set your default to the new directory and then go on your way to create or copy files. Note that you must have WRITE access in the directory under which the new directory is to be created; this is because CREATE/DIR will create a directory file in the current default directory.

Deleting Directories

Deleting a directory can be a bit more troublesome than creating one. To kill a directory, follow these steps:
1. Set your default to the directory you wish to delete:

```
$ SET DEF [.MYDIR]
```

2. Delete all of the files in that directory, or copy or rename them to another directory:

```
$ DELETE/LOG *.*;*
```

3. Set the default directory to one level above the one you wish to delete:

```
$ SET DEF [-]
```

4. Change the file protection for that directory to allow the delete privilege:

```
$ SET PROTECTION=OWNER:D MYDIR.DIR
```

5. Delete the directory:

```
$ DELETE MYDIR.DIR;
```

If you do not follow these steps, you will be likely to get a DCL error message such as

```
%DCL-F-INSPRIV - insufficient privilege for attempted operation
```

If you have done all of the steps correctly and still cannot delete your directory, call the system administrator. This is one of those occasions for which you have cultivated your friendly relationship with the system manager. You may not have sufficient privileges granted to you to delete your own directories. If your accounts are arranged in project groups and others have write privileges in your directories, the owner may be another person, not you, and you would not be able to delete the directory without special permission that only the system administrator has.

If all else fails or you do not have a system administrator, consult your manual. In the interim, you can rename your directory to some other location just to get rid of it. One of trick with a hard-to-kill directory is to rename it to the root directory using JUNK.DIR as the name. Then at least the doomed files are easy to identify when help finally arrives.

HOW TO DETERMINE STORAGE SPACE AVAILABLE

If you are running into storage space problems with your files, you can easily find out how much space is available both to you personally and to the entire system.

To display the attributes of the disk storage media, type

```
$ SHOW DEVICE D
```

This command will display the names of the drives whose device names begin with D (this includes most disk drives) and are connected to the system you are using.

Disk Quotas

Sometimes system managers will attempt to control the use of the disk storage media by establishing quotas for each user. These quotas don't have to add up to the total space available. Quotas work the way you might expect – you can't occupy more than your quota of disk space.

If you would like to see how much space has been allocated for your use, type

```
$ .i.SHOW QUOTA;
```

This command will either tell you how much space has been allocated to you on your current default device or will say that quotas are not in use.

To see quotas on other devices, just add the device specification to the command.

```
$ SHOW QUOTA DEVICE_NAME:
```

You don't really need the colon at the end of the device name specification. But it can remind you that you are referring to a device name.

If you find that you are well within your quota of storage space and the device is still filled, you will have to convince your system manager to clear some disk space for you.

SUMMARY

This chapter has covered the mechanics of basic file and directory manipulation with DCL. In the summary we now provide a table of default file types for various purposes and a more complete syntax for all of the DCL commands covered in the chapter.

Directory and File-Handling Commands

The following is a summary of the directory and file-handling commands introduced in this chapter, along with all of the command and positional qualifiers and their defaults.

COPY input-filespec[,...] output-filespec
Copy files anywhere in a system except onto magnetic tape.
Command Qualifiers
/BACKUP, /BEFORE=time, /BY_OWNER, /[NO]CONCATENATE,
/[NO]CONFIRM, /CREATED, /EXCLUDE=(filespec[,...]), /EXPIRED,
/[NO]LOG, /MODIFIED, /SINCE[=time]
Command Qualifier Defaults
/CREATED, /BEFORE=TODAY, /CONCATENATE, /NOCONFIRM, /NOLOG,
/SINCE=TODAY
Positional Qualifiers
/ALLOCATION=n, /[NO]CONTIGUOUS, /EXTENSION=n, /[NO]OVERLAY,
/PROTECTION=(code), /[NO]READ_CHECK, /[NO]REPLACE,
/[NO]TRUNCATE, /VOLUME=n, /[NO]WRITE_CHECK
Positional Qualifier Defaults
/NOOVERLAY, /NOREAD_CHECK, /NOREPLACE, /NOTRUNCATE,
/NOWRITE_CHECK

CREATE/DIRECTORY directory-spec[,...]
Used to create a new directory.
Command Qualifiers
/[NO]LOG, /OWNER_UIC[=option], /PROTECTION, /VERSION_LIMIT=n,
/VOLUME=n

Defaults
/NOLOG

DELETE filespec[,....]
Deletes any file(s) you have delete privileges to.
Command Qualifiers
/BACKUP, /BEFORE[=time], /BY_OWNER[=uic], /[NO]CONFIRM,
/CREATED, /[NO]ERASE, /EXCLUDE=(filespec[...]), /EXPIRED,
/[NO]LOG, /MODIFIED, /SINCE[=time]
Command Qualifier Defaults
/CREATED, /BEFORE=TODAY, /NOCONFIRM, /NOERASE, /NOLOG,
/SINCE=TODAY

DIRECTORY   [filespec[,...]]
Displays a listing of files in any number of directories any-
where you have read privileges.
Command Qualifiers
/ACL, /BACKUP, /BEFORE[=time], /BRIEF, /BY_OWNER, /COLUMNS=n,
/CREATED, /[NO]DATE[=option], /EXCLUDE=(filespec[,...]),
/EXPIRED, /FILE_ID, /FULL, /GRAND_TOTAL, /[NO]HEADING,
/MODIFIED, /[NO]OUTPUT=filespec, /[NO]OWNER, /PRINTER,
/[NO]PROTECTION, /SECURITY, /SELECT=(keyword[,...]),
/SINCE[=time], /[NO]SIZE[=option], /TOTAL, /[NO]TRAILING,
/VERSIONS=n, /WIDTH=(keyword[,...])
Command Qualifier Defaults
/CREATED, /BEFORE=TODAY, /BRIEF, /COLUMNS=4, /NODATE, /HEADING,
/OUTPUT=SYS$OUTPUT, /NOOWNER, /NOPROTECTION, /SINCE=TODAY,
/NOSIZE, /TRAILING

PRINT filespec[,...]
Prints a paper copy of the contents of your file(s).
Command Qualifiers
/AFTER=time, /[NO]BACKUP, /[NO]BEFORE[=time],
/[NO]BY_OWNER[=uic], /CHARACTERISTICS=(characteristic[,...]),
/[NO]CONFIRM, /[NO]CREATED, /DEVICE=queue-name[:],
/[NO]EXCLUDE=(filespec[,...]), /[NO]EXPIRED, /FORM=type,
/[NO]HOLD, /[NO]IDENTIFY, /JOB_COUNT=n, /[NO]LOWERCASE,
/[NO]MODIFIED, /NAME=job-name, /NOTE=string, /[NO]NOTIFY,
/OPERATOR=string, /PARAMETERS=(parameter[,...]), /PRIORITY=n,
/QUEUE=queue-name[:], /REMOTE, /[NO]RESTART, /[NO]SINCE[=time],
/USER=username

Command Qualifier Defaults

/NOAFTER, /CREATED, /BEFORE=TODAY, /NOCONFIRM,
/DEVICE=SYS$PRINT, /FORM=0, /NOHOLD, /IDENTIFY, /JOB_COUNT=1,
/NOLOWERCASE, /NONOTIFY, /SINCE=TODAY

Positional Qualifiers

/[NO]BURST[=keyword], /COPIES=n, /[NO]DELETE, /[NO]FEED,
/[NO]FLAG[=keyword], /[NO]HEADER, /PAGES=([lowlim,]uplim),
/[NO]PASSALL, /SETUP=module[,...], /[NO]SPACE,
/[NO]TRAILER[=keyword], /BACKUP, /BEFORE[=time],
/BY_OWNER[=uic], /[NO]CONFIRM, /CREATED, /[NO]ERASE,
/EXCLUDE=(filespec[,...]), /EXPIRED, /KEEP=n, /[NO]LOG,
/MODIFIED, /SINCE[=time]

Positional Qualifier Defaults

/COPIES=1, /NODELETE, /FEED, /NOHEADER, /NOPASSALL, /NOSPACE,
/CREATED, /BEFORE=TODAY, /NOCONFIRM, /NOERASE, /KEEP=1, /NOLOG,
/SINCE=TODAY

RENAME input-filespec[,...] output-filespec[,...]

Rename any number of files or directories to any other device
except a magnetic tape device.

Command Qualifiers

/BACKUP, /BEFORE[=time], /BY_OWNER[=uic], /[NO]CONFIRM,
/CREATED, /EXCLUDE=(filespec[,...]), /EXPIRED, /[NO]LOG,
/MODIFIED, /[NO]NEW_VERSION, /SINCE[=time]

Command Qualifier Defaults

/CREATED, /BEFORE=TODAY, /NOCONFIRM, /NOLOG, /NEW_VERSION,
/SINCE=TODAY

SET PROTECTION [=(code)] filespec[,...]

Sets file or directory protection.

TYPE filespec[,...]

Display the contents of one or more files.

Command Qualifiers

/BACKUP, /BEFORE[=time], /BY_OWNER[=uic], /[NO]CONFIRM,
/CREATED, /EXCLUDE=(filespec[,...]), /EXPIRED, /MODIFIED,
/[NO]OUTPUT=filespec, /[NO]PAGE, /SINCE[=time]

Command Qualifier Defaults

/CREATED, /BEFORE=TODAY, /NOCONFIRM, /OUTPUT=SYS$OUTPUT,
/NOPAGE, /SINCE=TODAY

5
Using Symbols

WHAT ARE SYMBOLS?

Symbols are a central feature of the VAX DCL command language. Although all symbols are handled alike by the DCL interpreter, their uses tend to fall into two major categories: command abbreviations and computational variables.

You can define your own symbols as abbreviations for other DCL commands or parts of commands. This use of a symbol can be thought of as causing a text substitution; it is sometimes called a macro function. Text symbols are extremely useful for shortening frequently used commands and will save you a great deal of typing.

The second use of symbols is more complex. It is as general-purpose variables that can hold either numeric or string data items. This feature enables DCL to perform calculations when needed and is responsible for giving DCL its characteristic programming language flavor and flexibility. Having a good understanding of this use of symbols is essential to writing effective DCL programs.

Symbol Attributes

A VMS DCL symbol is a data item having the following attributes:

Name – what the symbol is known by to the system and to the user.

Type – Determines whether the symbol contains a text string or a number.

Value – Holds the string or numeric value that the symbol is replaced by when it occurs in a DCL command.

Scope – Determines whether the symbol is global or local, that is, whether it's known outside the currently executing DCL context.

Using Symbols to Reduce Typing

Consider first the ubiquitous SET DEFAULT command. Suppose you are working on a project that frequently requires you to access files in a directory called

```
$DUA0:[FINANCE.PLAN]
```

In order to go to this directory from an arbitrary place in the VAX file structure, you
could type

```
SET DEFAULT $DUA0:[FINANCE.PLAN]
```

If you studied Chapter 4 on DCL concepts carefully, you'll realize that DCL will
permit you to shorten that command a bit by typing the unique command SET DEF.
The entire command would then be shortened to

```
SET DEF $DISK1:[FINANCE.PLAN]
```

This, however, is as far as you can get in plain vanilla DCL without invoking either a symbol or a logical name (logical names are introduced in Chapter 7). Symbols
were developed for DCL to enable users to set up abbreviations for virtually any command procedure or operation.

SYMBOL ASSIGNMENT OPERATORS

A symbol is defined using the =, ==, := or :== assignment operators and has one
of the following forms:

```
$ SYM =[=] "alpha" or numeric expression
$ SYM :=[=] "string expression"
```

where the left hand side of the expression is the symbol name and the right hand side is
the replacement or equivalent value for the name.

When DCL translates a symbol (left-hand side of the equation), it looks in the
appropriate symbol table and replaces your typed symbol with the expression it
represents (right-hand side). The selected operator defines the type of expression and
the scope of the symbol's effect.

Symbol Assignment Operator

The first form of symbol assignment operator (= or ==) works for either a literal (i.e., a quoted) alphabetic character string or a numeric expression.

The form

```
$ SYM =[=] "alpha" or numeric expression
```

defines a symbolic name for either a character string or an integer value. For this symbol assignment, using the single = creates a temporary, or *local*, symbol definition. This operator causes the symbol definition to be stored only with the currently executing DCL process. When the process terminates (e.g., when the defining .COM file ends), the symbol definition is deleted.

Using the double == causes the symbol to be entered as a *global* symbol, which remains in effect for your entire session or until you either log out or explicitly redefine or delete the symbol. Figure 5-1 illustrates the relationship between local and global symbols and those of parent processes to the process you are currently running.

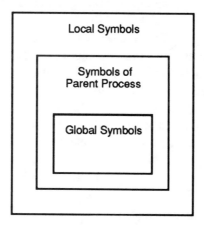

FIGURE 5-1.   The interrelationship of local, process and global symbols.

Both the symbol name and the expression can be 1- to 255-character alphanumeric strings. The expression can consist of any character, numeric, or alphanumeric string, including punctuation marks and blanks. All character strings must, however, be enclosed in quotation marks. In addition, if the expression contains an embedded symbol, that symbol's value will be translated at the time the symbol is used, unless it is embedded in a quoted string.

The symbol name can also contain any alphanumeric character combination, but it *must* begin with an alphabetic character, a dollar sign, or an underscore.

It is very important to observe that the type of the symbol is determined solely by the type of the expression on the right-hand side of the definition. If the right-hand side expression evaluates to a character string, then the symbol is of string type. If the right-hand side expression evaluates to a numeric value, the symbol has numeric type. Character string symbol values must be surrounded by double quotes.

String Symbol Assigment Operator

The second type of symbol assignment operator performs a string symbol assignment

```
$ SYM :=[=] string-expression
```

This assignment is used for string symbols only and has a few unique properties not belonging to the first assignment type. The single := defines a local process symbol, and the double :== defines a global process symbol having the same effects for definition of local and global process symbols as the previous type (= and ==). The symbol name is restricted, as always, to strings beginning with alphabetic characters, an underscore, or a dollar sign.

The difference between the first and second kinds of symbol assignment is essentially that the second form assumes that the expression being assigned is a character string, which is not quoted and can contain spaces or tabs. By default, string values are automatically converted to uppercase with leading and trailing white-space characters such as blanks and tabs removed. Each embedded consecutive white-space character is compressed to a single blank space.

As an example, consider the symbol assignment

```
$ LAMBS :=   Mary had   a    little    lamb!
```

The symbol LAMBS will now have the value

```
MARY HAD A LITTLE LAMB!
```

If these side effects are not desired, the uppercase conversion and compression of white space characters can be suppressed by enclosing the string in quotation marks.

WHAT HAPPENS DURING COMMAND PROCESSING

To better understand the use of symbols, it is important to understand the sequence of activities that take place when a DCL command is processed by VMS.

This is the order of events during symbol translation processing:

1. Symbol substitution – Symbol substitution takes place repeatedly until there are no more symbols to be replaced by their defined text.

2. Check validity of command verb – The command verb (the first word on the command line) is checked for validity. If it is a built-in DCL command, processing continues normally. If the verb is ambiguous or does not match any existing command, an error message is given.

3. Interpretation of the command verb – If the verb begins with @, it is interpreted as the name of a DCL command file to execute. DCL searches for the specified file (having a default extension of .COM if none is specified) and, if found, processes it. If the command file cannot be found in the current default directory, an error message is displayed.

4. Set up default parameters and qualifiers – Processing of normal DCL commands continues by setting up all the parameters and qualifiers with their default values. The remainder of the command line is then scanned by the DCL processor. All specified parameters and qualifiers are read in and will override the defaults.

5. Check commands for restrictions – Some commands have constraints on certain combinations of qualifiers, ranges of parameters, and so on. These restrictions are now checked, and any irregularities are reported to the user.

6. Execute the command – The completely analyzed command line is now executed. Results from the command are sent back to the user on the terminal.

USING GLOBAL SYMBOLS

Returning to the earlier SET DEFAULT example, an obvious shortcut might be to define a global symbol abbreviation for SET DEFAULT, which can be done as follows using a string-valued symbol:

```
$ SD :== SET DEFAULT
```

After entering the above command at any DCL prompt or within any command file, you can reduce a command such as

```
$ SET DEFAULT $DISK1
```

to

```
$ SD $DISK1:[FINANCE.PLAN]
```

Of course, this isn't terribly short yet, but defining SD in this manner has the advantage of creating a general-purpose command abbreviation that can be used anywhere it would be correct to type SET DEFAULT. Nearly every serious VAX user has some kind of abbreviation symbol for SET DEFAULT.

The same example can be shortened much further by defining a more specialized symbol by typing

```
$ PLAN :== SET DEFAULT $DISK1:[FINANCE.PLAN]
```

You can now set your default to the given directory merely by typing PLAN at the DCL prompt. This kind of symbol definition is very popular among users who must work with a large number of directories or who must change default directories often. Normally these directory symbol definitions are created as global symbols in a LOGIN.COM file, where they will be automatically activated every time you log in. Unless you need some intermediate symbol value for use within the LOGIN.COM command file, you'll want to make all symbols defined in LOGIN.COM global symbols since local symbols are destroyed when LOGIN.COM finishes.

Controlling Symbol Uniqueness Recognition

Symbols can be further shortened by using the asterisk (*) operator in their definition, which tells DCL that it need only scan a certain distance through the symbol before recognizing it as unique and rejecting other possibilities. A simple example of how this works is

```
$ TI*ME == "SHOW TIME"
$ TIMERS == "SET DEFAULT [SOURCECODE.TIMERS]"
```

In this case, the symbol for SHOW TIME will be recognized whenever the first two characters are typed. Other possibilities will not be considered when the input matches TI exactly, unless you define another symbol with the same beginning characters and an asterisk.

Using Symbols to Modify DCL Command Behavior

A common use of symbols is to redefine a normal command always to use certain options or switches, thereby modifying the default behavior of the command. Some of these redefinitions are practically standards in their own right. For example nearly all VAX FORTRAN programmers have used something like

```
$ F*ORTRAN == "FORTRAN/CONTIN=99"
```

in LOGIN.COM in order to bypass the usual FORTRAN limit of 19 continuation lines in a source statement. This lets the keystroke-conscious programmer type

```
$ F DIFEQ
```

to compile the program file DIFEQ.FOR with the 99 continuation line option. (Purists and other prudent programmers should note that the indiscriminate use of such options limits source file portability from one compiler to another.)

A more elaborate set of defaults often applied to the DIRECTORY command has a rich set of switches including width adjustment for most of the fields that can be displayed. A simple example is

```
$ DIR*ECTORY == "DIR /OWNER/PROTECTION/SIZE"
```

which will cause the results of normal DIR commands to be considerably more informative (while producing considerably more text on the screen) than the system default.

On some VAX installations such redefinitions may even be put into the system login command file as a way of promoting adherence to a system policy. One example that may sometimes be revealed by SHOW SYMBOL * is

```
$ LO*GOUT == "@SYS$MANAGER:SYLOGOUT.COM"
```

This causes the normal LOGOUT command to execute a system-defined command procedure that can perform housekeeping actions such as purging the user's directories, displaying estimated computer CPU time charges, blanking the terminal screen for security, and displaying a system logout message or bulletin. System administrators *must,* however, be aware that such system-wide symbols *do not* enforce their actions. A user can always redefine a symbol, whether it was defined by the system or not, thus defeating the intended action. The correct way to enforce specific desired actions is by using a *captive account* with the needed log-out-on-control/C and similar options activated.

NUMERIC SYMBOLS

So far in this chapter, you've seen only character-valued symbols, that is, those whose replacement value is a text string. It may come as no surprise to learn that there are also symbols whose value is some other form of data, such as a number. Such symbols are the basic variables of DCL and are often used within command procedures as counters and intermediate values. In contrast to character symbols, numeric symbols are frequently local, created with the intent of destroying them as soon as the command procedure is completed.

Numeric symbols are defined via statements like

```
$ [symbol_name] = [expression]
$ [symbol_name] == [expression]
```

Here the single and double equals sign operators carry the same meaning of local and global assignment as explained previously – the = operator creates a local symbol and the == operator produces a global symbol.

Numeric symbols are most frequently used as loop counters and to hold user-input values obtained with the INQUIRE statement. The following example shows a simple case of looping, controlled by a numeric variable. Don't worry about the location of this snippet of code, you'll get much more about command files and procedures in Chapter 6. Here's the example:

```
$!
$! Simple example of numeric symbols
$! This .COM fragment performs ten
$!   SHOW SYSTEM calls.
$!
$ loopIndex = 0
$TOP:
$         SHOW SYSTEM
$         loopIndex = loopIndex + 1
$         if loopIndex .LT. 10 then goto TOP
$!
$! End of loop
$!
```

LISTING DEFINED SYMBOLS

DCL provides a command that lists all of the symbols you have defined at the time the command is executed. It is

```
$ SHOW SYMBOL [sym-name] [switches]
```

where [sym-name] is either the name of a specific symbol or an * for all symbols, and the possible switches are as follows:

/ALL – Shows symbols from both the global and local symbol tables (default).

/GLOBAL – Shows only symbols from the global table for the current process.

/LOCAL – Shows only process-local symbols from the local symbol table.

/[NO]LOG – Controls whether or not the system will provide an informational message if the symbol's value is longer than 255 characters and must be truncated (the default is /LOG).

An example of a command file to define shortened command names for several common functions is the following:

```
$!
$! Symbols defining short commands
$!
$ sd        :== set default
$ ti*me     :== show time
$ ho*me     :== set default SYS$LOGIN
$ UP        :== set default [-]
$ DN        :== @SYS$LOGIN:DOWNDIR.COM
$ MONP      :== MONITOR PROCESS /TOPCPU
$ US        :== show users
$ SY        :== show system
$ V*DIR     == "DIRECTORY /OWN /PROTECTION /DATE=MOD"
$ F*ORTRAN  == "FORTRAN/CONTIN=99"
$ LO*GOUT   == "@SYS$LOGIN:LOGOUT.COM"
$!
$! Display a listing of global symbols
$!
$ SHOW SYMBOL * /GLOBAL
```

Note that caps and quotation marks are not needed for string symbol definitions using the :=[=] symbol assignment operators. Quotation marks are, however, required for the vanilla =[=] symbol assignment operators.

DELETING SYMBOLS

Frequently the need arises to remove an existing symbol definition. Perhaps it was mistyped, is obsolete, or is no longer needed in a command file. The DELETE/SYMBOL command will do just that. Various forms of the command permit you to delete a specific symbol or all symbols in either the local or global tables.

To get rid of a particular symbol, just type DELETE/SYMBOL followed by the name of the symbol you want to erase. For example,

```
$ DELETE/SYMBOL LAMBS
```

will remove the definition of LAMBS given in an example above.

Should you manage to create local and global symbols with the same name but different definitions, you'll want to remove one of them to avoid confusion. The /LOCAL and /GLOBAL switches let you specify which symbol table the given name should be deleted from. Thus,

```
$ DELETE /SYMBOL /GLOBAL LAMBS
```

would get rid of a global symbol named LAMBS but leave intact any local symbol named LAMBS. The default for DELETE/SYMBOL is to remove names from the local symbol table, so the /GLOBAL switch is frequently used.

To remove whole classes of symbols, use the /LOCAL or /GLOBAL qualifiers together with the /ALL switch. The following command will destroy all currently existing local symbols:

```
$ DELETE /SYMBOL /LOCAL /ALL
```

In addition, the /LOG switch is available; it causes an informational message to be displayed listing each symbol being deleted by the command.

Of course, an existing symbol definition can always be replaced by entering a new assignment for that symbol.

SYMBOLS TO EMULATE OTHER OPERATING SYSTEMS

A common use for DCL text substitution symbols is to create user-defined alternate command sets for VAX/VMS. Frequently these are borrowed nearly verbatim from other systems with which you are familiar. Examples of systems whose commands might be emulated include UNIX, MS-DOS, and RSX-11M.

The next example shows how an MS-DOS user might recreate some familiar comands in VMS:

```
$!
$! Sample MS-DOS command shell definitions
$!
$ CD == "SET DEFAULT"
$ MKDIR == "CREATE/DIRECTORY"
$ CLS == "@SYS$LOGIN:BLANK_SCREEN.COM"
$ DIR == "DIRECTORY /OWN /DATE /SIZE"
```

```
$ DATE == "SHOW DAYTIME"
$ TIME == "SHOW DAYTIME"
$ CHKDSK == "SHOW DEVICE $DISK1:"
$ RD == "@SYS$LOGIN:REMOVE_DIR.COM"
$ ATTRIB == "DIRECTORY /PROTECTION"
$!
$! Notes-
$!  You should resist any temptation to
$!  create an alias for the command "SET"!  Too
$!  many DCL commands depend on it.
$!
$!  The DEL and COPY commands have roughly the
$!       same functions in MS-DOS and VMS.
$
```

These MS-DOS command lookalikes do not work at all like their actual MS-DOS counterparts; they merely give DCL a slightly different face and help you avoid the mental hiccups that can occur when switching back and forth between operating systems.

The most important concept of this chapter is that symbols exist to make your life easier. By using them, you can create a more familiar and comfortable work environment. Symbols can also reduce typing errors and forgotten switches, such as those for the compiler or DELETE commands. The use of symbols can ease the transition from one computer to the other, such as MS-DOS to VMS or UNIX to VMS. As you gain familiarity and confidence with the use of symbols, they will save you considerable time and effort.

SUMMARY

Symbols can be used for shorthand conversion of any normal DCL programming task to improve and customize your work environment.

Symbols are defined through the use of either the =[=] or the :=[=] assignment statement.

String or Integer Symbol Assignment

The assignment statement

```
=[=] (Assignment Statement)
```

assigns a symbolic name for either a character string or an integer value. All character strings must be enclosed in quotation marks. The format for this assignment statement is

```
symbol-name =[=] expression
```

Character String Symbol Assignment

The assignment statement

```
:=[=] (Assignment Statement)
```

assigns a symbolic name for a character string. Strings with literal values must be enclosed in quotation marks. The format for this assignment statement for local symbols is

```
symbol-name = expression
```

its format for global symbols is

```
symbol-name == expression
```

Deleting Symbols

Symbols may be deleted using

```
DELETE/SYMBOL [name]
```

Qualifiers for DELETE/SYMBOL are as follows:
/LOCAL – Deletes a symbol from the local symbol table.

/GLOBAL – Deletes a symbol from the global symbol table.

/ALL – Deletes the symbol from all symbol tables.

/LOG – Prints an informational message to SYS$OUTPUT telling you which symbol(s) were deleted.

Showing Symbols

The following command can be used to display the existing values of various symbols:

SHOW   SYMBOL
/ALL
/GLOBAL
/LOCAL
/[NO]LOG

6

Command Files

USING DCL COMMAND FILES

Command files in VAX/VMS are a powerful means of automating your work. Also known as .COM files because of their standard file extension, they consist of ordinary DCL commands, which the VMS command processor generally executes in the order they are encountered.

Command files are simple text, meaning they can be read using the TYPE command, listed using the PRINT command, and created or modified with any standard VAX text editor like EDT. Comments may be imbedded within .COM files to improve their readability, and the overall impression is similar to some versions of BASIC. VMS command files are exact counterparts to UNIX shell scripts and MS-DOS batch files.

Using a DCL command file, you can perform any task you could accomplish from the $ prompt, as well as several additional jobs that cannot be directly done from the interactive prompt. DCL provides branching, label, and subroutine constructs that effectively make a full-fledged programming language available for use within command files. Some major tasks within the VAX system itself are implemented through .COM files. For example, the bulk of activity at system startup is controlled by the SYSTARTUP.COM file.

An additional bonus is that DCL command files can be SUBMITted as batch jobs that run in the background, leaving your terminal available for interactive tasks. At some installations there may be policies that require you to run long jobs in batch mode, making it well worth your while to learn the basics of command file usage.

Creating a Command File

When creating a .COM file, you have a choice of methods. The quick and dirty route is to use the CREATE command, which doesn't require learning or waiting for an editor but affords few correction features.

A simple example (which is about all the CREATE method is good for) is

```
$ CREATE TEST.COM
$SET NOVERIFY
$DIR *.TXT.*
$PURGE *.TXT
<CTRL/Z>
```

Recall that the CREATE command adds ASCII text to a file until you type CTRL/Z. When this sequence in the example is completed you will have a DCL command file called TEST.COM.

Here are a few rules for writing command procedures:

- All lines that are DCL commands must begin with a "$" in column 1.

- Data lines that are input to a program invoked by the command file (i.e. lines that are not DCL commands) must *not* contain a $ in column 1.

- The file type should be .COM. If it's not, you must enter the file type each time you run the command procedure.

- Commands and qualifiers should be spelled out completely.

Modifying Command Files

The recommended method for creating a command file is to use a regular text editor such as EDT, EMACS, or SED. Any editor or word processor capable of working with plain ASCII text files will do, but not all of these are present on all systems.

Avoid fancy word processors for command file editing since they usually are optimized for paragraph-level functions, not plain vanilla text file operations. If in doubt, ask the programmers on your system what editor they use. A good introduction to EDT, EVE and TPU editors (standard issue with VMS) can be found in DEC's *General User's Manual*, as well as in the user's manual for any editor your installation may have purchased.

Invoking Command Files

Now you are ready to invoke the test command procedure given above. Just type

```
$ @TEST
```

This will produce a listing of all your .TXT files and then purge the unwanted versions. SET NOVERIFY tells the system not to echo the command file lines as they are processed. The @ notation tells DCL that what follows is the name of a command file. Remember to always use the file type COM when naming command procedures. This practice is customary and helps others identify the purpose of the file. It also permits the file type to be omitted when you use the @ command to invoke the file.

Using Comments in Command Files

Any command procedure that is to be used more than once or that will be used by someone besides the procedure's author should be adequately documented using DCL comments. This is true for any programming language; it is axiomatic that undocumented code will nearly always be discarded rather than reused. The converse is also true; your command procedure will be much more likely to have a long life and wide use if it is succinctly documented.

Comments are added to a command procedure file using the exclamation point (!). The DCL command processor ignores everything to the right of the exclamation point on any line. A line that is pure comments or is to be blank should begin with a dollar sign ($) followed by an exclamation point (!), as in the following revised version of the test program:

```
$!
$!  TEST.COM - simple command procedure with comments
$!
$SET NOVERIFY
$DIR *.TXT.*
$PURGE *.TXT
```

DCL requires that blank lines in command files at least begin with $. A totally blank line (one without the $) is processed as a data line, which produces warning messages if a data line is not called for at that point in the procedure. For efficiency, DEC recommends the placement of the ! after the $, but this is not required by the DCL language.

The revised example illustrates a useful guideline for commenting command procedures: Always have at least one blank line above and below a block of comments. Comments with blank space around them are much more readable and lend an uncluttered look to the code.

CONDITIONAL AND BRANCHING COMMANDS; LABELS

A major difference between interactive DCL and command procedures is that the latter let you use branching constructs similar to those found in high-level programming languages. Although DCL does not provide a complete set like those found in C, DCL under VMS 5.0 has an IF-THEN-ELSE facility that is quite convenient. Figure 6-1 illustrates one method for constructing a loop within a DCL command file.

The IF...GOTO syntax enables you to simulate any other high-level mechanism including the C constructs switch(), for(), and while(). (FORTRAN equivalents of these are CASE, DO and DO WHILE).

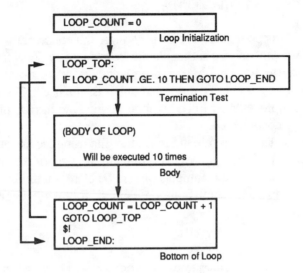

FIGURE 6-1.   A method for constructing a DCL command loop.

Before going any further, you should learn about the IF, IF-THEN-ELSE-ENDIF, and GOTO commands, plus labels. There are two forms of the IF statement – a single line version that is schematically represented by

```
$ IF <condition> THEN <single-statement>
```

and the new VMS 5.0 form that allows multiple statements to be executed upon a true condition, which looks like this:

```
$ IF <condition>
$      THEN <statements>
$           <...>
$      ELSE
$           <more statements>
$           <...>
$ ENDIF
```

The major difference between the two kinds of IF statements is that the IF-THEN-ELSE version must have the THEN keyword on a separate line after the IF line. This syntax will seem a bit unnatural to programmers, but is necessitated by the requirement that DCL be able to recognize the old-style single-line IF. (There is a fundamental rule at work here that says that you should never change the already-established syntax of a command or programming language; often it is called the rule of backward compatibility.)

An example of the first kind of DCL IF statement is

```
$IF J .GT. 5 THEN GOTO ILLEGAL_J_VALUE
```

Command Labels

Programmers will recognize the meaning of command labels right away. In order to introduce things properly, though, here is the definition of a label. A *label* is a marker in the DCL procedure that identifies a location that may be referred to by another DCL statement. Labels can appear in front of any other DCL statement, but normally they are placed on lines by themselves. The label referred to by the above statement might be defined by

```
$ILLEGAL_J_VALUE:
$!
$! The following is executed after a GOTO ILLEGAL_J_VALUE
$!
$TYPE SYS$INPUT
Error - value of J is out of bounds
$...
```

The rules for label definitions are as follows:

- Labels must be the first item on a DCL command line.

- Labels must end with a colon.

- Labels must not contain any embedded blank characters.

- Labels must not contain more than 255 characters.

- Any legal DCL statement may appear after a label on the same line.

- If a label is encountered more than once in processing a command procedure, the first instance is replaced by the second.

The GOTO command is defined by

```
$GOTO <label>
```

When DCL encounters this command, it immediately proceeds to the statement at or immediately following the specified label. Normally the GOTO command should only be used as part of the simulation of a more fundamental flow-control construct (see below). Indiscriminate GOTOs, especially the backward GOTO where the DCL inter-preter must jump upward to a previous point in the procedure logic, detract greatly from the intelligibility of a procedure and must be avoided.

The general syntax of the first (old) form of the IF command is

```
$IF <condition> THEN <DCL_command>
```

Here <condition> is a DCL expression that evaluates to a logical TRUE or FALSE, and <DCL_command> is any other legal DCL command, possibly consisting of sev-eral words. Typically, <condition> will consist of two numeric or string expressions connected by a relational operator. These relational operators are patterned after FORTRAN. Their definitions are as follows:

```
Operator  Meaning
.EQ.      numeric Equals
.NE.      numeric Not Equal To
.GT.      numeric Greater Than
.LT.      numeric Less Than
.GE.      numeric Greater Than or Equal To
.LE.      numeric Less Than or Equal To
.EQS.     string Equals
.NES.     string Not Equal To
.GTS.     string Greater Than
.LTS.     string Less Than
.GES.     string Greater Than or Equal To
.LES.     string Less Than or Equal To
```

Returning to the example of a realistic IF statement and extending it a bit gives

```
$ IF J .GT. 5 THEN GOTO ILLEGAL_J_VALUE
$    WRITE SYS$OUTPUT "Value of J is legal!"
$ GOTO END_OF_ROUTINE
$ ILLEGAL_J_VALUE:
$    WRITE SYS$OUTPUT "???Value of J is out of bounds!"
$ END_OF_ROUTINE:
```

As you see, the IF statement tells the DCL command processor to examine the value of the symbol J and jump to the statement following the label ILLEGAL_J_VALUE if J is 6 or more. An error message defined by the WRITE command will then appear on the terminal. Should J be 5 or less, the IF command has no effect and DCL processing continues at the line immediately after the IF, emitting a message saying that the value of J is fine.

IF-THEN-ELSE CONSTRUCTS

A more precise definition of the syntax of the IF-THEN-ELSE command form is given next, where square brackets [] denote optional elements of the construct:

```
$ IF <condition>
$     THEN <statement(s) done when condition is true>
$         <...>
$     [ELSE
$         [<statement(s) done when condition is false>
$         <...>]]
$ ENDIF
```

This syntax is similar to the method of writing the same algorithm in FORTRAN, except for the requirement that the THEN clause stand on a line by itself. As may be expected, the ELSE clause and its false-condition statements are optional. They may also be nested, as in

```
$ IF <condition1>
$   THEN IF <condition2>
$     <statements done when condition2 is true>
$         <...>
$   ELSE
$     <statements done when condition2 is false>
$         <...>
$   ENDIF
$ ELSE
$     <statements done when condition1 is false>
$         <...>
$ ENDIF
```

When trying to determine what IF an ELSE goes with, remember the standard programming rule that an ELSE belongs logically to the nearest unterminated IF above it.

SUBROUTINES

Like many other programming languages, DCL provides subroutine-calling features that encourage partitioning of complex tasks into small, manageable chunks. There are two subroutine calling mechanisms with subtly different properties, GOSUB and CALL. Both kinds of subroutines can only be used inside command procedure files; they cannot be used in interactive mode from the $ prompt. Figure 6-2 illustrates one method of constructing a subroutine in DCL.

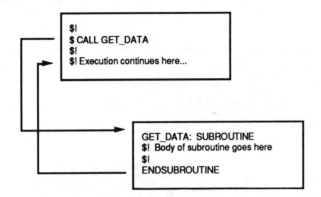

FIGURE 6-2.   Constructing a subroutine in DCL.

The forms of declaration for the subroutines themselves are different and are not interchangeable. The aim in using subroutines should be to group logically related commands together, not blindly chopping up a long procedure into arbitrary short ones. Sequences of commands that are executed more than once are particularly good candidates for subroutines.

Subroutines are invoked using either the CALL or GOSUB statement. When DCL sees a CALL, control transfers to the beginning of the subroutine, proceeds to the ENDSUBROUTINE statement, then returns to the command immediately following the CALL. The CALL form of subroutine is defined by placing a SUBROUTINE command immediately after a normal label. The subroutine extends from there to the next ENDSUBROUTINE statement encountered by the command processor. A simple example is

```
$DO_DIRECTORY: SUBROUTINE
$   WRITE SYS$OUTPUT "Directory Listing Follows:"
$   DIR/SIZE/DATE=MODIFIED/OWNER *.*.*
$ENDSUBROUTINE
```

An important point to realize is that all DCL commands between a SUBROUTINE statement and its ENDSUBROUTINE statement are executed only as the result of a CALL. Should your procedure merely fall through and reach a SUBROUTINE statement, the statements within the subroutine will be skipped; execution resumes at the statement following the ENDSUBROUTINE command.

If you read the definition of GOSUB subroutine processing carefully, you might ask whether the normal structure of a subroutine could be subverted by exploiting the fact that control will return to the caller at the next RETURN command *encountered* rather than the next one to occur sequentially in the file. This can in fact be done, but it is a strongly discouraged programming practice. If combined with backward GOTOs, some especially impenetrable procedures could be written that way.

Some guidelines for writing DCL command subroutines are as follows:

- Subroutines of the GOSUB variety should have a single entry point and a single exit point.

- The statements in a subroutine should be logically related to each other.

- The subroutine's name or label should be closely related to its purpose.

- Each subroutine should be preceded by a block of comments explaining its functions.

- The body of the subroutine should be indented with respect to the opening label.

- Subroutines should not be excessively long – no more than 50-100 lines.

A MENU SYSTEM SKELETON

Armed with your knowledge of branching constructs and subroutines, you have enough information to put together a very generalized DCL menu system that will let a user repeatedly (in a loop) select one of several operations (subroutines) to perform. In the interest of providing a general-purpose procedure that you can type and use, the sample menu system uses some commands which haven't been introduced yet. In creating your own menu-driven system, you'll want to replace the subroutine bodies with commands of your own choosing, probably renaming the subroutines in the process.

A worthwhile improvement over previous examples that blindly SET NOVERIFY is to use commands that remember the state of VERIFY at entry to the procedure and restore it upon exit. That restoration is done unconditionally by installing an ON CONTROL_Y<> handler. If you were so inclined, you could make things almost bulletproof by installing an ON <CONTROL_C> statement as well. The main disadvantage of using ON conditions for both CONTROL_C and CONTROL_Y is that there is no way of interrupting such a procedure should the ON handlers wind up in an infinite loop (unlikely) or if the procedure does a SET NOON and forgets to reenable the ON conditions (quite possible).

One real application for trapping all interrupt conditions is to provide strict limitations on what commands a captive account user can access. If you use ON CONTROL_C THEN LOGOUT and a similar command for CONTROL_Y, the user is unable to exit the menu shell without getting logged out. The following example could easily be converted to a captive user shell just by adding an ON CONTROL_C command and placing a LOGOUT command at label CLEANUP:

```
$ SAVED_VERIFY = F$VERIFY(0)
$!
$! The preceding sets NOVERIFY and saves the prior state
$! This comment comes afterward so it won't be VERIFY'd
$! before we can shut it off.
$!
$! MENUSHELL.COM - sample menu/subroutine shell
$!
$! Take over CTRL/Y handling for clean exit
$!
$ ON CONTROL_Y THEN GOTO CLEANUP
$!
$! Top of main menu loop
$!
$ MENU_TOP:
$!
$!    Display the menu
$!
$     TYPE SYS$OUTPUT


                        Main Menu

              1.   List all .COM files
              2.   Change to home directory
              3.   Change to working directory
              4.   Exit to VMS


$!
$!    Get user's selection and analyze it
$!
$     INQUIRE RESP "Enter choice [1]: "
$!
$     IF RESP .EQS. "" THEN RESP = 1
$     IF RESP .EQ. 1 THEN CALL DIR_COM_FILES
$     IF RESP .EQ. 2 THEN CALL RUN_MAIL
$     IF RESP .EQ. 3 THEN CALL RUN_PHONE
$     IF RESP .EQ. 4 THEN GOTO CLEANUP
$!
$     GOTO MENU_TOP                          ! end of main loop
$!
```

```
$! Control comes here when we are ready to exit
$!
$ CLEANUP:
$ IF SAVED_VERIFY THEN SET VERIFY    ! restore verify
$ EXIT
$!
$!------------------------
$! MENU HANDLER SUBROUTINES
$!------------------------
$!
$! DIR_COM_FILES - produces a directory of .COM files
$!
$ DIR_COM_FILES: SUBROUTINE
$    IF F$SEARCH("*.COM") .EQS. "" THEN GOTO NO_COM_FILES
$    DIR/SIZE/OWNER *.COM
$    GOTO DIR_COM_END
$ NO_COM_FILES:
$    WRITE SYS$OUTPUT "No .COM files are present"
$ DIR_COM_END:
$ ENDSUBROUTINE
$!
$! RUN_MAIL - invokes VMS MAIL facility
$!
$ RUN_MAIL: SUBROUTINE
$    SET DEFAULT SYS$LOGIN
$    MAIL
$ ENDSUBROUTINE
$!
$! RUN_PHONE - runs the VMS PHONE utility
$!
$ RUN_PHONE: SUBROUTINE
$    SET DEFAULT SYS$LOGIN
$    PHONE
$ ENDSUBROUTINE
```

SIMULATION OF HIGH-LEVEL CONTROL CONSTRUCTS

We previously claimed that you shouldn't use GOTO commands except to simulate an accepted structured programming construct such as IF-THEN-ELSE or WHILE.

This section gives the major constructs and shows exactly how to emulate them using the IF and GOTO facilities provided by DCL. Although some questions of style are purely subjective, adherence to the algorithms given here and to some reasonable form of procedure commenting will produce readable, maintainable DCL command files.

The techniques shown are identical to those used to emulate FORTRAN-77 structured constructs with older FORTRAN IV implementations (not surprising since the raw commands available are essentially identical.) Notice that the IF conditions are usually inverted from the structured version; that is, if the structured test is IF (A .EQ. B) the actual DCL test will read IF A .NE. B. This is because in DCL you can only jump away from a test with a GOTO, instead of having the true-condition commands right after the test. Here's an example showing the technique of inverted IF conditions:

```
$!
$! IF-THEN-ELSE - simulates
$! IF (RESP .EQS. "Y") THEN ... ELSE ... ENDIF
$!
$ IF RESP .NES. "Y" THEN GOTO ELSE_CLAUSE
$!
$!   Code for RESP .EQS. "Y" goes here
$!
$    GOTO END_IF
$ ELSE_CLAUSE:
$!
$!   ELSE case code goes here
$!
$ END_IF:
$!
$! DO-WHILE - simulates
$! DO WHILE (COUNT .NE. 0)
$!
$ WHILE_TEST:
$ IF COUNT .EQ. 0 THEN GOTO END_WHILE
$!
$!   Body of while loop code goes here
$!   It had better modify COUNT!
$!
$    GOTO WHILE_TEST
$!
$ END_WHILE:
$!
$! DO LOOP - simulates
```

```
$!     DO K = 1, 10
$!     ENDDO
$!
$ K = 0
$ DO_LOOP_TOP:
$ K = K + 1
$ IF K .GT. 10 THEN GOTO DO_LOOP_END
$!
$!    Body of DO loop goes here
$!
$      GOTO DO_LOOP_TOP
$!
$DO_LOOP_END:
$!
$! REPEAT UNTIL - simulates
$!    REPEAT
$!        X = X + 1
$!    UNTIL (X > 4)
$!
$! REPEAT UNTIL is considered a nonstandard
$! construct, but is included here for
$! completeness.
$!
$ RU_TOP:
$!
$!    Body of REPEAT UNTIL goes here
$!
$      X = X + 1
$      IF X .LE. 4 THEN GOTO RU_TOP
$!
```

Passing Parameters to the Command File

After writing a few DCL command procedures, you'll probably find that you want to reuse the same command file to process different files, access a different directory, and so forth. You'll also find that going into EDT every time to change the .COM file is tedious. As you have probably guessed, there's a better way. This is where command file *parameters* come into the picture.

Parameters are a way of passing information from the original DCL command line where you invoked the command procedure down into the procedure as local symbols.

By now it should not come as a surprise that a command procedure can find out what else you typed on the command line besides the name of the .COM file.

Suppose, for example, that you typed

```
$ @findit tangent secant.pas
```

Each addtional word on the command line (after the @xxxxxx.COM) is a separate parameter. Parameters are numbered from left to right on the command line as P1, P2, and so forth, up through P8. They are separated by blanks and/or tabs and may not contain embedded separators unless the parameter consists of a quoted string.

In the example, the command file FINDIT.COM would find that the local symbol P1 contained the string tangent and P2 contained secant.pas. The command procedure might look like this:

```
$!
$! FINDIT.COM - parameter passing example using SEARCH
$!
$ IF 'P1' .EQS. "" THEN GOTO NO_SEARCH
$   SEARCH 'P2' 'P1'
$ EXIT
$ NO_SEARCH:
$   WRITE SYS$OUTPUT "?Nothing to search for"
```

If FINDIT.COM were called with the above command line, it would search the file SECANT.PAS for the string TANGENT (see the following list of rules for the reason why this example would search for TANGENT in uppercase text). This command procedure could also search the file SINH.FOR for the string Result without being modified. Note the use of single quotation marks around the 'P1' and 'P2'. It causes the local symbols to be evaluated prior before used in the command procedure line.

There are a few special rules about procedure parameters that are a little odd and must be remembered:

- Parameters specified as integers on the command line are converted to string values before being stored in Pn.

- Parameters containing lowercase letters are forced to upper-case unless they are surrounded by quotation marks on the command line.

- Attempting to pass nine or more parameters causes an error message to be emitted and the command file to not run.

Here's a useful example of a .COM file that will compile, link, and run a FORTRAN program specified on the command line:

```
$!
$! FL.COM - FORTRAN compile/link/run procedure file
$!
$ FORTRAN/CONTIN=99 'P1'
$ LINK 'P1'
$ RUN 'P1'
```

Using Nested Command Files

A natural question to ask at this point is, Can a command file invoke another command file? That is referred to as command nesting, and you'll be happy to know the answer is yes, up to 16 levels deep. To invoke a second command procedure from within another, just add a command line with the normal @file.COM syntax; for example,

```
$!
$! NESTED.COM - trivial nested command
$! procedure example
$!
$ @SYS$LOGIN:DIRSAVE.COM ! runs another file
$ EXIT
```

This example runs DIRSAVE.COM from your system login directory (the same one where LOGIN.COM is kept). If you wished, DIRSAVE.COM could invoke yet another command file, and so on. The same limits on nesting depth apply to interactive and batch jobs. In both situations you can have up to 16 nested procedures running on top of the fundamental interactive job or SUBMITted file.

Be aware that a new set of local parameter symbols P1 - P8 is created for each level of nested procedure files. Each command procedure receives values for P1 - P8 that were specified by its immediate parent file's command that invoked the new procedure. When a nested .COM file exits, control returns to the parent .COM file at the line following the @ command, and the former child's local symbols (including its P1 - P8) are destroyed irrevocably.

SUBMITTING BATCH COMMAND FILES

An additional useful feature of DCL command files is that they can be used to run batch jobs with very little extra effort. A *batch job* is one that runs in the background and does not normally have an interactive terminal assigned to it. Creating batch files is no more difficult than creating other command files. Batch files are just one step further on the development curve for command files. Figure 6-3 illustrates the pro

gressive automation of DCL functions from the command line to the command file to
the batch file.

You create a batch job using the SUBMIT command followed by the name of a
DCL .COM file. VMS begins executing the .COM file in a background mode, and you
immediately regain control of your terminal for other, more people-oriented tasks. If
you select the /NOTIFY option, a message appears on your terminal when the batch
job is done.

Checking Batch Job Results

Batch results can be monitored in two ways. One is by periodically typing SHOW
QUEUE to see where the batch queue is at the moment. SHOW QUEUE
SYS$BATCH will show you the progress in the default batch queue. Not all batch
queues have this name, however, so a simple SHOW QUEUE may be the most convenient way to check all batch queues.

If your job has been held up by others, the SHOW QUEUE message will specify
that it is behind some number of other batch jobs. If your job is currently executing, it
will tell you that also. If your job has either bombed or finished, you will see nothing
in the queue.

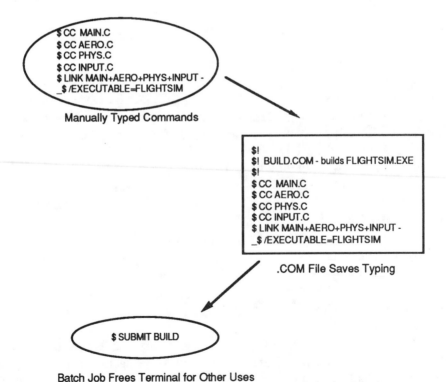

Manually Typed Commands

.COM File Saves Typing

Batch Job Frees Terminal for Other Uses

FIGURE 6-3.   *Automation of DCL functions – from command line to batch job file.*

The second way to monitor the progress of your batch jobs is by examining the .LOG files generated by the system. An explanation of batch log files comes next.

Batch Log Files

Batch job results are usually found in the batch log file, given the filename of the .COM file you used to run it and the type .LOG. The file will contain a copy of your batch LOGIN.COM, your run statistics, and any error messages you would ordinarily have seen on the terminal screen.

You can specify the file you would like to send your batch results to by using the SUBMIT qualifier /LOG_FILE=file-spec. You can use this parameter to send the log file to some other device.

Another method for specifying where specific batch log results go is to use a batch LOGIN.COM to reassign the logical names for SYS$INPUT, SYS$OUTPUT and SYS$ERROR. You can name the default output and error output specifiers to be either the same or different. SYS$INPUT can be set to any input file you like. Your batch job will treat the newly assigned filename as if it were accepting keyboard inputs.

SUMMARY

In this chapter you learned the basics of writing and using DCL command files. The topics discussed were

- Conditional and branching commands – DCL provides for several methods to create emulations of all the traditional high-level language looping constructs.

- IF-THEN-ELSE constructs.

- Subroutines – They are similar to subroutines used in the BASIC language.

- A simple menu system skeleton.

- Simulation of high-level control constructs like DO, DO WHILE, REPEAT UNTIL, CASE, and SWITCH.

- Submitting batch command files.

Part 3
Working with DCL

As you move into more complicated topics, the material gets a little more intense and the sections contain more chapters. The group of six chapters in Part Three contain all of the material you will need to work competently in DCL. If you never get beyond the contents of this part, you will have as much material as many software professionals have learned in years of experience with the VAX.

Chapter 7, Logical Names, introduces some basic variables for more effective use of many VMS features not found in other operating systems.

Chapter 8, Lexical Functions, gets into some of the ways you can use DCL to check system and process parameters. For example, you can find out your terminal type and test for the time from within a DCL command file by using lexical functions.

Chapter 9, Tactics for LOGIN.COM, lets you in on one of many programmers' favorite features of VMS. Through the use of a carefully tailored LOGIN.COM file, you can customize your operating environment to your liking, and have your environment set up automatically every time you log in on a terminal.

Chapter 10, File and Terminal I/O From DCL, introduces you to methods using DCL to perform file and terminal I/O tasks without using a traditional programming language.

Chapter 11, Success With BACKUP, helps you gain control over the way VMS saves and restores bulk data on disk and tape devices. Although this chapter borders on being geared toward the system manager, keep in mind that with the advent of the new DEC workstations and the increasing use of the MicroVAX, more and more of you are now your own system manager.

7

Logical Names

Logical names are defined by equating one character string to an equivalence name, which can be a file specification, another logical name, or any other character string. Once the logical name has been equated to an equivalence name, you can use the logical name instead of that equivalence name. As an example, you can assign the logical name HOME to your default directory and disk. Logical name assignments can be useful for a number of applications, both in the VMS operating environment and in the programming environment it is designed to support.

The reasons for using logical names are as varied as the names themselves. Programmers use them to represent directory and file specifications inside their source code when writing programs. That use creates source files that are independent of directory structure, as long as a command file is executed that assigns the logical name before compilation. One easy way to do this is to define some static location for certain types of files, for example, a file of parameters representing physical constants and conversion factors in a directory called PARAMETERS:

```
$ DEFINE PARAM [200101.PARAMETERS]
```

This would allow you to include the specification for this directory in source code without having to spell out the UIC and full directory specification. This could be used in a FORTRAN source file with the syntax

```
INCLUDE 'PARAM:PHYSICAL_CONSTANTS.INC/LIST'
INCLUDE 'PARAM:CONVERSION_FACTORS.INC/LIST'
```

Notice the colon (:) separator between the logical name and the rest of the file specification. You must separate logical names from file specifications with a colon for them to be recognized as a logical name. You do not need the colon if you are not appending a file or directory specification to the end of the logical name, however. For this reason, logical names are said to be used with the same syntax as a device name.

HOW LOGICAL NAMES AND SYMBOLS DIFFER

The primary difference between logical names and symbols is that they are handled differently by DCL. A logical name is used as a descriptor of some physical *thing*, such as a device or directory specification. You could think of it as an an *adjective* in DCL. Logical names are translated directly into their lowest counterpart by DCL's expression translator.

When you use a symbol, it can represent just about anything. Symbols can be used to execute a command. When you type an expression at a DCL command prompt, the first thing that happens is a scan through your symbol tables. If no match is found in your symbol tables, DCL looks for a match in the command parser. If there is still no match, you will get an error message after the command line of the form

```
DCL-W-NOCOMD, no command on line - reenter with alphabetic
first character
```

DCL will not recognize a logical name typed by itself on a command line as a valid command. Logical names can be used as a parameter of a command, however.

You can perform arithmetic and logical operations on symbols, such as

```
$ FLOWERS = ROSES + CARNATIONS
```

You cannot do this with logical names, however. Symbols can be treated like variables, whereas logical names can only be established with the ASSIGN or DEFINE commands.

CREATING LOGICAL NAMES

Logical names can be created using either the ASSIGN or the DEFINE command. The syntax differs for the two commands in some significant ways, although the logical name created behaves in an identical manner no matter which command is actually used for its creation.

DIFFERENCES IN THE DEFINE AND ASSIGN COMMANDS

The primary difference in the use of the DEFINE and ASSIGN commands involves the positions of the logical and equivalence names in the command line. The DEFINE statement is easier to use because it does not strip characters from the logical name string, so it is used for the examples in the remainder of the chapter. But the translation between the two types should be possible through the use of these explanations of the syntactic rules:

```
$ DEFINE logical-name equivalence-name[,...]
$ ASSIGN equivalence-name[,...] logical name[:]
```

Notice that you can assign a logical name to a string of equivalence names. Doing this creates a *search list* through the specified list of devices, directories, or other objects. This is similar to the MS-DOS PATH command. One use of a logical name search list is to create a search path for source code shared in two directories like this:

```
$ DEFINE SOURCE [200101.ROCKETSIM],[200101.FLIGHTSIM]
```

The logical name SOURCE now represents a search list through the two directories ROCKETSIM and FLIGHTSIM in the root directory represented by the UIC 200101. To use this search list to recompile FORTRAN source code, you could type

```
$ FORTRAN SOURCE:*
```

In this case, the FORTRAN compiler would search the two directories ROCKETSIM and FLIGHTSIM in the order specified for all occurrances of files with default file type .FOR. The creation of search lists could save you a great deal of time for repetitive operations on files located in several different directories.

Another difference in the DEFINE and ASSIGN commands is the use of the colon as a terminator for the logical name in the ASSIGN command. If a colon is used at the end of the logical name in the ASSIGN command, it will be removed by DCL. Therefore, if you wish to save the terminating colon on the logical name, you must use two colons. The DEFINE command does not remove the trailing colon, so a single colon should be used for this command if you wish the colon to be part of the logical name.

SYNTAX RULES FOR CREATING LOGICAL NAMES WITH THE DEFINE COMMAND

The following rules apply when creating a logical name with the DEFINE command:

- The logical name and its equivalence name are limited to a maximum of 255 characters.

- Valid characters are all alphanumeric characters, the dollar sign ($), the underscore (_), and the hyphen (-).

- The equivalence name must include all of the punctuation marks (such as colons, brackets, and periods) that would be required if it were a part of a valid file specification. This ensures that DCL will interpret it as a file specification if that is what is intended. For example, device names must be terminated by a colon, directory specifications must be terminated by brackets, and file types must be preceded by periods.

Logical names can be optionally terminated by a colon. Remember that the ASSIGN command will remove the colon when placing the logical name in the appropriate logical name table, and the DEFINE command will not. As a general rule, however, do not terminate a logical name with a colon, since you often will want to use a colon to separate the logical name from the rest of the file specification.

When a logical name represents a part of a file specification, it must be the leftmost part of that specification and must be separated from the rest of the file specification with a colon. Remember that when the logical name represents the complete file specification, the terminating colon is not required as a separator. Both of the following commands are valid:

```
$ SET DEFAULT PARAM
$ EDIT PARAM:PHYSICAL_CONSTANTS.INC
```

You can equate more than one logical name to the same equivalence string. You can also define a logical name more than once with different equivalence names. If these assignments occur one after the other, the second definition will ordinarily supercede the first. You can use several assignments for the same logical name, however, if they each appear in different logical name tables. You can even have different definitions for the logical name appear in the same table if they are created in different access modes.

One further note for logical name users: If at any time you cannot access a file and the command you have specified used apparently correct syntax, check that the leftmost component of the file specification is not defined as a logical name with SHOW LOGICAL like this:

```
$ SHOW LOGICAL PARAM
  "PARAM" = "[200101.PARAMETERS]"
```

Since DCL's first priority in analyzing a command line's directory specification is to translate logical names, your filename may not represent what you expect.

DISPLAYING LOGICAL NAMES

You can display a logical name's equivalence name with either the SHOW TRANSLATION or the SHOW LOGICAL command.

The SHOW TRANSLATION command causes the system to search all the logical name tables for the specified logical name and display the first definition it finds along with the table in which this definition was found:

```
$ SHOW TRANSLATION PARAM
  "PARAM" = "[200101.PARAMETERS]"
```

The SHOW TRANSLATION command does not translate logical names iteratively. It will provide only the first-level equivalence name. Try defining a logical name a couple of levels deep to see how this works:

```
$ DEFINE    PARAM      [200101.PARAMETERS]
$ DEFINE    CONSTANTS  PARAM:PHYSICAL_CONSTANTS.INC
```

Now the CONSTANTS logical name can be translated two levels deep. If you were to type a SHOW TRANSLATION, this is the result:

```
$ SHOW TRANSLATION CONSTANTS
  "CONSTANTS" = "PARAM:PHYSICAL_CONSTANTS.INC"
```

The SHOW LOGICAL command will perform the iterative translation to show you the root level of what the logical name is really representing. The same example you saw above now becomes

```
$ SHOW LOGICAL CONSTANTS
  "CONSTANTS" = "[200101.PARAMETERS]PHYSICAL_CONSTANTS.INC"
```

DELETING LOGICAL NAMES

Deleting logical names can be done interactively using the DEASSIGN command.

```
$ DEFINE CURRENT [RSIM.UTILITY]
        •
        •
        •
$ DEASSIGN CURRENT
```

All logical names in your process and job tables are automatically deassigned or deleted when your process terminaltes. You can, however, create another behavior by specifying the /USER_MODE qualifier to the DEFINE command when you create your logical name. This will cause the logical name to be placed in the process logical name table and executed once before the logical name is deleted.

LOGICAL NAME TABLES

There are four logical name tables; you will want to be familiar with the functions of each. When you type SHOW LOGICAL *, you will get a list of all entries in each. If you wish to see the logical names in a particular table, use the table name with the SHOW LOGICAL command like this:

```
$ SHOW LOGICAL/TABLE=TABLE_NAME
```

The Process Table

The process logical name table is named LNM$PROCESS_TABLE. This table contains names that are local to your process and any subprocesses you create. This is the table in which your logical name definitions using DEFINE and ASSIGN end up in by default. You can refer to this table with the logical name LNM$PROCESS. To display the logical names in this table only, use the command

```
$ SHOW LOGICAL/PROCESS
```

The Job Table

The job table contains logical names that are local to the processes in your job tree. The name of the job table is in the form LNM$JOB_XXX, with the logical name LNM$JOB. In this case, the XXX is an identifier for the address defined by your system. When you type SHOW LOGICAL/JOB you will get a display similar to

```
$ SHOW LOGICAL/JOB
(LNM$JOB_8021AA80)
  "SYS$LOGIN" = "$DISK1:[200101]"
  "SYS$LOGIN_DEVICE" = "$DISK1:"
  "SYS$REM_ID" = "LEISNER"
  "SYS$REM_NODE" = "MOZART::"
  "SYS$SCRATCH" = "$DISK1:[200101]"
```

The Group Table

Your group logical name table contains the logical names that are available to all of those with the same group number; it is named LNM$GROUP_XXX, with the logical name LNM$GROUP. In this case, the XXX represents the group number in your user identification code, usually the first three digits in your UIC.

In the example, you would display this logical name table with the command

```
$ SHOW LOGICAL/GROUP
(LNM$GROUP_200)
```

In this case, there were no logical names in the group logical name table.

The System Table

Your system logical name table contains the logical names available to everyone authorized to use the system. The table is named LNM$SYSTEM_TABLE, with the logical name LNM$SYSTEM. You can look at it by typing

```
$SHOW LOGICAL/SYSTEM
```

Unlike the other tables, there is only one system logical name table. This table contains the logical names for your devices, such as printers, terminals, disk drives, and start-up logicals. You are unlikely to have the privileges to alter the logical names contained in this table.

Default Logical Names

Default logical names are those assigned by DCL or the system manager. These include SYS$INPUT, SYS$OUTPUT, SYS$ERROR, and SYS$COMMAND. Occasionally it's useful to reassign these to point to a file.

CREATING A LOGICAL NAME TABLE

The CREATE/NAME_TABLE command will create a logical name table and enter it into one of the directory logical name tables. You can use this command to create a logical name table that is private to your process by placing it in the LNM$PROCESS_DIRECTORY. If you want to share it, you will require special system privileges. Read more about this in the DEC *General User's Manual* if you are interested.

TRANSLATION AND USES OF LOGICAL NAMES

Each time the system reads a device name or file specification in a command line, it examines the leftmost component to determine if it is a logical name. If this component ends with a recogized DCL punctuation mark such as a colon, comma, space, or a carriage return, DCL will attempt to translate it as a logical name.

Iterative Translation

Logical names are translated in an iterative manner to decode the equivalence names of any imbedded logical names found in the first pass of DCL logical name translation. This is the process that happened with the SHOW LOGICAL example.

The number of levels of translation DCL will perform to translate a single logical names varies from installation to installation and is under the control of the system manager. The minimum number of translation levels is nine. Don't worry too much about exceeding that limit, though, because if you attempt to create a logical name with more embedded layers than the system can handle, an error will occur when the name is used. This error condition will also occur if you create a circular definition. You can avoid problems by always testing the logical name after creation, thereby allowing DCL to catch the errors early.

Defaults for Logical Name Translation

The system fills in any missing fields in a file specification when it translates a logical name. This includes the current default device name, the directory, and the version number. For example, when you use a logical name and specify an input file for a command, the command will also assign a file specification to the output file, giving it the same file name and file type. If the name does not contain a file type, a default type is used. The file type used will depend on the default for the command in use. For example, the result of the COPY command using the logical name CONSTANTS would be to create a new file with the same file name and file type as follows:

```
$ COPY/LOG CONSTANTS
  DUA0:[200101.PARAMETERS]PHYSICAL_CONSTANTS.INC;1 copied to
DUA0:[200101.PARAMETERS]PHYSICAL_CONSTANTS.INC;2 5 blocks
```

This behavior is unique when using logical names as file specifications.

Modifications to Logical Name Translation

At the time you first create a logical name you can specify translation attributes to modify system behavior when it translates and interprets the equivalence name string. This is done by using the /TRANSLATION_ATTRIBUTES qualifier on the DEFINE command. This positional qualifier can be interpreted as applicable to all or only certain translation attributies, depending on its placement on the command line. The two translation attributes that can be specified for this qualifier are CONCEALED and TERMINAL.

The CONCEALED attribute displays the logical name of the device rather than the actual physical name in all system messages except the SHOW LOGICAL message display. This attribute is usally used for defining logical names for devices such as printers and disk drives. The CONCEALED attribute allows you to write programs and command procedures and perform various other operations without concern for exactly which device is actually holding the disk or tape file. It also lets you use names that are more meaningful to the average user than the actual physical device names.

The TERMINAL attribute turns off the iterative translation of a logical name. (Note that the word TERMINAL here refers to the end of a translation, not to a display device.) This means that the first equivalence name for the logical name being translated is not examined any further to decode the logical name. The translation is therefore TERMINAL after the first iteration. This is useful in instances such as when the translation time for the logical name is a factor in the speed of execution of a command contained within a tight iterative loop.

LOGICAL NODE NAMES

Your CPU is referred to as a NODE, especially when networked with other NODEs (CPUs). You can assign logical names to your nodes that make some sense to you using the DEFINE or ASSIGN statement like this:

```
$ DEFINE KRISNODE "MOZART::"
$ DEFINE DAVENODE "CHOPIN::"
```

or, using ASSIGN:

```
$ ASSIGN "MOZART::" KRISNODE
$ ASSIGN "CHOPIN::" DAVENODE
```

Note that node names used in equivalence names will have characters that are not in the normally acceptable character set of the alphanumeric characters, the dollar sign ($) or the underscore (_). For this reason, the node name character string must be enclosed in quotes.

SYSTEM-CREATED LOGICAL NAMES

Your logical name system table contains lots of logical names endorsed by either DEC or your system manager.

If you are curious about your system logical name table, try typing the following to see all of the logical names in all of of the logical name tables:

```
$ SHOW LOGICAL *
```

Be ready with the no scroll key, <CTRL/S> for this one, since the logical name list will probably be quite long.

Process-Permanent Logical Names

The process-permanent logical names are created by DCL at the time you log in and remain for the entire duration of your process. It is not possible to deassign these logical names, but they can be redefined by specifying the same name in a DEFINE command. If the same name is later DEASSIGNed, then the process-permanent name is reestablished.

There are four process-permanent logical names available to all users at the process level:

- SYS$INPUT – Specifies the default input device or file.

- SYS$OUTPUT – Specifies the default output device or file.

- SYS$ERROR – Specifies the destination output device or file where system error messages will be sent.

- SYS$COMMAND – Refers to the value for SYS$INPUT at the time of log in.

Redefining Process-Permanent Logical Names

Sometimes it is convenient to reassign or redefine the system's process-permanent logical names to redirect input from or output to files you specify.

SYS$INPUT – SYS$INPUT can be redefined to allow a command procedure to read interactive and other input from either the terminal or another user-defined file. For example, to run a program from a command file but still take input from the terminal, you can include an extra line in the command file as follows:

```
$ DEFINE/USER_MODE SYS$INPUT SYS$COMMAND
$ RUN ANY_IMAGE
```

In this type of example, the default for SYS$INPUT is the command file. Here SYS$INPUT is redefined to be SYS$COMMAND so that the image will look for its input from the terminal rather than the command procedure file. SYS$COMMAND is the terminal input device or the input device on which you logged in. The /USER_MODE qualifier redefines SYS$INPUT for the duration of the next command image only.

When the command RUN ANY_IMAGE is finished, SYS$INPUT will revert to its default value – the command file.

DCL will ordinarily ignore any attempt to redefine SYS$INPUT, assuming you will always want to provide input using your default input stream, the login terminal. DCL will allow SYS$INPUT to be redefined for images such as command files only for the duration of the command.

SYS$OUTPUT – You can redefine the default SYS$OUTPUT to be anything you like. This can be especially useful for redirecting output from the standard sources like the BATCH log file to any file specification. You can redirect SYS$OUTPUT with a normal ASSIGN or DEFINE statement:

```
$ DEFINE SYS$OUTPUT [200101.BATCH]OUTPUT.TXT
```

When this command is inserted in your LOGIN.COM for use when in the BATCH mode, all outputs from BATCH jobs will go to successive files named OUTPUT.TXT. You can then print them if you want or throw them away if you like.

SYS$ERROR – You may find it convenient to reassign or redefine SYS$ERROR occasionally to direct error messages to some other file. If you assign SYS$ERROR to a file that is different from SYS$OUTPUT, DCL will send error messages to each. The result is that you will receive all of your error messages twice. This condition is overridden if you run an image referencing SYS$ERROR, with error messages being sent only to SYS$ERROR, even if it is different from SYS$OUTPUT.

SYS$COMMAND – Although it is possible to redefine SYS$COMMAND, the redefinition is often ignored by DCL. Each time you execute a command from the DCL command line, DCL uses the default definition for your initial input stream. This condition is overriden when you execute an image that references SYS$COMMAND internally. For this case only, the executed image can use your new definition.

SUMMARY

In this chapter you learned about the methods of assignment and uses of logical names. As a result, you can

- Create logical names with either the ASSIGN or DEFINE commands.

- Delete logical names with DEASSIGN.

- Have a good understanding of how logical names and symbols differ.

- Display logical names with

   SHOW LOGICAL – Translates logical names to their lowest level with the following qualifiers and the asterisk (*) wildcard:

```
/PROCESS
/SYSTEM
/JOB
/GROUP
```

SHOW TRANSLATION – Displays a logical name translation only one level down.

- Use and display of the standard logical name tables:

PROCESS

JOB

GROUP

SYSTEM

8

Lexical Functions

DCL lexical functions were originally intended to perform lexical analysis of strings, as the term for them implies. As the DCL command language has grown, however, the term *lexical function* has come to refer to any of a family of built-in functions that, in addition to processing strings, also return information about the system and process environment, find the types of symbols, set the command procedure verification state, run SEARCH, set privileges, obtain system queue information, and so on. In VMS 5.0, DCL lexical functions consist of a mixed bag of utility functions commonly used in DCL programs.

A distinguishing feature of lexical functions is that their names all begin with F$ and must always be followed by a pair of parentheses. The use of an unusual character in the names helps to differentiate them from ordinary DCL variables. It should be evident that to avoid confusion, you should not create any variables of your own with names starting with F$. Also keep in mind that the parentheses must always be furnished, even if no arguments are passed to the lexical function; for example "F$TIME()".

Lexical functions fall into one of several categories based upon what the functions accomplish:

- String manipulation

- Environment information

- Process control

- File/directory information

- Variable type conversions

- Miscellaneous

Lexical functions are treated as DCL expressions that have values. The kind of value returned by the lexical function depends upon what sort of function it is and may be either a string or an integer. In some cases (e.g. F$GETSYI, F$GETQUI) a key word item argument will determine what type of value is returned. The lexical function can therefore be used in an expression just as any other variable of the same type.

An example of the use of lexical functions is:

```
$! Example of simple lexical function use
$!
$ A := F$EXTRACT(1,3,"THE QUICK") + " DOG"
$ WRITE SYS$OUTPUT A
```

It will send the string "THE DOG" to SYS$OUTPUT. The F$EXTRACT() function returns a string value extracted from its third argument (the word "THE"), which is concatenated with the literal string " DOG" to form the value of the string variable A.

A more useful example is the following, which sets the DCL prompt to be the current host nodename:

```
$!
$! Set DCL prompt to contain current nodename,
$! that is, if you are currently logged in to THOR::
$! the new DCL prompt will be
$!             THOR>
$!
$ nodenm = F$ENVIRONMENT("NODENAME") + ">"
$ SET PROMPT nodenm
THOR>
```

This code fragment is often used in LOGIN.COM for installations in which you have accounts on several machines on different clusters and use the SET HOST command frequently to switch between them. If you are logged in through a terminal server that supports multiple simultaneous sessions, having a nodename prompt can become almost mandatory.

WILDCARDS AND SEQUENCES OF LEXICAL CALLS

Some of the lexical functions have the ability to process wildcard characters (* and ?) in their input arguments. An example is F$SEARCH, where you can write:

```
$ FILESPEC = F$SEARCH("*.DAT")
$ SHOW SYM FILESPEC
  FILESPEC = "AARDVARK.DAT"
```

What is returned in this case? Here F$SEARCH returns the full filespec of the *first* file it finds that matches *.DAT. It then remembers the context; the next call to F$SEARCH produces the next filespec that matches the wildcard string:

```
$ FILESPEC = F$SEARCH("*.DAT")
$ SHOW SYM FILESPEC
  FILESPEC = "BRATWURST.DAT"
```

This process continues until no more files are found that match *.DAT, at which point F$SEARCH will return a null string (""). This feature is very handy, since it lets you construct a DCL loop that will process all files matching a certain wildcard-containing expression.

To illustrate the use of this feature, suppose you wanted to run SCRAMBLE.COM on each .DAT file:

```
$!
$! LOOP TO PROCESS A GROUP OF FILES
$!
$ LOOP_TOP:
$    DATFILE = F$SEARCH("*.DAT")
$    IF DATFILE .EQS. "" THEN GOTO END_LOOP
$    @SCRAMBLE 'DATFILE'
$    GOTO LOOP_TOP
$!
$ END_LOOP:
$!
```

Another feature of the F$SEARCH function could be used to allow you to maintain two or more parallel wildcard search channels. The default behavior of F$SEARCH when you only give one argument is to maintain the wildcard context only as long as successive calls to the lexical function have the identical filespec argument. Any F$SEARCH with a different filespec will revert the search to the top of the directory list.

This is where the second argument (the stream_id) comes into play. When this argument is specified, all F$SEARCH calls with the same stream_id will use a search pointer independent of a series of calls with any other stream_id. The stream_id argument must be a positive (nonzero) integer.

Now try to exploit this feature with another example. If the previous example were expanded to include pairs of files with different file types, you could write the loop as follows:

```
$!
$! LOOP TO PROCESS TWO GROUPS OF FILES IN PARALLEL
$!
$ LOOP_TOP:
$    DATFILE = F$SEARCH("*.DAT", 1)
$    AUXFILE = F$SEARCH("*.AUX", 2)
$    IF (DATFILE .EQS. "") THEN GOTO END_LOOP
$    IF (AUXFILE .EQS. "") THEN GOTO MATCH_ERROR
$    @SCRAMBLE2 'DATFILE' 'AUXFILE'
$    GOTO LOOP_TOP
$!
$ END_LOOP:
$!
$ EXIT
$!
$ MATCH_ERROR:
$    WRITE SYS$OUTPUT "?? Ran out of AUX files before DAT"
$!
```

KINDS OF FUNCTIONS OFFERED BY THE LEXICALS

This section categorizes all the lexicals by functional group and gives a thumbnail description of each function. A complete listing of the lexicals, including their arguments and return types, is given in Appendix C.

String manipulation functions are used as an extended set of string operators. Capabilities include substring extraction, length finding, blank compression or removal, substring location, filespec expansion, and multifile searching for text.

Here are capsule summaries of the string manipulation routines:

- F$EXTRACT(startpos, length, string) – Extracts a substring from *string* beginning at *startpos* and extending for *length* characters.

- F$LENGTH(string) – Finds the length of *string* in characters.

- F$EDIT(string, edit_list) – Compresses *string* according to keywords in *edit_list*. Can remove blanks, tabs, and so on.

- F$ELEMENT(element_num, delimiter, string) – Extracts element (text word) number *element_num* from *string*, where the elements are separated by *delimiter*.

- F$LOCATE(substring, string) – Locates the first occurrence of *substring* within *string*.

- F$PARSE(filespec[,default_spec][,related_spec][,field][,type]) – Expands a partial filespec into a fully qualified filespec, with substitution of defaults for omitted fields. Can handle wildcards in the filespec.

- F$SEARCH(filespec [,stream_id]) – Searches for files matching *filespec*. Great with wildcards for processing groups of files. Argument *stream_id* permits multiple streams of searching.

Environment information lexicals are among the most-used functions. They will tell you almost anything you want to know about the VAX/VMS environment surrounding your process. The F$GETXXX functions have a host of option keywords for obtaining information about VMS devices (F$GETDVI), job and process information (F$GETJPI), system data (F$GETSYI), and batch/print queue information (F$GETQUI). You can also find out about the current DCL command interpreter environment with F$ENVIRONMENT(). F$MODE, F$TIME, and F$USER round out the group; these don't take any arguments and return simple values.

One important point to be aware of when dealing with lexicals that expect item keywords is that the item argument must be a character expression. If you use a string literal it must be enclosed in quotes. Error messages about undefined symbols often result from forgetting the quotes.

Short descriptions of the environment information functions follow. Refer to Appendix C for detailed descriptions of the items available, especially for the F$GETXXX series.

- F$ENVIRONMENT(item) – Produces information about the DCL command environment existing at the time you call it. Has numerous item keywords. All but DEPTH and MAX_DEPTH return string values. A sample F$ENVIRONMENT call showing how to obtain the current DCL nesting depth is:

```
$ DCL_DEPTH = F$ENVIRONMENT("DEPTH")
$ SHOW SYM DCL_DEPTH
  DCL_DEPTH = 2
```

- F$GETDVI(dev_name, item) – Produces information about a particular VMS device. Has a large number of item keywords, including most of the repertoire from SET TERMINAL. Returns both integer and string values depending upon the item selected.

- F$GETJPI(PID, item) - Obtains information about the job and process having the specified PID. LIke F$GETDVI, has numerous item selection keywords and can return either integer or string values depending on the item.

- F$GETSYI(item[,node]) – Obtains information about the local system or a node in the local cluster. There is a group of item keywords that apply only to the local CPU and another group that can apply to either the local CPU or another cluster member. The following example shows how to find your local nodename:

```
$ LOCAL_NODE = F$GETSYI("NODENAME")
$ SHOW SYM LOCAL_NODE
  LOCAL_NODE = "MOZART"
```

- F$GETQUI(function,[item],[object_id],[flags]) – Produces information about sys-
  tem queues, including batch queues, print queues, and the generic queues that feed
  execution queues. F$GETQUI has an enormous number of item keywords (well
  over 100). It can be used, for instance, to analyze the reason why a given print job
  is being held by the system.

- F$MODE() – Tells what command mode the current process is in; returns one of
  BATCH, INTERACTIVE, NETWORK, or OTHER.

- F$TIME() - Produces a string giving the current system time. Result is always a
  23-character string in absolute time format; for example

```
$ SYSTIME = F$TIME()
$ SHOW SYMBOL SYSTIME
  SYSTIME = "10-NOV-1988 23:37:55.44"
```

F$USER() – Produces the alphanumeric UIC of the current process, as in

```
$ ALPHA_UIC = F$USER()
$ SHOW SYMBOL F$USER
  F$USER = "[ENGR,COOK]"
```

Process control and status functions return information about the current process
state and privileges. F$PID and F$PROCESS obtain your PID and process name, respectively, whereas F$PRIVILEGE and F$SETPRV let you determine what privileges
you have enabled and attempt to set those that are not currently enabled.

- F$PID(context_symbol) – Produces the Process ID (PID) for all processes you
  have enough privilege to see. Can handle concurrent search streams through use
  of the context_symbol argument.

- F$PRIVILEGE(privilege_list) – Tells you whether the privileges given in privi-
  lege_list are all currently enabled. Does not give you a list of enabled privileges.

- F$PROCESS() – Produces the name of the current process; for example

```
$!
$! Result of F$PROCESS() when in a subprocess
$!
$ PROC_NAME = F$PROCESS()
```

```
$ SHOW SYMBOL PROC_NAME
  PROC_NAME = "COOK_1"
```

- F$SETPRV(privilege_list) – Attempts to set all privileges specified in privilege_list. Gives no indication of success or failure; you must use F$PRIVILEGE for that.

File/directory information lexical functions let you find out the current default device and directory (F$DIRECTORY), obtain any of the RMS attributes for a file (F$FILE_ATTRIBUTES), and translate logical names (F$TRNLNM and the obsolete F$LOGICAL).

- F$DIRECTORY() – Provides the same output as a SHOW DEFAULT command. The result can be used in a subsequent SET DEFAULT.

- F$FILE_ATTRIBUTES(filespec, item) – Obtains any of the VMS Record Management System (RMS) file information fields for the specified file. Wildcards cannot be used in the filespec. Has a lot of keywords. Very useful for command procedures that analyze file statistics.

- F$LOGICAL(logical_name) – Produces the equivalence name associated with the given *logical_name*. This routine is obsolete; DEC recommends using F$TRNLNM instead, which offers the same basic functions with more options.

- F$TRNLNM(logname[,table][,index][,mode][,case][,item]) – Translates a logical name to one of its equivalence names. Unlike F$LOGICAL, it can handle logicals with more than one equivalence name. Also can deal with the various logical name tables. Use this function to find out to what physical device, directory, or file a given logical name actually points.

Variable type conversion lexicals are routines that facilitate the conversion of DCL symbols from one data type to another. Two of them – F$CVSI and F$CVUI – can extract bit fields from a symbol and convert them to signed and unsigned integers, respectively. F$TYPE will tell you which type a given symbol has (integer or string). F$IDENTIFIER is a special-purpose function that converts a rights database identifier to a regular integer. The F$INTEGER and F$STRING functions are used for conversion of a symbol to the opposite type.

- F$CVSI(startbit, nbits, string) – Produces a signed integer from a bitfield extracted from *string*. This is a little confusing; the entry in Appendix C for this routine gives an example.

- F$CVUI(startbit, nbits, string) – Produces an unsigned integer from a bitfield in *string*.

- F$IDENTIFIER(rights_identifier, convert_type) – Converts a system rights identifier from the rights database into a number and vice-versa.

- F$INTEGER(expression) – Produces an integer value from *expression*. If *expression* has a string value, it gets converted to an integer if possible; otherwise it gives 0 or 1, depending on whether the string begins with T or Y (either uppercase or lowercase). Examples follow:

```
$!
$ INT1 = F$INTEGER("351")
$ INT2 = F$INTEGER("this is a test")
$ SHOW SYMBOL INT1
  INT1 = 351
$ SHOW SYMBOL INT2
  INT2 = 1
```

Since the string "this is a test" begins with a lowercase t, F$INTEGER returns a 1.
- F$STRING(expression) – Produces a string equivalent for *expression*. When *expression* has an integer value, the integer is converted to a decimal string. String-valued expressions are merely evaluated.

- F$TYPE(symbol_name) – Tells you what type the given symbol has. Gives the string values INTEGER and STRING.

Miscellaneous useful lexicals include the following
- F$FAO(control_string [,arg1,arg2...,arg15) - A complex, workhorse function that effectively does formatted string output based on the control string and the supplied arguments.

Essentially what happens is that the arguments *arg1* through (possibly) *arg15* are formatted through commands embedded in *control_string*. The resulting formatted string becomes the F$FAO return value. This routine serves like a FORTRAN WRITE statement or a C language printf() call.
- F$MESSAGE(status_code) – Produces the English system message text that matches the specified numeric *status_code*.

- F$VERIFY([procedure_val][,image_val]) – Lets you both query and set the state of the PROCEDURE_VERIFY and IMAGE_VERIFY variables. The return value is the current state of PROCEDURE_VERIFY.

SUMMARY

Lexical functions are used to secure process-specific or character string information. They are identified by the F$ prefix. The following is a summary of all of the VMS lexical functions current with VMS 5.0:

```
F$CVSI (start_bit,number_of_bits,string)
F$CVTIME ([input_time][,output_time_format][,output_field]
F$CVUI (start_bit,number_of_bits,string)
F$DIRECTORY ()
F$EDIT (string,edit_list)
F$ELEMENT (element_number,delim_char,string)
F$ENVIRONMENT (item)
F$EXTRACT (startpos,length,string)
F$FAO (control_string [,arg1,arg2...,arg15])
F$FILE_ATTRIBUTES (filespec,item)
F$GETDVI (device_name,item)
F$GETJPI (pid,item)
F$GETSYI (item[,nodename])
F$GETQUI (function,[item],[object_id],[flags])
F$IDENTIFIER (identifier,conversion_type)
F$INTEGER (expression)
F$LENGTH (string)
F$LOCATE (substring,string)
F$LOGICAL (logical_name) - use F$TRNLNM instead!
F$MESSAGE (status_code)
F$MODE ()
F$PARSE (filespec[,default_spec][,related_spec][,field][,type])
F$PID (context_symbol)
F$PRIVILEGE (priv_states)
F$PROCESS ()
F$SEARCH (filespec[,stream_id])
F$SETPRV (priv_states)
F$STRING (expression)
F$TIME ()
F$TRNLNM (log-name[,table][,index][,mode][,case][,item])
F$TYPE (symbol_name)
F$USER ()
F$VERIFY ([procedure_val][,image_val])
```

9

Tactics for LOGIN.COM

A properly constructed LOGIN.COM can simplify your work environment and provide specialized facilities for your personal projects. It is not unusual among serious VAX users to find log in procedures containing dozens or hundreds of lines of DCL. This chapter explains some advanced techniques that are useful in creating good LOGIN.COM programs and discusses some of the subtleties that must be addressed in order to avoid undesired effects.

What Is a LOGIN?

In designing your log in procedure, the first thing to note is that a LOGIN.COM is always executed at any log in. In addition to log-ins occurring when you sit down at a terminal and hit <return> a couple of times, they also occur whenever you SUBMIT a batch command file and whenever you SET HOST, even if it is to the same node. Therefore it's important to remember what constitutes a log in.

Why Create a Special LOGIN.COM?

Each time you initiate a LOGIN procedure, VMS looks for a file named LOGIN.COM in your root or home level directory. If this file is not found there, or has some other name, the system will use its own default. This means that if you have not created a personal LOGIN.COM file, the VMS operating system will execute its default file for you, and you lose your opportunity to customize your environment automatically.

Many DCL operations that are great for interactive sessions at a terminal are time wasters or even downright problems if executed in a batch environment in which there is no physical terminal attached to the job (i.e., SYS$OUTPUT is connected to a file, not a terminal screen or other TXnn device).

Considerable thought should be given to sensibly partitioning your log in procedure. Being organized doesn't matter much if the file is only 20 lines long. But as it grows past 100 lines a disorganized file becomes inconvenient, and at 500 lines it is probably not maintainable if not properly documented and structured. Log in file organization means keeping like commands together and grouping DCL operations that are parts of the same logical function. For instance, DEFINE/KEY commands should be kept together. Not everything is cut and dried, however.

A general rule might be to keep symbol assignments together, but in many cases it will make more sense to keep all the commands that go with a given project together, even if they are quite varied. This makes it easy to add a new project or remove an old one.

Another point to consider is the kind of VAX environment in which you are working. For a stand-alone MicroVAX system, you (as the potential sole user) will probably want some system management commands built in to your LOGIN.COM. If you don't you will get very tired of typing routine system management commands like SET DEF SYS$MANAGER over and over.

If you regularly use several nodes on a large network, you will very likely want more emphasis on remembering what node you are logged into (by setting the prompt to the current nodename) and what your current disk quotas are on different devices.

TAILORING THE LOGIN.COM FOR THE OPERATING MODE

VMS provides various facilities for letting a running DCL command procedure determine what its environment looks like, that is, on what node the program is running, what version of VMS is in use, whether the program is an interactive log in or a batch (SUBMIT) job, and so on. This last item is particularly useful to the LOGIN.COM procedure, which is executed by the operating system for all log ins, both batch and interactive.

Environment reading features are implemented through some of the lexical or F$ functions built into DCL. Although the main body of lexical functions is concerned with string manipulations (F$EXTRACT being a universally used workhorse), some simply return string values containing information of use to the command procedure.

DCL commands in LOGIN.COM can be categorized according to whether they should be done for interactive jobs, batch jobs, or both. There is, for example, no need to solicit a terminal type with SET TERM/INQUIRE from a batch job nor to execute any DEFINE/KEY assignments (although they are actually harmless in batch mode).

At a more sophisticated level, if you have a complex menu system that is automatically started for interactive jobs, you will definitely not want this system to run in batch mode. On the other hand, batch processes that don't have a user available to type different setup commands or to run project-related command procedures may need some extra things done at log in time. Some guidelines for selecting what kinds of commands to do in each mode are given later in this chapter.

Testing for Interactive Versus Batch Mode with F$MODE

One of the first things a LOGIN.COM procedure should do is determine the mode of the task that is logging in. This is accomplished through the F$MODE lexical function, which returns a string specifying what kind of log in is occurring. (This and other lexical functions are covered in greater depth in Chapter 8, Lexical Functions.) The value will be "INTERACTIVE" for terminal log ins, and "BATCH" for processes run via the SUBMIT command. The result of the F$MODE function should be used to call subroutines to handle each case. A skeletal LOGIN.COM based on this idea is

```
$! LOGIN.COM skeleton showing use of F$MODE
$!
$ ourmode = F$MODE()
$
$ if ourmode .eqs. "INTERACTIVE" call terminal_login
$ if ourmode .eqs. "BATCH" call batch_login
$ call all_logins
$ exit
$!
$! terminal_login - subroutine done for interactive jobs
$!
$terminal_login: SUBROUTINE
$!...
$ENDSUBROUTINE
$!
$! batch_login - subroutine done for batch jobs
$batch_login: SUBROUTINE
$!...
$ENDSUBROUTINE
$!
$! all_logins - subroutine done for all jobs
$all_logins: SUBROUTINE
$!...
$ENDSUBROUTINE
```

CONTENTS OF A LOGIN.COM FILE

Try to put things in LOGIN.COM that enhance your overall work environment in a permanent fashion. Often this means using terse shortcuts for the commands you use most frequently. The more you use a command, the shorter you'll want its symbolic equivalent to be.

One of the most common (and well-used) abbreviations for UNIX, MS-DOS and TOPS-20 converts is the symbol

```
$ CD == SET DEFAULT
```

This shortcut reduces the minimum amount of typing for a directory change from 7 characters (SET DEF) to only 2 (CD). By the way, the mnemonic for the symbol CD is Connect to Directory. Some other common symbols are

```
$ ANS       == PHONE /ANSWER
$ AUTH      == RUN AUTHORIZE
$ DEV       == SHOW DEVICE
$ DN        == @SYS$LOGIN:DOWN.COM
$ ED*IT     == EDIT/EDT/COMMAND=SYS$LOGIN:EDTINI.EDT
$ FAU*LTS   == MONITOR PROCESS/TOPFAULT
$ F         == FORTRAN/CONTIN=99
$ FD        == FORTRAN/CONTIN=99/DEBUG/NOOPT/CHECK=ALL
$ HO*ME     == SET DEFAULT SYS$LOGIN
$ MD        == CREATE/DIRECTORY
$ MGR       == SET DEFAULT SYS$MANAGER
$ PRIV      == SHOW PROCESS/PRIVILEGE
$ PROCS     == MONITOR PROCESS/TOPCPU
$ PU*RGE    == PURGE/KEEP=3/LOG
$ RD        == DELETE/DIRECTORY/LOG
$ ROOT      == SET DEFAULT SYS$SYSTEM
$ SYS       == SHOW SYSTEM
$ UP        == SET DEFAULT [-]
$ US        == SHOW USERS
```

Please notice that the list contains only those system level commands that you will use constantly as long as you are working with a VAX/VMS system. Items that *don't* belong in LOGIN.COM are project specific or temporary definitions. Project symbol and logical name assignments should absolutely be kept in the project directories where they can be maintained by the person responsible for the project. The best way to reference them in your own LOGIN.COM is simply to call the project specific setup procedure via the @ command, as in

```
$ @$DISK2:[ROCKET_SIM]SETUP.COM
```

This is in keeping with the programming principle that information (in this case the project's DCL definitions) should only be kept in one place, as far as practical.

SYMBOLS TO EMULATE OTHER OPERATING SYSTEM ENVIRONMENTS

There are lots of VAX users out there who are familiar with operating systems other than VMS. Without arguing the merits of various systems and command languages (we'll admit that VMS can be quite wordy), the following groups of command definitions can be used to provide minimal shells or emulations of UNIX or MS-DOS. These definitions only emulate the first-level commands; very complex DCL command procedures are required, for example, to have the CD command understand the UNIX directory and file syntax.

UNIX COMMAND DEFINITIONS

```
$!
$! .COM FRAGMENT FOR MINIMAL UNIX COMMAND EMULATION
$!
$ CD == SET DEFAULT
$ PWD == SHOW DEFAULT
$ LS == DIRECTORY
$ CAT == TYPE
$ RM == DELETE
$ MKDIR == CREATE/DIRECTORY
$ RD == DELETE/DIRECTORY
```

MS-DOS COMMAND DEFINITIONS

```
$!
$! .COM FRAGMENT FOR MINIMAL MS-DOS COMMAND EMULATION
$! Note that some MS-DOS commands are the same:
$!    DEL   TYPE   LINK  DEBUG
$!
$ CD == SET DEFAULT
$ DIR == DIRECTORY/DATE=MODIFIED
$ MD == CREATE/DIRECTORY
$ RD == DELETE/DIRECTORY
```

```
$ ERASE == DELETE
$ FF == DIR [*]          ! File Find from Norton Utilities
$ EDLIN == EDIT          ! editor substitution
$ ATTRIB == DIR/PROTECTION
```

GUIDELINES FOR INTERACTIVE AND BATCH MODE LOGIN FUNCTIONS

The primary separation of LOGIN functions is made between batch and interactive sessions. Since batch jobs are run without human intervention, and do not usually interact with a terminal for either input or output, it makes sense to partition your LOGIN.COM for these two functions. Specific suggestions for partitioning LOGIN.COM functions according to the job type follow.

Batch Job

- SET TERMINAL is not needed.

- Avoid terminal-oriented displays, especially those containing escape sequences.

- Be sure to include all DEFINE and ASSIGN statements needed by your program.

- DEFINE/KEY macros are unnecessary.

- Custom prompts aren't needed. (Don't SET PROMPT.)

- INQUIRE statements don't make sense.

- Symbols used as command abbreviations are not required unless used by subsidiary batch files. Note the use of command abbreviations in command files is not recommended; for maximum clarity you should always spell out the commands you use in .COM files – you never know who will need to read your files later on.

- Format WRITE SYS$OUTPUT statements with the .LOG file in mind, not a terminal.

Interactive Jobs

- Be sure to SET TERMINAL/INQUIRE (unless you have a very good reason for doing otherwise such as dialing in to a computer having terminal emulator software that does not respond to the normal terminal ID interrogation).

- Include symbol definitions for command abbreviations. Unlike the recommendation for .COM files, using abbreviations in this context is recommended – you are not creating files that may later be read by someone unacquainted with your abbreviations.

- DEFINE/KEY commands are fine.

- In a networked environment, you may want to announce the host on the terminal or do a custom SET PROMPT containing the nodename.

SUMMARY

LOGIN.COM is a file executed every time you log in to a terminal with your user ID and password. VMS looks for a file with this name and invokes it to set up your process environment to suit your work requirements automatically. Its use can make your life easier and your work more accurate and faster. Practice using a variety of parameters in your personal LOGIN.COM to find the system that works best for you.

A Comprehensive LOGIN.COM.

The example given here is a comprehensive LOGIN.COM file modeled after the one that Kristyne Leisner, a VAX programmer, uses for her VAX/VMS tasks. Modify it as you like for your own use. Command files referenced in this LOGIN.COM can be found in Appendix D, Command File Library.

```
$!-------------------------------------
$! Kristyne Leisner's personal LOGIN.COM
$!-------------------------------------
$ krismode = F$MODE()
$!
$ if krismode .eqs. "INTERACTIVE" call terminal_login
$ if krismode .eqs. "BATCH" call batch_login
$ call all_logins
$ exit
$!-------------------------------------
$          interactive_login: SUBROUTINE
$!-------------------------------------
$!
$! Directory and file navigation symbols
```

```
$!
$! Working symbols
$!
$ cd      :==       create/directory
$ del*ete      :==    delete/log/confirm
$ deln   :==    delete/log/noconfirm
$ ed*it  :==    edit/edt/com=sys$login:edtini.edt-
                login.com
$ el*ogin:==    edit/edt/com=sys$login:edtini.edt-
                login.com
$ f       :==    fortran
$ fd      :==    fortran/debug/noopt/check=all
$ fl      :==    fortran/lis
$ pri*nt :==    print/header
$ prn    :==    print/noheader
$ pu*rge :==    purge/log
$ rd      :==    delete/directory
$ re*log :==    @sys$login:login.com
$!
$! System and system manager symbols
$!
$ ans     :==    phone/answer
$ aut*hor:==    run authorize
$ dev*ice:==    show device
$ fau*lts:==    monitor process/topfault
$ mgr     :==    set default sys$manager
$ pri*vil:==    show process/privilege
$ pro*cs :==    monitor process/topcpu
$ sys     :==    show system
$ us      :==    show users
$!
$ ENDSUBROUTINE
$!-------------------------------------
$ batch_login: SUBROUTINE
$!-------------------------------------
$!
$ show time
$ set verify
$!
$ ENDSUBROUTINE
```

```
$!--------------------------------------
$ all_logins: SUBROUTINE
$!-------------------------------------$!
$   @PROJECT          ! Invoke the current project's
$                     !"login.com"
$ lo*gout:==          @sys$login:mylogout.com
$!
$ ENDSUBROUTINE
$ EXIT
```

10

File and Terminal I/O from DCL

One of the things that makes DCL complete as a computer working environment is its ability to access VMS files directly. Many less-sophisticated operating systems have very primitive file-management functions, generally limited to commands like COPY, APPEND, and DELETE, which really belong in the category of directory handling. Normally, there is no means of access to the *contents* of a file on a byte-by-byte basis. DCL, on the other hand, gives you complete access to the data inside files through its READ and WRITE commands.

Furthermore, since the VMS standard names SYS$INPUT and SYS$OUTPUT are treated exactly like files, DCL can get complete access to a terminal by doing READs and WRITEs to those identifiers. Combine this with the fact that the symbol-manipulation operators make it possible to generate ANSI escape sequences compatible with the VT100, VT200 and VT300 series of terminals, and it becomes possible to generate some very fancy screen displays entirely within DCL – no FORTRAN, C or COBOL programming required.

BASIC METHODS OF FILE ACCESS

The essential sequence of operations for doing any kind of file work from DCL is
* OPEN the file.

* Use READ and WRITE to access data inside the file.

* CLOSE the file.

The SYS$INPUT, SYS$OUTPUT, SYS$COMMAND and SYS$ERROR logical names are preopened for you when you log in and are closed automatically when you log out. Normally, therefore, you won't need to OPEN or CLOSE any of them.

Here's an example that creates a file and writes some data to it:

```
$ OPEN/WRITE OUT_FILE TEXT.DAT
$ WRITE OUT_FILE "Here is a bit of text"
$ WRITE OUT_FILE "A second line of text too"
$ CLOSE OUT_FILE
$ WRITE SYS$OUTPUT "File write example is finished"
```

This example illustrates some facts about the file access commands: First, each file opened has a logical name assigned to it by the OPEN statement. In the example, the logical name is OUT_FILE. This logical name is placed in the process logical name table, where it remains until the file is closed. Second, if you want write access to a file, it must be opened with the /WRITE qualifier.

In this case, the file need not exist already; it will be created automatically if it doesn't exist yet. If it does exist, a new generation will be created. The default OPEN is for read-only access, in which case the file *must* already exist. Lastly, each WRITE statement places one record or line in the output file identified by the logical name following the WRITE command. Conversely, each READ statement will fetch one record. You can WRITE to SYS$OUTPUT and SYS$ERROR just like normal files.

FINDING OUT YOUR TERMINAL TYPE

Before sending hardware-dependent terminal control sequences to SYS$OUTPUT, it's a good idea to make sure what kind of terminal you're dealing with. As the Digital terminal product line has evolved from the VT52 through the VT100, VT200, and VT300 families, the size and power of the terminal command set has steadily increased. Unfortunately, the older terminal families do not recognize the new command codes and will interpret them in strange and unwanted ways.

Recall that your LOGIN.COM command file can contain a SET TERMINAL/INQUIRE command to cause VMS to interrogate your terminal about its type. Your command procedure can then find out the exact terminal type established by using the F$GETDVI lexical function as in the following example:

```
$ TTYPE = F$GETDVI("SYS$COMMAND", "DEVTYPE")
```

The F$GETDVI function, when called with the above arguments, returns a number specifying the device type of the terminal – one of the types listed in Table 10-1.

Be careful using device type specification references – the list given in DEC's new VMS [5.0] *General User's Manual* is not complete – several device types were not included.

One thing you should *not* do is issue a new SET TERMINAL/INQUIRE command in command procedures that will be used by others. Unless you have a compelling reason for doing so, this operation should be left up to each user. This permits compensation for unusual terminal types and non-Digital terminals. If you forge right ahead and do the SET TERMINAL/INQUIRE in command procedures for use with your software, your command will negate any SET TERMINAL/DEVICE=xxxxx commands previously issued by the user, often replacing a meaningful device type with "UNKNOWN". Once this has been done, the revised setting persists throughout the session, even after your command procedure has finished. The user may notice later that the terminal type has been clobbered and wonder why.

TABLE 10-1.   *Device type specifications returned from the lexical function F$GETDVI.;*

Terminal Type	Number
UNKNOWN	0
FT1 - FT8	16-23
LA12	36
LA24	37
LA34	34
LA36	32
LA38	35
LA100	37
LA120	33
LA210	40
VT5X	64
VT52	64
VT55	65
VT100	96
VT101	97
VT102	98
VT105	99
VT125	100
VT131	101
VT132	102
VT173	3
VT200	110
VT300	(not listed in DEC's VMS 5.0 *General User's Manual*)

While at first blush it may seem attractive to write a complicated terminal-identification routine with separate code to handle every possible terminal type, in practice there's usually no reason to do that. If the performance improvement from using the VT200/300 block edit modes is important, you should be writing your application in a standard programming language that generates high-performance machine code, not in DCL, which is interpreted at a much more modest pace. Usually the only distinction you'll need to make in DCL command procedures is between those terminals that understand at least the VT100 control codes and those that don't.

With the current allocation of device codes, any terminal device with a type greater than or equal to the VT100 code (96) is guaranteed to accept the VT100 escape sequences. The only issue that remains is what to do about terminals that return "UNKNOWN" or a device type less than 96. Usually the solutions are either to refuse to operate with the offending terminal (unfriendly but sometimes necessary with very screen-intensive procedures) or to treat the device as a dumb teletype, where the only available control sequence is a carriage return <CR> to start a new line.

A command procedure fragment to interrogate the system about the terminal type and set a flag according to whether it's a VT100-compatible terminal follows:

```
$!
$! Command procedure showing terminal type determination
$!
$ TTYPE = F$GETDVI("SYS$COMMAND", "DEVTYPE")
$ IF TTYPE .GE. 96
$ THEN
$    VT100_FLAG = 1
$ ELSE
$    VT100_FLAG = 0
$    WRITE SYS$OUTPUT "Working in dumb terminal mode"
$ ENDIF
$!
$! Blank screen on terminal
$!
$ IF VT100_FLAG .EQ. 1
$ THEN
$    ESCSEQ[7,8] = 27               ! <esc> character
$    ESCSEQ[31,24] = 0              ! rest is NULLs
$    WRITE SYS$OUTPUT ESCSEQ, "[2J" ! ANSI erase cmd
$ ELSE
$    WRITE SYS$OUTPUT " "  ! blank line for dumb TTY
$ ENDIF
```

HOW TO DO FANCY TERMINAL OUTPUT FROM WITHIN DCL

The previous example introduced an additional concept that is needed for effective terminal displays: how to create a string symbol containing nonprintable characters such as <escape>. So-called *escape sequences* are needed so often that the term is considered standard. The square bracket symbol notation always means an [offset, length] pair. There are two interpretations of offset and length, depending on whether the expression on the right hand side of the = evaluates to a string or to a number. The one used above is a bit-wise overlay that must obey the following rules:

- The right-hand side expression must be numeric, not a string.

- When the name of the symbol on the left hand side has already been defined as a string, or is undefined, the result of the assignment is a string. Otherwise the resulting symbol is a number. (In the example a string is needed and is gotten by having ESCSEQ be previously undefined.)

- The offset is treated as a starting bit position. It must be between 0 and 31, inclusive. Bits are counted from right to left in the data word, where the rightmost bit is called bit 0. The length can be in the range 1 to 32, inclusive. It does not make sense to have the length exceed (offset + 1).

In the example, the symbol ESCSEQ is set to contain the ASCII <esc> character in its rightmost 8 bits (offset 7, length 8) and ASCII NULLs in the high 3 bytes (offset 31, length 24). Thus, the final sequence that gets sent to the terminal is

```
<NULL><NULL><NULL><ESC>[2J
```

which amounts to a "clear screen" command preceded by three nulls. Since the terminal ignores nulls, the net effect is to blank the screen.

The other form of the square bracket overlay assignment performs a bytewise string replacement rather than a bitwise overlay. A code fragment illustrating this method is

```
$ WORD_A := "ALPHA BRAVO CHARLIE DELTA"
$ WORD_A[0,5] = HOTEL
$ SHOW SYMBOL WORD_A
```

Itwill display the following message on the terminal screen:

```
A = "HOTEL BRAVO CHARLIE DELTA"
```

As you can see from the example, here the offset is the character position counting from the left end of the string, and the length is how many characters to replace.

The general rules for the construction of a DCL string assignment statement are as follows:

- The assignment operator must be the string assignment :=

- The right-hand side of the assignment must be a character string.

- The offset and size can range from 0 to 768.

- Offset denotes the starting position in characters (bytes), counting from the left end of the string. Offset 0 is the first character of the string.

- Length is how many characters (bytes) of the string symbol are to be replaced.

- If the symbol is undefined at the outset, the symbol will be created and padded with sufficient leading or trailing blanks to accommodate the replacement request.

SUMMARY

This chapter introduced the concept of controling the functions of your terminal using DCL commands and escape sequences rather than through the brute-force terminal SETUP screen. The chapter began with a discussion of the SET TERMINAL command. The following is a complete list of SET TERMINAL command switches:

```
SET   TERMINAL
/[NO]ADVANCED_VIDEO              /FRAME=n
/ALTYPEAHD                      /[NO]FULLDUP
/[NO]ANSI_CRT                   /[NO]HALFDUP
/APPLICATION_KEYPAD             /[NO]HANGUP
/[NO]AUTOBAUD                   /[NO]HARDCOPY
/[NO]BLOCK_MODE                 /[NO]HOSTSYNC
/[NO]BRDCSTMBX                  /INQUIRE
/[NO]BROADCAST                  /INSERT
/CRFILL[=fill-count]            /LFFILL[=fill-count]
/[NO]DEC_CRT[=(val1,val2,val3)] /[NO]LINE_EDITING
/DEVICE_TYPE=terminal-type      /[NO]LOCAL_ECHO
/[NO]DIALUP                     /[NO]LOWERCASE
/[NO]DISCONNECT                 /MANUAL
/[NO]DISMISS                    /[NO]MODEM
/[NO]DMA                        /NUMERIC_KEYPAD
/[NO]ECHO                       /OVERSTRIKE
/[NO]EDIT_MODE                  /PAGE[=lines-per-page]
/[NO]EIGHT_BIT                  /[NO]PARITY
/[NO]ESCAPE                     /[NO]PASTHRU
/[NO]FALLBACK                   /PERMANENT
/[NO]FORM                       /[NO]PRINTER_PORT
```

```
/PROTOCOL=DDCMP                /SPEED=(input-rate,output-
/PROTOCOL=NONE                   rate)
/[NO]READSYNC                  /SWITCH=DECNET
/[NO]REGIS                     /[NO]SYSPASSWORD
/[NO]SCOPE                     /[NO]TTSYNC
/[NO]SECURE_SERVER             /[NO]TYPE_AHEAD
/[NO]SET_SPEED                 /UNKNOWN
/[NO]SIXEL_GRAPHICS            /[NO]UPPERCASE
/[NO]SOFT_CHARACTERS           /WIDTH=characters-per-line
                               /[NO]WRAP
```

Other commands covered in this chapter dealt with file I/O. The following is a complete listing of the command switches are:

CLOSE   logical-name[:]
```
/ERROR=label                   /[NO]LOG
```

OPEN   logical-name[:]   filespec
```
/APPEND
/ERROR=label                   /SHARE[=option]
/READ                          /WRITE
```

READ   logical-name[:]   symbol-name
```
/DELETE                        /MATCH=option      /MATCH=EQ
/END_OF_FILE=label             /NOLOCK
/ERROR=label                   /PROMPT=string
/INDEX=n          /INDEX=0     /[NO]TIME_OUT=n    /NOTIME_OUT
/KEY=string
```

WRITE   logical-name   expression[,…]
```
/ERROR=label                   /UPDATE
/SYMBOL
```

11

Success with BACKUP

WHY USE BACKUP?

Often, it seems that backing up files is relegated to the system manager, and users never learn the procedures required for the successful use of the BACKUP command. DEC doesn't really help all that much either. The DEC manual set buries the instructions for BACKUP in the dark recesses of the *System Manager's Manual*, assuming mere users will either never do their own backups or have the desire to retrieve files from months or years back.

But BACKUP is easily the one utility that can save your hide in a crunch. Imagine a situation in which your boss or a customer requests assistance on a project you haven't worked on for months or even years. Since you have a limit on your available disk storage, you had removed the necessary files from disk. The people needing answers have made a number of changes to your work, and you need your last working copy to help you debug it. You don't have a backup, and the system manager's backups are hard to access. Even worse, your files are buried with those of all the other users of your VAX system. You can't even remember the date of the backup, that you need to locate your old files. What are you going to do now?

You can avoid all that by learning to use BACKUP to keep copies of your work in all the critical stages and archive them once delivery has been made of the completed software.

Rationale for BACKUP

We want to impress you with this: The two best reasons for backing up your files are (1) to protect your valuable files from loss during catastrophic crashes or fits of simple absentmindedness and (2) to delete old files from everyday memory while still maintaining the ability to restore and reuse them at will.

You may think there is no real possibility for loss because the system you use is rarely if ever at risk, but a lot can happen. Someone may accidentally get access to shared files, which is what happened at a friend's office once. Several important, unsaved files were lost when another team member was doing some file cleanup and delete housekeeping, mistakenly believing she was cleaning up her own directory. You may even misuse a wildcard during a DELETE command, wiping out megabytes of valuable work. At any rate, for your own peace of mind, learn about and use the BACKUP facility. At some point in the not-too-distant future it will probably save many hours of work and maybe even your professional hide.

The second reason for backups, to archive your work is just as important. You cannot and should not save copies of all the tests you run during a software development exercise, but you can save backups of these runs when redoing them is not a worthwhile venture for the inevitable questions. Problems do come up that can be solved very quickly through the use of early backups.

BACKUP is sometimes used instead of the DCL COPY command, since it can create an exact duplicate of your original files and directories, with the original creation dates and file protections intact. It is especially useful for disk-to-disk copy operations that are often used for moving files to a less-filled disk on systems with limited memory.

BACKUP OPTIONS

BACKUP can be used in a number of modes to create identical or functional copies of all or a part of the files in your directories. The options are defined below and will be discussed in the following pages.

Physical

The physical backup operation creates an exactly identical bit-by-bit duplicate of your volume, while ignoring file structures.

Image

Creates a functional equivalent rather than an identical copy of your original volume. You can use an image backup for bootable volumes, like the VAX/VMS system boot disk. You might also use the /IMAGE qualifier to compress a volume, making all the files contiguous (i.e., occupying consecutive space on the disk with no intervening blocks belonging to other files).

Selective

A selective backup is useful for creating backups of specific files or for choosing files using specified criteria with switches (such as /DATE and *.FOR) to specify file types, version numbers, or date of creation or modification.

File by File

In file-by-file mode, file copy facilities are available that the DCL COPY command cannot do, such as directory creation during the execution of the BACKUP command. Backup copies individual files, an entire directory, or an entire disk volume, depending on the specifications given.

Incremental

Incremental backups save files created since your most recent backup. On some installations, the incremental backup is the one most often done by the system manager on a daily or weekly basis. If you have the privileges, you should also do incremental backups, with occasional complete physical backups.

USING BACKUP

The usual BACKUP tasks are to save files, restore files, and list tape contents. The specific task THAT BACKUP performs is determined by the input and output specifiers in the command line and any qualifiers modifying the default behavior of the command.

You enter the BACKUP command at the DCL command prompt. VMS then evaluates the input and output specifiers to determine which type of BACKUP operation to perform. BACKUP uses the input file spec to identify the input to the utility, then directs the output to the destination named by the output file spec. This output can be a file or a save-set (a collection of backed-up files) on either disk or magnetic tape. After execution, the BACKUP utility returns to the DCL command prompt. The command can be interrupted like any other with the CTRL/Y command, stopping it in midstream.

To test the BACKUP command, start with a simple file-to-file BACKUP copy. The syntax is

```
$ BACKUP input-file-spec output-file-spec
```

Input File Specifier

You specify the input for the BACKUP operation with an input-file-spec. This specifier can be a BACKUP save-set specification, a standard VMS file specification, or a device name. For input save-set file specifiers located on a disk, the command line must also include the /SAVE_SET qualifier. Save-set qualifiers must also be used if the input file specification is a DEC-net-VAX node name. Wildcards are permitted for all standard VMS file specifications and in save-set specifications only if they are on magnetic tape.

Output File Specifier

An output file specifier can also be a save-set specification, a standard VMS file specification, or a device name. As for the input specifier, save-set qualifiers must be used for save-sets that are on disk but are not necessary for save-sets on magnetic tape. Save-set qualifiers must also be used if the input file specification is a DECnet-VAX node name. Wildcards are permitted for all standard VMS file specifications. Wildcards are not permitted, however, for either output BACKUP save-sets or for volumes created with the BACKUP/PHYSICAL or the BACKUP/IMAGE commands.

Single File Backups

The BACKUP command works the same from either direction. For example, suppose you want to create a copy of a file on a tape mounted on device MUA0: (a default name for a TK50 drive). You would name the file you wish to copy as the input-file-spec, or the source, and the output would have the same name, on device MUA0:

```
$ BACKUP anyfile.sav MUA0:anyfile.sav/SAVE_SET
```

In this case, the file anyfile.sav from your default directory will be copied to the tape mounted on device MUA0: with the filename as specified. If you do not specify the full name of the destination file, DCL will assume the copy will have the same name as the source file. When you specify a tape drive with the MUA0 or other default disk drive device name, DCL will assume that the specified file is a SAVE_SET. It is usually good form to use the parameter, however, since when doing a disk-to-disk copy that default does not apply.

To reverse the operation, simply reverse the order of the file names. Now you will say the MUA0:anyfile.txt is the source and give the filename for the destination as follows:

```
$ BACKUP MUA0:anyfile.txt/SAVE_SET anyfile.sav
```

As usual, wildcards can be used anywhere that wildcards would ordinarily work. For example, any of these

```
$ BACKUP MUA0:anyfile.sav/SAVE_SET anyfile.sav
$ BACKUP MUA0:anyfile.sav anyfile.sav
$ BACKUP MUA0:anyfile.sav/SAVE_SET *.*
$ BACKUP MUA0:anyfile.sav
```

would work the same way. Experiment, if you can, with a tape or cartridge drive to see what the behavior is so you will be ready for the examples to come. They are a little difficult to grasp the first time through.

Multiple File Backups

The BACKUP command for multiple files is facilitated the same way as the COPY command. Use the ellipsis [...] to specify multiple directories, and wildcards for the filename, type, and version numbers at will. The save-set qualifier refers to a collection of files related to a single BACKUP operation, so wildcards are meaningless for save-sets as output. For input, wildcards are treated as though the operation executes for each named save-set in series.

BACKUP MEDIA HANDLING

The most commonly used media for storing BACKUP save sets is magnetic tape. It is less expensive than disk storage, conveniently portable, and easily storable, making its use fairly painless. Intelligent use of tape media will greatly reduce the time used by the critical work- and sanity-saving tool, BACKUP.

INITIALIZE

Magnetic tapes must be initialized before their first use. The INITIALIZE command prepares the tape to receive data and can be used to write a volume label, volume protection data, and a tape expiration date into the tape's volume header. The INITIALIZE operation destroys any data recorded on a used magnetic tape, so it is useful for recycling used tapes as well. INITIALIZE can change the volume label, tape expiration date, and volume protection data on the tape.

Magnetic tapes can be initialized using either the DCL INITIALIZE command or by invoking the /REWIND output save-set qualifier in the BACKUP command line. When /REWIND is used in an output save-set qualifier, BACKUP rewinds the output tape to the beginning-of-tape marker, then initializes the output tape. Using a /NOREWIND qualifier (the default) causes the tape to wind forward to the end of the last save-set stored on the tape and begin writing the new save-set there.

Be careful about using the /REWIND output qualifier since you can inadvertently destroy the files you have previously backed up by writing new data on top of them.

MOUNT/DISMOUNT

The MOUNT utility is used to make a magnetic tape or disk volume available for use by the system. You can invoke MOUNT at the DCL command prompt or in a command file.

The syntax is for invoking the MOUNT utility is

```
$ MOUNT device-name[:][,...] [volume-label[,...]] [logical-
name[:]]
```

Figure 11-1 shows the sequence of events when using tape drives for backup with /REWIND.

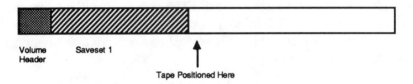

Tape After BACKUP / REWIND /SAVESET...

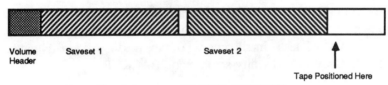

Tape After Subsequent BACKUP /SAVESET...

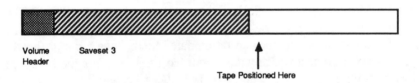

Tape After Another BACKUP / REWIND /SAVESET...
Note that Savesets 1 and 2 have been lost

FIGURE 11-1.   Tape Operations Under BACKUP/REWIND.

The volume label parameter is optional if the tape has been mounted with the /FOREIGN, /NOLABEL, or /OVERRIDE=IDENTIFICATION qualifiers. The logical name parameter is totally optional. If you forget a parameter, DCL will prompt you for all those that are required. A magnetic tape can have one or more volume labels and one or more logical names.

Automatic mounting is one of the bonuses of the VMS 5.0 BACKUP command. In the earlier VMS versions, magnetic tapes had to be mounted as a foreign volume using the /FOREIGN volume qualifier.

Backups to Disk

If you wish to use disk storage rather than or in addition to magnetic tapes, you can do so by adding the /SAVE_SET qualifier to the save-set specifier in the BACKUP command line. This example BACKUP command will create a single file physical backup save-set of anyfile.txt on DISK1 named anyfile.sav. The command will not work as intended without the /SAVE_SET qualifier.

```
$BACKUP anyfile.sav DISK1:anyfile.sav/SAVE_SET
```

SUMMARY

BACKUP   input-specifier   output-specifier

Command Qualifiers	Defaults
/[NO]ASSIST	/ASSIST
/BRIEF	/BRIEF
/BUFFER_COUNT=n	/BUFFER_COUNT=3
/COMPARE	
/DELETE	
/FAST	
/FULL	/BRIEF
/IGNORE=option	
/IMAGE	
/INCREMENTAL	/BY_OWNER=ORIGINAL
/[NO]INITIALIZE	
/INTERCHANGE	
/JOURNAL[=filespec]	
/LIST[=filespec]	
/[NO]LOG	/NOLOG
/PHYSICAL	
/RECORD	
/[NO]TRUNCATE	/NOTRUNCATE
/VERIFY	
/VOLUME=n	

```
Input  File-Selection  Qualifiers      Defaults
/BACKUP
/BEFORE=time
/BY_OWNER[=[uic]]
/CONFIRM
/CREATED
/EXCLUDE=(filespec[,...])
/EXPIRED
/MODIFIED
/SINCE=time


Input  Save-Set  Qualifiers            Defaults
/[NO]CRC                               /CRC
/[NO]REWIND                            /NOREWIND
/SAVE_SET
/SELECT=(filespec[,...])


Output  File  Qualifiers               Defaults
/BY_OWNER[=option]                     /BY_OWNER=DEFAULT
/NEW_VERSION
/OVERLAY
/REPLACE


Output  Save-Set  Qualifiers           Defaults
/BLOCK_SIZE=n
/BY_OWNER=[uic]
/CEMENT=string
/[NO]CRC  /CRC
/DENSITY=n
/GROUP_SIZE=n                          /GROUP_SIZE=10
/LABEL=(string[,…])
/PROTECTION[=(code)]
/[NO]REWIND                            /NOREWIND
/SAVE_SET
/TAPE_EXPIRATION
```

Part 4
Advanced Topics

The information in this six-chapter part is what many experienced professionals never get into at all, much less go beyond. Therefore, if you get to know the material, you will be well on your way to becoming your group's DCL ace.

Chapter 12, Terminal Characteristics, will give you the knowledge to use your DCL prompt line or command files to change terminal display characteristics instead of having to resort the the terminal's often slow and confusing setup menu.

Chapter 13, File Protection, Privileges, and Access Control Lists, enables you to alter the protections and priveleges for files you create and to find out what privileges your system manager has given you.

Chapter 14, Process Control and Monitoring, tells you how the VAX runs your processes. You will learn to create and manage new processes using SPAWN and to monitor the processes that both you and other users create.

Chapter 15, Network Access, gives you a fundamental knowledge of the use of DECNET and Ethernet for enhanced performance and delves into the differences between networking and clustering VAX CPUs.

Chapter 16, VMS 5.0 Changes, gives you an overview of the significant changes in the latest major system release, along with a few pointers on behavior changes to watch out for in this and later VMS releases.

12

Terminal Characteristics

STANDARD TERMINAL FEATURES

In its simplest form, a terminal is just a replacement for the dumb teletype printers that were once the standard devices for communicating with a computer. On those original machines, you simply typed a line of commands to the machine, and one or more lines of output on paper came back. Video display terminals have ended the massive use of teletype paper rolls, but the basic means of interacting with a large operating system such as VMS have remained largely the same.

Fortunately, modern character-based terminals such as DEC's VT300 series have a lot more capability than a mere electronic typewriter. Their capabilities are quite different, however, than those of a PC display. Character-based terminals are essentially always attached to the host VAX by a serial line, over which the command and screen display data are sent at speeds typically in the range of 4800 to 19,200 bits per second (bps). These data are coded in ASCII, 1 byte per character.

In a PC, the display is generated directly from the computer's memory, with no serial link. Screen graphics are much easier to generate on a PC than character-based graphics terminals that require a complicated serial character protocol to achieve the same result.

Terminals can be attached to a VAX either directly through a serial port or across an Ethernet network through a terminal server. Direct connection is typical for smaller installations where there may not be more than one computer or where budget constraints won't allow terminal servers. Figure 12-1 illustrates how directly connected terminals are arranged.

Network terminal connections through a terminal server are usually much more convenient than those that are directly connected. The terminal server can be attached anywhere on an Ethernet trunk, providing access for eight or more terminals. Through the terminal server you can access any VAX on the network. DEC's terminal servers provide a unique capability that enables you to have more than one simultaneous session; that is, the server will maintain connections for you to more than one VAX. You can flip back and forth between sessions using special keystroke sequences from your terminal. Figure 12-2 illustrates network-connected terminals.

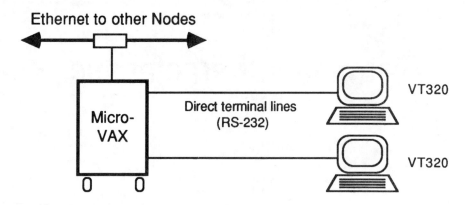

FIGURE 12-1.   Directly Connected Terminals.

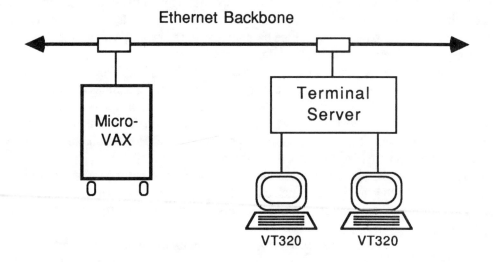

FIGURE 12-2.   Network Terminal Connections.

Character-based terminals come in many different forms, but they nearly all have one universal feature: When you send them ordinary ASCII-encoded letters, numbers, and punctuation marks (the so-called printing characters) those are what appear on the screen. In ASCII encoding, each letter, digit, and punctuation character is assigned a unique byte-wide value that represents the character. (For a complete chart of the ASCII coding scheme, see Appendix D.)

If just spewing out characters were all the terminal could do, however, you couldn't even backspace over a typing error at the terminal. Much of the power of character display terminals stems from how they react to the nonprinting characters. These characters are defined so that they cause the terminal to take some action other than just putting a character up on the screen. For example, sending a BEL character (CTRL/G, ASCII code 07 hexadecimal) will cause the terminal to beep.

Some of the single output characters that cause some special action in the terminal are as follows:

- Carriage return (0D hex) – causes the cursor to return to be beginning of the current line. Normally followed by a linefeed.

- Linefeed (0A hex) – causes the cursor to move directly downward one line. If the cursor is already at the last line of the screen, the display scrolls up one line, leaving a blank line at the bottom.

- Bell (07 hex) – emits a beep.

- Backspace (08 hex) – causes the cursor to move left one position. Does not erase the previous character. To erase a character, use <backspace> <space> <backspace>.

- Tab (09 hex) – advances the cursor to the next tab stop. Default tab stops are at 8-character intervals.

ESCAPE SEQUENCES

Even with the control granted by TAB, BS, and so forth, terminal displays are difficult. For one thing, the normal ASCII character set does not provide any way to write a specific character at a specific location on the terminal screen. Nor does it let you erase the screen, create inverse video characters, or any of the other fancy things you've probably seen on your display.

In order to do more advanced terminal functions, escape sequences are needed. An *escape sequence* is a command to the terminal rather than just text to the screen for display. Escape sequences consist of a string of data preceded by the ESC character. Of course, this mechanism presupposes that the terminal is set up to understand the sequences being sent and has the ability to perform the specified commands.

Since the host computer and terminal must agree on the meaning of escape sequences, there is actually an ANSI-standard set of them that covers most of the basic terminal display functions. Some ANSI escape sequence formats are shown in Figure 12-3.

Many sequences take parameters. In this case a parameter is a nonnegative number composed of the ASCII digits 0 through 9. Omitted parameters always default to a value of 1. Some of the most commonly used escape sequences are defined in the following list:

```
<ESC> [ 2 J          Blanks entire screen
<ESC> [ 1 J          Blanks screen from top to cursor
<ESC> [ 0 J          Blanks screen from cursor to end
<ESC> [ 2 K          Blanks current line
<ESC> [ 1 K          Blanks from start of line to cursor
<ESC> [ 0 K          Blanks from cursor to end of line
<ESC> [<P1>A         Moves cursor up P1 lines
<ESC> [<P1>B         Moves cursor down P1 lines
<ESC> [<P1>C         Moves cursor right P1 characters
<ESC> [<P1>D         Moves cursor left P1 characters
<ESC> [<P1>;<P2>H        Moves cursor to row P1, column P2
<ESC> [ 0 m          Resets to normal video attributes
<ESC> [ 1 m          Turns on Bold attribute
<ESC> [ 4 m          Turns on Underline attribute
<ESC> [ 5 m          Turns on Blinking attribute
<ESC> [ 7 m          Turns on Inverse Video attribute
<ESC> [ 1 ; 4 m      Turn on Bold + Underline (etc.)
<ESC> [ ? 3 l        Sets 132-column display width
<ESC> [ ? 3 h        Sets 80-column display width
<ESC> # 6                Turns on double width characters
<ESC> # 5                Back to single width characters
<ESC> # 3                Double height characters (upper half)
<ESC> # 4                Double height characters (lower half)
<ESC> ( 0                Switch to graphic character set
<ESC> ( B                Switch to standard US ASCII character
set
```

In addition to the ANSI-standard control sequences, Digital Equipment Corp. has added several of its own sequences that invoke various DEC-specific terminal features. The number and complexity of these increase from the VT100 series terminals onward to the VT200 and VT300 series. The later models feature block editing and other advanced functions. For a complete listing of escape sequences, refer to the documentation for the particular terminal. The set listed above works on all DEC ANSI-compatible terminals and their clones (basically anything later than a VT52).

Simple DCL WRITE statements can be used to send escape sequences to a terminal. The following example blanks the screen, moves the cursor to row 20, column 30, and displays a message:

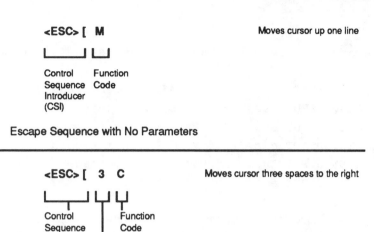

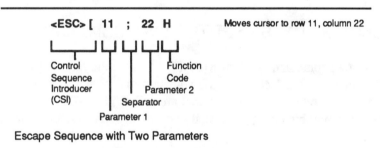

FIGURE 12-3.   ANSI Escape Sequence Formats.

```
$! demo of terminal escape sequence capabilities
$!
$ ESC[0,8] = %X1B              ! ASCII <ESC> character
$!
$ WRITE SYS$OUTPUT esc,"2J"    ! blank screen
$!
$ WRITE SYS$OUTPUT esc,"20;30H"      ! position cursor
$!
$ WRITE SYS$OUTPUT "Hello!"    ! output message
$!
```

The next listing shows how to do the same thing as above but in blinking, boldface characters:

```
$!
$! louder demo of terminal escape sequence capabilities
$!
$ ESC[0,8] = %X1B                   ! ASCII <ESC> character
$ WRITE SYS$OUTPUT esc,"[2J"   ! blank screen
$ WRITE SYS$OUTPUT esc,"[20;30H"    ! position cursor
$ WRITE SYS$OUTPUT esc,"[1;5m"      ! blink+bold
$ WRITE SYS$OUTPUT "Hello!"   ! output message
$ WRITE SYS$OUTPUT esc,"[0m"   ! restore normal video
```

The graphic character set is quite useful for generating boxes and lines. In order to use any characters from this set, you must first put the terminal into graphics mode. When you are finished drawing boxes, and so on, remember to reinvoke the standard U.S. ASCII character set.

INTRODUCTION TO THE SET TERMINAL COMMAND

Many system commands such as MONITOR use some terminal features beyond typing text. In order for VMS to handle your terminal properly, you must be able to specify what the attributes of your terminal are. SET TERMINAL takes care of this (and quite a bit more) by letting you specify almost any conceivable attribute for a display device.

The most-used variant of SET TERMINAL is the simple SET TERMINAL/INQUIRE command. This command, which causes VMS to interrogate the terminal via a special escape sequence, belongs in your LOGIN.COM. VMS analyzes the response and sets appropriate terminal attributes for you. A seldom-noticed side effect of SET TERMINAL/INQUIRE is that the typeahead buffer gets flushed out. This is done so that VMS can have a good expectation that the reply it analyzes came from the terminal and not from the user's typing.

If your terminal does not reply to the system's interrogation or gives an unintelligible answer, you will find (via SHOW TERMINAL) that the device type has been set to "UNKNOWN". If you know that your terminal is similar to an existing DEC model, you can force the device type to be what you want using SET TERMINAL/DEVICE_TYPE=name. A list of the device types known to DCL is given in the chapter summary. If you have a basic, plain-vanilla, mostly ANSI terminal, try

```
$ SET TERMINAL /DEVICE_TYPE=VT100
```

If for some reason you need to change your terminal serial I/O speed, you must tell the system about it *beforehand*, as in

```
$ SET TERMINAL /SPEED=19200
```

After you set the new terminal speed through DCL, you can physically change your terminal using the SETUP function. Notice that doing these two things in the wrong order will prevent DCL from receiving the SET TERMINAL/SPEED command.

A few of the SET TERMINAL qualifiers actually cause a response from the terminal. The one most often encountered is the /WIDTH control. When you do a SET TERMINAL/WIDTH=132 or SET TERMINAL/WIDTH=80, DCL will actually transmit the correct escape sequences to put your terminal into that display width. This sequence is shown here:

```
$! Terminal width changing example
$!
$ SET TERMINAL /WIDTH=132
$! terminal now is in wide display mode
$!
$ SET TERMINAL /WIDTH=80
$! Terminal is back in normal character mode
```

Another setting that directly affects the terminal is /NUMERIC_KEYPAD or /APPLICATION_KEYPAD. Invoking either one of these settings will actually cause the terminal to be set to the specified state. Be warned that in order for any DEFINE/KEY macros to work, your terminal must be in the /APPLICATION_KEYPAD state.

You can specify characteristics for a terminal other than your own by using the appropriate device name as a parameter to any SET TERMINAL command. Of course, you cannot affect any other user's terminal without the proper privileges. Usually LOG_IO or PHY_IO are needed. To set the port TXA5: to be a dialup line, you might use

```
$! set a dialup line
$!
$ SET TERMINAL TXA5: /PERMANENT /DIALUP
```

ESTABLISHING SPECIAL SERIAL LINES

The last example illustrates an operation that is frequently done during system startup: setting /PERMANENT terminal characteristics on various physical devices.

The use of /PERMANENT causes the settings to persist across different log in sessions by several users. Several situations frequently demand special permanent settings:

- Establishing dialup lines.

- Invoking the SYSPASSWORD protection on less-secure lines.

- Configuring output ports for serial printers (e.g. most low-end laser printers).

- Setting up async DDCMP DECNET lines.

An example showing how to set up a dialup modem line with most security features enabled is as follows:

```
$!
$! Set permanent dialup line
$!   we enable /HANGUP, /SYSPASSWORD, etc., for protection
$!
$ SET TERMINAL TXB3: /PERMANENT /DIALUP /HANGUP /SYSPASS -
_$ /DISCONNECT /SPEED=2400
$!
```

Several of the most important qualifiers to SET TERMINAL are as follows:

- /[NO]ADVANCED_VIDEO – Says whether the terminal is capable of a full 132-column x 24 line display.

- /[NO]ANSI_CRT – Says whether the terminal obeys the ANSI standard escape sequences.

- /[NO]AUTOBAUD – Controls whether the system will do speed recognition on the device. When AUTOBAUD is enabled you must press <CR> a few times slowly to let the hardware determine your terminal speed.

- /[NO]BROADCAST – Enables or disables reception of broadcast messages from MAIL and PHONE. Setting /NOBROADCAST is often useful on graphics terminals.

- /DEVICE_TYPE=name – Allows you to specify all characteristics for most DEC terminals with one qualifier. See chapter summary for a list of valid names.

- /[NO]DIALUP – Controls whether the terminal is treated as a dialup line.

- /[NO]ECHO – Controls whether DCL echoes input from the terminal.

- /[NO]FULLDUP – Says whether the terminal operates in full-duplex or half-duplex mode.

- /[NO]HANGUP – Causes the terminal modem to be hung up when a job logs out. Good security feature; should be set for dialup lines.

- /[NO]HARDCOPY – Says that the terminal is a hardcopy device (e.g., LAXXX) causes the DELETE key to echo as a backslash ("\").

- /INQUIRE – Causes the terminal to be interrogated for its device type.

- /[NO]MODEM – Says whether the line is connected to a modem. When /MODEM is set, any attempt to set it to /NOMODEM causes you to be logged out.

- /PAGE=number – Specifies the number of lines per page on hardcopy terminals.

- /[NO]PASTHRU – Controls whether all keyboard input is passed unfiltered to an application program. If you leave /NOPASTHRU in effect, VMS intercepts <CR>, <LF>, <tab>, and all control characters.

- /PERMANENT – Causes the specified settings to become permanent terminal characteristics that last until the VAX is rebooted. PHY_IO or LOG_IO privilege is required.

- /[NO]SET_SPEED – Controls whether users can alter the terminal speed with /SPEED. PHY_IO or LOG_IO is required.

- /SPEED=rate – Sets both the input and output speeds to the specified rate. Rates of 9600 and 19,200 bps are typical.

- /SPEED=(in_rate, out_rate) – Allows separate setting of input and output rates.

- /[NO]SYSPASSWORD – controls whether the system demands that the system password be entered before the regular log in prompts appear. LOG_IO privilege is needed.

- /[NO]TYPE_AHEAD – controls whether a typeahead buffer is enabled for the terminal. Setting /NOTYPE_AHEAD creates a dedicated terminal; no log ins are allowed.

- /UNKNOWN – used when you have a device that does not match any defined /DEVICE_TYPE. DCL supplies default terminal parameters.

- /WIDTH=n – specifies the display line width, in characters, not to exceed 511. If n = 132 or n = 80, ANSI terminals will be commanded to the appropriate display width. See also /[NO]WRAP

- /[NO]WRAP – when /WRAP is set, a <CR><LF> is automatically emitted when /WIDTH characters have been output on one line. /NOWRAP causes output to be lost at the right edge of the screen.

SUMMARY

The main purpose of this chapter is for you to become familiar with the SET TERMINAL and DEFINE/KEY commands. Their definitions are as follows:

DEFINE/KEY key-name equivalence-string

/[NO]ECHO	/[NO]LOCK_STATE
/[NO]ERASE	/[NO]SET_STATE[=state-name]
/[NO]IF_STATE[=(state-name,...)]	/[NO]TERMINATE

SET TERMINAL [device_name[:]]

/[NO]ADVANCED_VIDEO	/[NO]BLOCK_MODE
/ALTYPEAHD	/[NO]BRDCSTMBX
/[NO]ANSI_CRT	/[NO]BROADCAST
/APPLICATION_KEYPAD	/CRFILL[=null_count]
/[NO]AUTOBAUD	/[NO]DEC_CRT

/DEVICE_TYPE=type

UNKNOWN	LA100	PRO_SERIES	VT102
FT1-FT8	LA120	VT05	VT105
LA12	LA210	VT52	VT131
LA34	LN01K	VT55	VT173
LA36	LN03	VT100	VT200
LA38	LQP02	VT101	VT300

/[NO]DIALUP	/[NO]HARDCOPY
/[NO]DISCONNECT	/[NO]HOSTSYNC
/[NO]DISMISS	/INQUIRE
/[NO]DMA	/INSERT
/[NO]ECHO	/LFFILL[=null_count]
/[NO]EDIT_MODE	/[NO]LINE_EDITING
/[NO]EIGHT_BIT	/[NO]LOCAL_ECHO
/[NO]ESCAPE	/[NO]LOWERCASE
/[NO]FALLBACK	/MANUAL
/[NO]FORM	/[NO]MODEM
/FRAME=n_data_bits	/NUMERIC_KEYPAD
/[NO]FULLDUP	/OVERSTRIKE
/[NO]HALFDUP	/PAGE[=line_count]
/[NO]HANGUP	/[NO]PARITY[=option]

/[NO]PASTHRU
/PERMANENT
(LOG_IO or PHY_IO req'd)
/[NO]PRINTER_PORT
/PROTOCOL=NONE
/PROTOCOL=DDCMP
/[NO]READSYNC
/[NO]REGIS
/[NO]SCOPE
/[NO]SECURE_SERVER
/[NO]SET_SPEED
(LOG_IO or PHY_IO req'd)
/[NO]SIXEL_GRAPHICS

/[NO]SOFT_CHARACTERS
/SPEED=(input_speed, out-
put_speed)
/SPEED=speed
/SWITCH=DECNET
/[NO]SYSPASSWORD
/[NO]TAB
/[NO]TTSYNC
/[NO]TYPE_AHEAD
/UNKNOWN
/[NO]UPPERCASE
/WIDTH=chars_per_line
/[NO]WRAP

13

File Protection, Privileges, and Access Control Lists

VMS offers a very complete set of file and device access control mechanisms. As the operating system has matured over the last several years, these access controls have grown more sophisticated (and more bulletproof). This improvement has been motivated in part by the desire to make the VAX more suitable for government secure computing and in part to satisfy the needs of commercial customers with sensitive business data.

Originally, there was only the System-Owner-Group-World (SOGW) protection controls, also known as UIC-based protection. Any user who wanted to access a certain file was assigned to one of those categories. The main kinds of access were Read, Write, Execute, and Delete, which led to the familiar protection specifiers seen in

```
$SET FILE /PROTECTION=(S:RWED, O:RWED, G:RE, W:) filespec
```

With a few moments' reflection, you can probably see some of the shortcomings of this approach. The two greatest limitations were (1) since every user apart from the owner was either a member of group or world, there was no way to give a specific user access to one particular file and (2) the file's owner could grant access to absolutely anyone using the following:

```
$ SET FILE /PROTECTION=(W:RWED) myfile.txt
```

In many cases, security managers want to restrict the authority of a file's creator to expose the file to the outside world, and at the same time, keep the flexibility to give as-needed access to certain users who have a specific need for a certain file. Unfortunately, the traditional file access controls simply do not provide the desired features.

Thus was born the Access Control List, or ACL for short. The ACL is a new security feature that DEC added on top of the old SOGW protection codes. ACLs permit extremely specific control over access to files, directories, and even output devices such as printers. In addition, they provide selective control according to whether the user is interactive, batch, dialup, and so forth.

ACCESS CONTROL METHODS

There are three distinct ways to gain access to an object under VMS 5.0:

1. Through the Access Control List attached to that object – If there is no ACL or if the ACL denies access, then you may obtain access via (2).

2. The UIC-based protection for the object – Only the SYSTEM and OWNER categories will override an ACL denial of access. If the UIC codes also afford no access, you might still obtain access through (3).

3. Privileges – The following privileges may suffice to access an object even if both the ACL- and UIC-based protections deny access: SYSPRV, BYPASS, READALL, and GRPPRV.

It's important to understand how these three features interact so that you can trace through the access control logic. If you are responsible for the management of your system, knowing that UIC SYSTEM and OWNER access supercedes ACL denial and that sufficient privileges overcome both UIC and ACL denials is critical.

TYPES OF OBJECTS AND THEIR PROTECTION

VMS applies protection to the following kinds of objects:

- Files

- Directory descriptor files

- Queues (batch and print)

- Global sections

- Logical name tables

- Devices

Each kind of object will have a UIC-based protection mask and may optionally have an ACL. In general, when manipulating the protection for these objects it is not necessary to worry about that kind of object with which you are working. The SET PROTECTION and SET ACL commands are mostly symmetric across all the object types.

BASIS OF THE UIC SYSTEM

A UIC is a two-part code that identifies a group of users and a specific user within that group. It is normally written as [GROUP_ID, MEMBER_ID].

There are two kinds of UICs that you may see:

- Numeric, as in [462,12]

- Alphanumeric, for example [ENGR, COOK]

Numeric UICs are the fundamental identifier used by VMS. The two numbers for group and members are always in octal (base eight) format. The limiting bounds on these numbers are as follows:

TABLE 14-1. The limiting bounds for user identification codes imply a large number of unique codes.

ID Type	Lower Limit	Upper Limit
GROUP	0	37776
MEMBER	0	177776

Group numbers in the range 1 through 10 (octal) are reserved for SYSTEM objects. The actual upper bound of the SYSTEM group IDs is configurable by the system manager but is rarely changed in practice.

Subscribers to the Compuserve online information service may have noticed by now that your Compuserve user ID looks suspiciously like a DEC UIC code. This should give you some idea of how many users (a maximum of 37776 x 177776 = 6715666176) the UIC system is capable of supporting.

Alphanumeric UICs are mapped by VMS back onto the numeric UICs. Names in an alphanumeric UIC can consist of no more than 31 characters and may include only the letters A-Z, numerals 0-9, the dollar sign ($), and the underscore (_). As usual, embedded blanks are not allowed. In the sample given above, the UIC [ENGR,COOK] could be identical to [462,12]. For most practical purposes, the alphanumeric and numeric UICs are totally equivalent; either form may be used at will.

One additional point about the alphanumeric UICs is that the member portion taken alone must be unique to the system. This means that there could not be both a [ENGR,COOK] and a [ADMIN,COOK] on the same VMS node. The good thing about this feature is that merely specifying [COOK] is equivalent to either [ENGR,COOK] or [462,12]. Figure 13-1 shows the general layout of numeric and alphanumeric UICs.

A user's fundamental UIC is recorded more or less immutably in the system User Authorization File (UAF). Whenever you log in, this UIC is fetched and attached to your process, becoming the UIC that is used for any files or other objects that your process may create.

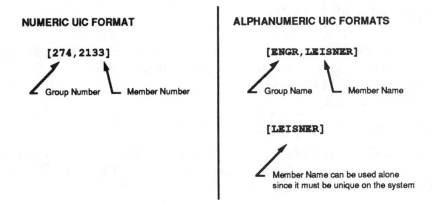

FIGURE 13-1.   UIC Formats.

UIC PROTECTION METHODS

Any object that is created by a process will, by default, be assigned the UIC of the creating process. This is of the greatest practical concern for files and directories. Once created, the UIC for an object is the one that is compared with the UIC of any user attempting to access the object.

In determining access rights to an object, the following criteria are used in matching the user process UIC to the target object UIC:

WORLD – Any user UIC on the system.

GROUP – The group number portion of the accessing process UIC and that of the target object are identical. May be overridden via the GRPPRV privilege.

OWNER – The complete UIC (both group and member) of the accessing process and the target object are identical.

SYSTEM – The group portion of the accessing process UIC is in the range 1 through 10 (octal). The same rights are granted if the accessing process has the SYSPRV privilege.

Should a process qualify for access under more than one of these criteria, it obtains the most favorable treatment. For example, if the process qualifies both as GROUP and OWNER, it will be treated as having OWNER access (which is generally more permissive).

There are four types of access controlled by the UIC-based protection mechanisms:

READ - Read a file or disk volume; allocate a non-file device.

WRITE - Write a file.

EXECUTE - Execute a program (.EXE) file; create files on a disk device; view directory entries specified without the use of wildcards.

DELETE - Delete files from a file device.

Under the UIC-based protection scheme, each kind of access (READ, WRITE, EXECUTE, and DELETE) may be selectively granted or denied to each of the four user classes (SYSTEM, OWNER, GROUP, and WORLD). Default protection for files is assigned as follows:

```
(S:RWED,O:RWED,G:RE,W)
```

The UIC-based scheme requires that users specify parameters satisfying the SYSTEM or OWNER criteria can do anything to the file. Other members of the creator's group can read or execute the file, and the general population has no access at all.

Default file protections for files within a given directory can be changed by using the SET PROTECTION/DEFAULT command on the enclosing directory file. For example, if you type:

```
$ SET PROTECTION=(S:RWED,O:RWED,G,W)/DEFAULT ROCKETSIM.DIR
```

The command would change the default protection for all files created within [ROCKETSIM] to prohibit any group or world access. In this case, a prerequisite would be the ability to connect to and manipulate the parent of [ROCKETSIM], which is the [000000] root directory.

For queues, the default protection is (SYSTEM:E, OWNER:D, GROUP:R, WORLD:W), allowing anyone to submit a job to the queue (WRITE access for WORLD) but only letting the owner delete a job from the queue (DELETE access for OWNER).

Once created, the UIC-based protection for an object can be modified by certain commands. For files, the SET FILE, BACKUP, and CREATE commands can affect the owner UIC of the file. Use the /OWNER_UIC qualifier with the SET FILE command to modify the UIC of the owner. Should you be an unprivileged user, you can't change the UIC to anything except your own. If you have the GRPPRV privilege, you can alter a UIC to specify any member of your process UIC group. With SYSPRV, you can change the UIC of any object to any other legal UIC (be careful!).

For directories, the /OWNER_UIC qualifier is used with the SET DIRECTORY command to alter the owner UIC of the directory.

Terminals and other devices that normally carry no owner UIC can also have one assigned using the /OWNER_UIC qualifier with the SET PROTECTION/DEVICE command, although this is unusual unless you wish to reserve a terminal for the exclusive use of one particular user.

The process UIC for your current process can also be modified using the SET UIC command. CMKRNL privilege is required to do this. Child processes created with SPAWN, RUN, or SUBMIT will always inherit the same UIC as their parent process.

The only exception to this is that the RUN command can take a /UIC qualifier so that the image being run can operate under a different UIC than the parent (DETACH privilege is required).

ACL PROTECTION METHODS

An ACL, or Access Control List is composed of a list of Access Control Entries (ACEs), each of which grants or denies access to a particular object by a specific user or set of users. For the purposes of ACLs, the concept of a user identifier is expanded: Users are identified not only by who they are (i.e., by UIC) but also by their mode of usage. This means that network users logged in remotely may be treated differently than users logged in at locally connected terminals.

ACLs can be set up for the same types of objects as are covered by UIC-based protection: files, directories, queues, global sections, devices, and logical name tables. As for UIC-based protection, the manner of assigning access is generally independent of the kind of object involved. The SET ACL command is the most straightforward way of creating an ACE for an object:

```
$ SET ACL/OBJECT_TYPE=FILE SECRET_METHOD.C -
_$   /ACL=(IDENTIFIER=REMOTE,ACCESS=NONE)
```

This example creates an ACL for SECRET_METHOD.C that categorically denies access to any user who is logged in over the network. This prevents the sensitive data from being transmitted over a channel that may not be secure.

For any significant editing of ACLs, you should learn and use the ACL Editor utility, called ACLEDIT. ACLEDIT provides context sensitive help and is a real time saver for security intensive operations that may involve a dozen or more user and group identifiers. It also helps you avoid lots of repetitive typing – SET ACL tends to be one of the most verbose DCL commands around.

Recall that the ACL concept of an identifier goes beyond the UIC notion of merely [group,member]. In the ACL world, there are actually three kinds of identifiers, of which the UIC-based codes are only one element.

These identifiers are:

- UIC identifiers

- General (group) identifiers

- System-defined (aspect) identifiers

UIC identifiers used with ACLs may be of either the numeric or alphanumeric variety, with exactly the same syntax as previously explained. The following example grants read-only access to [LEISNER] for a specific file:

```
$ SET ACL/OBJECT_TYPE=FILE AERO_FORCE.FOR -
_$  /ACL=(IDENTIFIER=[LEISNER],ACCESS=READ)
```

General identifiers are mainly used to create special-purpose groups of user IDs that lie outside the regular UIC groups. These identifiers are created by your system manager with the AUTHORIZE utility. You might, for example, create the general identifier C_WIZARDS with members [JOHNSON], [JONES] and [RITTER], and then use the command

```
$ SET ACL/OBJECT=FILE WHIZBANG.C -
_$  /ACL=(IDENTIFIER=C_WIZARDS,ACCESS=READ+WRITE+EXECUTE)
```

This ACL gives the C programming aces all the necessary rights to hack up WHIZBANG.C, but not enough rights to delete it outright. (They could, however, leave the file empty – the preceding example is more of a hedge against an inadvertent DEL *.*.* command.)

The so-called system-defined identifiers really specify aspects of using the VAX/VMS system. They are categories of jobs, classified according to the type of log in. The system-defined identifiers are as follows:

BATCH – batch job user.

DIALUP – logged in on dialup line.

INTERACTIVE – interactive (not BATCH).

LOCAL – direct-connect terminal.

NETWORK – network process.

REMOTE – remote process (not LOCAL).

These identifiers may be used in conjunction with either UIC or general identifiers by using the same plus sign notation used to grant more than one kind of access. Normally you should not use more than one system-defined identifier in a single ACE since most of them are mutually exclusive.

PRIVILEGE IDENTIFIERS AND WHAT THEY AUTHORIZE

The classes of privilege managed by ACLs are as follows:

READ – Read a file or disk volume; allocate a nonfile device.

WRITE – Write a file.

EXECUTE – Execute a program; create files on a disk device; view directory entries specified without the use of wildcards.

DELETE – Delete files from a file device.

CONTROL – Priveleges enabling control over another user's access to an object.

The first four (READ, WRITE, EXECUTE and DELETE) are functionally identical to those used with UIC-based protection. The CONTROL attribute is different; It determines whether you can affect someone else's ability to access an object. In the UIC-based security mechanisms, having WRITE access to an object is enough to let you use SET FILE/PROTECTION or SET ACL to grant or deny access to other users (subject to any protection applied to parent directories).

Suppression of the CONTROL attribute in an ACL enables you to grant someone WRITE access to a file without enabling that person to change who can access it. This feature is useful for making shared or public files available to everyone who is supposed be to able to reach them. Please recall, however, that people with SYSTEM or OWNER access to an object are not subject to an ACL-based denial of CONTROL access.

SUMMARY

This chapter has dealt with the commands that allow a user to alter the priveleges of other users to read, modify, execute or delete files over which the user has control. The specific commands and qualifiers discussed are as follows:

SET ACL object-name

/ACL[=(ace[,...])]

/AFTER=ace

/BEFORE[=time]

/BY_OWNER[=uic]

/[NO]CONFIRM

/CREATED

/DEFAULT

/DELETE

/EDIT

/EXCLUDE=(filespec[,...])

/[NO]JOURNAL=[filespec]

/LIKE=(OBJECT_TYPE=type, OBJECT_NAME=name)

/[NO]LOG

/MODE-[NO]PROMPT

/NEW

/OBJECT_TYPE=type

/[NO]RECOVER[=filespec]

/REPLACE=(ace[,...])

/SINCE[=time]

SET FILE filespec[,...]

/ACL

/[NO]BACKUP

/BEFORE[=time]

/BY_OWNER[=uic]

/DATA_CHECK[=([NO]READ,[NO]WRITE)]

/ENTER=new-filespec

/ERASE_ON_DELETE

```
/[NO]CONFIRM                    /EXCLUDE=(filespec[,...])
/CREATED                        /[NO]EXPIRATION_DATE[=date]
/EXTENSION[=n]                  /REMOVE
/GLOBAL_BUFFER=n                /SINCE[=time]
/MODIFIED                       /[NO]STATISTICS
/[NO]LOG                        /TRUNCATE
/NODIRECTORY                    /UNLOCK
/OWNER_UIC[=uic]                /VERSION_LIMIT[=n]
/PROTECTION[=(code)]
```

SET   FILE/ACL[=(ace[,...])]   filespec[,...]

SET   PROTECTION[=(code)]   filespec[,...]

SET   PROTECTION   [=(code)]/DEFAULT

SET   PROTECTION   =(ownership[:access],...)/DEVICE
device-name[:]

```
/OWNER_UIC=uic                       /OWNER_UIC=current uic
```

14

Process Control and Monitoring

CONCEPT OF A VMS PROCESS

The notion of a process is very important to understand when you're trying to comprehend the workings of VMS. In the simplest terms, you can think of a process as what goes on during the execution of any program. A process may own system resources such as memory and I/O devices. When a process terminates, all of its resources are released for reuse by the system. A VAX computer is capable of running numerous processes more or less simultaneously.

One of the most common kinds of processes is the DCL interpreter, which is run whenever you log in to the system. Although many people don't really think of DCL as a program, it is. DCL has the special mission of interacting with users through the command prompt/response mechanism, but at heart it's just another program. When you examine the system process information (the method is described below), you'll find at least one process for each logged-in user.

There are also several other processes typically running in a VMS system that don't belong to any particular user. These processes (e.g., SWAPPER) are usually permanently resident (detached) and are owned by the system. Processes can own *child processes*, technically known as *subprocesses*. Subprocesses inherit most of the privileges and attributes of their parent process and are automatically terminated if the parent process is terminated. Subprocesses are often used to interrupt execution of one program to do something else without destroying the context of the interrupted program. Figure 14-1 shows the relationship between the various types of processes.

OBTAINING INFORMATION ABOUT CURRENT PROCESSES

Three main commands are used for getting information about processes currently active: SHOW SYSTEM, SHOW PROCESS, and SHOW STATUS. SHOW SYSTEM is used for obtaining a summary of all processes in the system, whereas

SHOW PROCESS provides information about a specified process. SHOW STATUS gives a quick summary of I/O and CPU usage for your current process only.

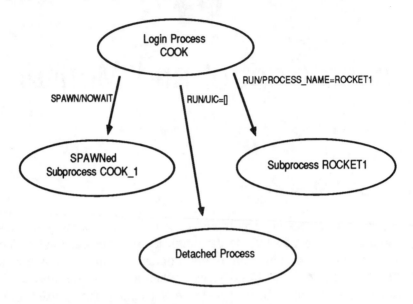

FIGURE 14-1.   Process Relationships.

SHOW SYSTEM produces a table listing all processes currently active in the CPU on which you are logged in. For each process, the PIDnumber, process name, priority, I/O operation count, CPU usage, page fault count, and physical memory occupied are shown. There is also an indicator as to whether each process is a batch job, network process, or a subprocess of another process. A sample SHOW SYSTEM listing is reproduced in Figure 14-2.

The SHOW SYSTEM command takes no parameters, but it has a few qualifiers that can be used to select a subset of the processes to show, to route output to a file rather than SYS$OUTPUT, or to generate a two-lines-per-process listing showing the UIC code associated with each process.

The SHOW SYSTEM qualifiers are enumerated below:

/BATCH – Displays only batch processes.

/FULL – Causes the UIC code associated with each process to be shown beneath the process name.

/NETWORK – Displays only network processes.

/OUTPUT[=filespec] – Sends output to a file. In the absence of this qualifier, output goes to SYS$OUTPUT.

/NOOUTPUT – Suppresses all output. This is not a very useful qualifier.

```
VAX/VMS V5.1  on node BACH  2-AUG-1989 22:53:20.04   Uptime   8 10:34:36
   Pid    Process Name    State  Pri    I/O       CPU      Page flts Ph. Mem
00000021 SWAPPER          HIB    16       0     0 00:01:19.78       0       0
00000082 COOK             CUR     4  392031     0 00:18:16.39   70787     189
00000024 ERRFMT           HIB     8    6294     0 00:01:15.98      76      97
00000025 OPCOM            HIB     8     682     0 00:00:05.31     241      85
00000026 JOB CONTROL      HIB     8     350     0 00:00:03.10     149     336
000000A7 LEISNER          HIB     4   12518     0 00:09:14.72   59509     150
00000028 NETACP           HIB     9    4470     0 00:00:39.07     198     357
00000029 EVL              HIB     6      55     0 00:01:02.56  188709      43
0000002A REMACP           HIB     9      84     0 00:00:00.55      79      44
000000AD _RTA2:           LEF     4     361     0 00:00:11.73    2129     150
00000098  TXA1:           COM     4  266862     0 00:17:19.09   81481     331
```

FIGURE 14-2.   Sample SHOW SYSTEM Listing.

/PROCESS (default) – Lists all processes in the system. This is a superset of what would be obtained by using /BATCH, /NETWORK and /SUBPROCESS in tandem.

/SUBPROCESS – Displays only subprocesses.

A typical SHOW SYSTEM command that lists all processes in the system, including UIC codes, and sends its output to a file would be

```
$ SHOW SYSTEM /FULL /OUTPUT=PROCS.TXT
```

SHOW PROCESS is a more specific command that gives various information about either the current process or the process whose name is given as a parameter to the command. Simply typing SHOW PROCESS produces a display similar to the following:

```
$ SHOW PROCESS
10-NOV-1988 14:12:58     TXB0:        User: LEISNER
Pid: 24200082   Proc. name: LEISNER   UIC:  [GRP,LEISNER]
Priority:   4   Default file spec: $DISK1:[LEISNER]
Devices allocated: TXB0:, MUA0:
```

SHOW PROCESS takes several different qualifiers, which produce different kinds of displays. The /ALL qualifier gives, in addition to the basic information shown above, the following:

1. The accounting statistics for the current session.

2. All current privileges.

3. All resource quotas and limits currently in effect.

4. Information about all subprocesses.

There are also individual switches for each of these categories:

/ACCOUNTING

/PRIVILEGES

/QUOTAS

/SUBPROCESSES

/ALL; (Gives basic information plus all of the above.)

These switches allow DCL to show the requested category of information *without* the basic summary. The /SUBPROCESSES switch is peculiar because it can be used only on the current process, that is, it is not compatible with the /IDENTIFICATION qualifier or the process-name parameter to SHOW PROCESS.

You can examine another process belonging to you or your group by using the process name as a parameter to the command; for example,

```
$ SHOW PROCESS ROCKET_1
```

In order for this to work, the UIC of the specified process must have the same group code as that of the current process. This feature is mainly useful for looking at your own subprocesses. You need the GROUP privilege to examine another process in the same group that does not belong to you.

You can, armed with the right privileges, examine any process in the system using the /IDENTIFICATION qualifier to SHOW PROCESS. The identification number needed is the PID revealed by SHOW SYSTEM. (Now you know why we presented SHOW SYSTEM first.) Leading zeros can be omitted from the PID when you type the command. The WORLD privilege will be required in order for you to access any process outside your group. An example of this would be

```
$ SHOW PROCESS /IDENTIFICATION=384
```

As usual, you can use the /OUTPUT switch to route the output from the SHOW PROCESS command to a file other than SYS$OUTPUT. As noted, this is not allowed in combination with the /CONTINUOUS qualifier.

The /CONTINUOUS qualifier to SHOW PROCESS is fancy. This qualifier causes a continuously updated display of process information to appear on your terminal. It's worth a try just for entertainment. Furthermore, once you have SHOW PROCESS /CONT running, you can switch to a virtual memory map display by typing V. The original process display returns when you press the space bar. To get out of the continuous display, type E. The SHOW PROCESS/CONTINUOUS display makes use of your terminal type to generate its output and thus is incompatible with the /OUTPUT qualifier.

The final flourish to SHOW PROCESS is the /MEMORY qualifier, which shows the dynamic memory usage of the current process. This qualifier is permitted only for the current process; it does not work with /IDENTIFICATION or the process-name parameter.

The last command used for obtaining process information is SHOW STATUS. This is a very simple (some might claim primitive) command with no parameters and no qualifiers. It gives a very short summary of I/O statistics for the current process, which looks like this:

```
$ SHOW STATUS
Status on          10-NOV-1988 13:18:17     Elapsed CPU:       0
00:00:20.03
Buff. I/O:4008     Curr. ws.:  900   Open files: 1
Dir. I/O:          458   Phys. Mem.: 186   Page Faults:
         1298
```

An even smaller subset of this process information can be obtained anytime from your terminal by typing CTRL/T. Typing that key combination interrupts the running task very briefly and sends some statistics to the terminal. The displayed line looks something like this:

```
CHOPIN::COOK 10:09:44 FLIGHTSIM CPU=00:01:22.04 PF=1049 IO=5334
MEM=806
```

Here CPU gives the CPU time used since the process began (or logged in), PF denotes page faults, IO stands for I/O operations performed, and MEM is the currently occupied memory, in pages.

INTERRUPTING A PROCESS

The CTRL/Y command is used to interrupt a running process. When you type CTRL/Y, the executing task is suspended and a DCL prompt appears. All information about the current task is preserved as long as you only issue built-in DCL commands. Afterward you can use the CONTINUE command to resume execution of the interrupted task.

Any execution of a nonbuilt-in command or program or execution of a DCL command (.COM) file will replace all information about the interrupted task with information about the new task, effectively destroying the interrupted task.

SPAWNING A SUBPROCESS

The main usefulness of subprocesses at the DCL command level is when you want to interrupt a long-running program from your terminal to do some small but pressing task. By SPAWNing a new process, you can preserve the entire context of the executing program and then CONTINUE it as if it had never been interrupted. Using SPAWN/NOWAIT you can even run several programs at once.

The SPAWN command gives you some control over the source and destination of input and output for the subprocess. Input to the subprocess can be furnished in three ways: 1. The command string parameter to the SPAWN command. 2. From a .COM file by using the /INPUT= qualifier. 3. From SYS$INPUT by neither giving a parameter to SPAWN nor using the /INPUT qualifier.

Output normally goes to SYS$COMMAND, but it can be redirected using the /OUTPUT= qualifier.

Two methods of running the subprocess are available, depending on whether you want to insist that the subprocess finish its work before the parent process can resume. Waiting for the subprocess is controlled by the /[NO]WAIT qualifier. The /WAIT setting (the default) indicates that the parent process should be suspended until the spawned subprocess terminates. The /NOWAIT qualifier lets you type new commands to the parent process while the subprocess is still running. This qualifier may be used only to execute commands that do not require any input from the terminal.

One thing to watch out for is that under SPAWN/NOWAIT, output from *both* the parent process and the subprocess will appear on your terminal at the same time. DEC recommends that you use the /OUTPUT= qualifier with any SPAWN/NOWAIT command to avoid confusion when both processes assume they control the terminal screen. Another thing to be aware of is that a CTRL/Y typed to the parent process will cause a /NOWAIT subprocess, in addition to the parent, to abort.

Another qualifier that comes in handy in conjunction with /NOWAIT is /NOTIFY. Turning on /NOTIFY causes a message to be broadcast to the terminal when the subprocess terminates. Obviously this isn't very useful unless you also set /NOWAIT. /NOTIFY is not meaningful for and should not be issued from a batch job or noninteractive task.

For the sake of showing a simple example, assume you're running a large numerical integration program when you suddenly realize you'd like to have a short PHONE conversation with another user. The command sequence might look something like this:

```
$ RUN FLIGHTSIM
   (half an hour passes)
   <CTRL/Y>
$ SPAWN PHONE
  (PHONE conversation takes place)
```

```
PHONE> EXIT
$ CONTINUE
   (FLIGHTSIM execution continues where it left off)
```

Of course, you need to be careful – as noted, running any image or a command file in the context of the parent process (the interrupted FLIGHTSIM) will destroy the FLIGHTSIM results. Notice that the subprocess ends when you finish the command string specified in the SPAWN statement. Should you want to create another entire DCL session underneath the interrupted process, just issue the SPAWN command alone and use LOGOUT to terminate the subprocess. An example of this follows (showing the system responses):

```
$ RUN FLIGHTSIM
  (time passes)
  <CTRL/Y>
$ SPAWN
%DCL-S-SPAWNED, process COOK_1 spawned
%DCL-S-ATTACHED, terminal now attached to process COOK_1
$   [this prompt now belongs to the subprocess COOK_1]
  (do some commands)
$ LOGOUT
  Process COOK_1 logged out at 17-NOV-1988 19:27:03
%DCL-S-RETURNED, control returned to process COOK
$ CONTINUE
```

A subprocess will automatically receive many of the attributes of its parent process. The most important of these are symbol definitions, logical name definitions, privileges, and defaults. The subprocess also will inherit some some less significant items such as the state of the VERIFY flag, any DEFINE/KEYs existing in the parent, the current system message format, control character definitions, and the current DCL prompt.

There are two major process-context items that are not passed intact to a subprocess: the possible privileges (as opposed to those currently enabled) and commands established with SET COMMAND. Since use of the SET COMMAND feature is relatively uncommon, this limitation will probably not prove to be much of an annoyance. You do, however, need to know how privileges are passed.

The subprocess receives only the privileges *currently enabled* in the parent process; once you are inside the subprocess, you cannot enable any additional privileges even though the parent process might be entitled to enable them. The effect of this is that if you need a privilege in the subprocess, you must first enable it in the parent process using

```
$ SET PROCESS/PRIVILEGES=(...).
```

Every subprocess is assigned a unique name, which is derived from the name of the parent process by appending an underscore followed by a numeral. Thus, the first subprocess created under process COOK would be COOK_1, the next SPAWN command will produce COOK_2, and so on. You can override the default naming of the subprocess by using the /PROCESS=name qualifier to the SPAWN command. The SPAWN command with this qualifier will create a subprocess with the given name instead of COOK_1.

```
$ SPAWN /PROCESS="COOK_SUB"
```

Each subprocess is also assigned a unique Process ID number (PID), which VMS uses internally to identify the subprocess. The PIDs of subprocesses can be seen in the SHOW SYSTEM display. As is the case with all PIDs, you have no control over what particular number is assigned.

You can control the prompt used by the subprocess using the /PROMPT= qualifier to SPAWN. The subprocess prompt defaults to that of the parent, but it can be modified using this qualifier. As usual, the string specified must be quoted if it has any embedded blanks or other special characters or if you want the displayed prompt to contain any lowercase characters. To create a subprocess whose prompt mimics its name, follow this sample:

```
$ SPAWN /PROCESS="ROCKET2" /PROMPT="Rocket2>"
```

USING THE RUN COMMAND

Many DCL users are unaware that the RUN command actually has two forms, depending upon what qualifiers are specified. The simple form of the RUN command just runs an executable image (.EXE file) in the context of the current process. When this kind of command is executed, the image being RUN obtains control of SYS$INPUT and SYS$OUTPUT. The example simulation program would be run with

```
$ RUN FLIGHTSIM
```

The RUN command is unique in that it can be abbreviated with the single character R. Therefore, the following example works exactly the same as the previous:

```
$ R FLIGHTSIM
```

Only one qualifier is available for use with this kind of RUN command: /[NO]DEBUG. The /[NO]DEBUG qualifier is used to override the default behavior of the image set by the state of the LINK/[NO]DEBUG qualifier. Normally, if an image was built using LINK/DEBUG, it will run under the control of VAX DEBUG; if it was built using LINK/NODEBUG, it will run without the debugger. The primary usefulness of RUN/NODEBUG is to run an image that was linked with debug information without having to fiddle with the debugger at program startup.

Using RUN/DEBUG on an image linked with /NODEBUG is of limited use because the debugger will not have its normal symbol tables with which to work.

The following example shows how you might use the /NODEBUG qualifier in conjunction with LINK:

```
$ LINK/DEBUG FLIGHTSIM
$ RUN/NODEBUG FLIGHTSIM
```

In the example, FLIGHTSIM will execute as if it had been linked without the use of the /DEBUG qualifier.

Executable images subject to use with the RUN command are built in a defined manner using VMS development tools. A schematic diagram of this process is shown in Figure 14-3.

No matter what compiler is used, the .EXE file is always built with VMS LINK, as in the above example.

There is an important trick to the use of RUN that arises when using it with installed images such as MAIL. If you specify the name of an installed image by simply using the name and extension with no explicit version number, the image will be run with whatever privileges it was *installed*. If you give an explicit version number (or semicolon) on the RUN command line, however, the image will be run with the privileges of the *current process*. For example, in

```
$ RUN FLIGHTSIM.EXE;
$ RUN FLIGHTSIM.EXE
```

the first line would run the installed version of FLIGHTSIM.EXE with your current privileges, whereas the second would run it with the installed privileges. As an ordinary user, your current process privileges will *not* be adequate for most system programs. Therefore, you should avoid specifying version numbers or semicolons in the RUN command.

The second form of the RUN command causes a subprocess to be created in which to execute the specified image instead of running the image in the current process. Subprocess creation occurs when any qualifier except /[NO]DEBUG is applied to the

RUN command. Any of the following would cause an image to be run in a subprocess:

```
$ RUN /PROCESS_NAME=Joe FIN_DESIGN
$ RUN /INPUT=saturn5.dat FLIGHTSIM
$ RUN /SCHEDULE=15:30:00.00 ROCKET_X
```

In the first line of the example, the program FIN_DESIGN.EXE is run as a subprocess named Joe. The second line runs the image FLIGHTSIM with input from the file SATURN5.DAT. The third line causes the ROCKET_X image to hibernate and begin running at 3:30 P.M.

There are many qualifiers that apply to the subprocess-creating form of RUN. Two of them, the /UIC=uic_code and /DETACHED, cause the specified image to run as a detached process rather than a subprocess. Some of the more important qualifiers for the RUN command are enumerated below. A complete listing is given in the summary at the end of this chapter.

/DELAY=time_delta – Specifies how long the process should hibernate until its *first* wake-up. All wake-ups after the first are controlled by the value of /INTERVAL.

/[NO]DETACHED – Specifies that the created process should be a detached process, not a subprocess.

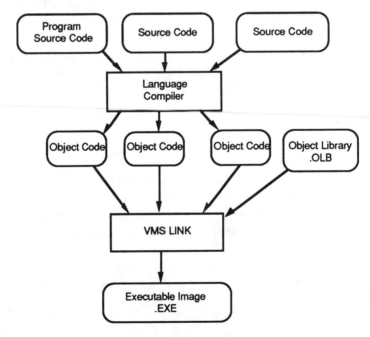

FIGURE 14-3.   VAX/VMS Software Development Cycle.

/ERROR=filespec – Routes the output of SYS$ERROR to the given equivalence name. Limit is 63 characters.

/FILE_LIMIT=file_quota – Specifies maximum number of files that the created process may have open simultaneously. Must be at least two.

/INPUT=filespec – Causes the created process to take SYS$INPUT from the specified equivalence name. Limit is 63 characters.

/INTERVAL=time_delta – Causes the created process to be given wake-ups at the specified interval. Unless you also use /DELAY or /SCHEDULE, the first wake-up occurs immediately.

/MAILBOX=mbox_unit - Gives the unit number of a mailbox that is notified whenever the created subprocess terminates. This is the only way to notify the parent process of the end of the created process.

/OUTPUT=filespec - Redirects SYS$OUTPUT for the created process to the specified equivalence name. Limit is 63 characters.

/PRIVILEGES=(priv[,...]) - Defines privileges for the created process. SETPRV is needed to specify privileges that the current process does not have. If not specified, the created process has the same privileges as its creator.

/PROCESS_NAME=name – Assigns a name to the created process. Commonly used, rather than RUN, to cause process creation.

/SCHEDULE=abs_time – Causes the created process to hibernate until the given absolute time. Works just like /DELAY, except /SCHEDULE takes an absolute time rather than a delta time.

/TIME_LIMIT=time_delta – Sets the CPU time limit for the created process. A zero value permits unlimited CPU time, assuming the creator has unlimited CPU time. If not specified, detached processes get unlimited CPU, whereas subprocesses get half the time limit of the creator.

/UIC=uic_code – Causes the created process to be a detached process and assigns it a specific UIC.

SUBPROCESS SYMBOLS AND LOGICALS

The default behavior of a SPAWN is to copy all process logical names plus all global and local symbols from the parent process to the child subprocess. The only items that are not passed are the $STATUS, $SEVERITY, and $RESTART symbols and any logical names defined with the CONFINE attribute. If your subprocess won't need them, you can accelerate the spawning procedure by using the

/NOLOGICAL_NAMES and/or the /NOSYMBOLS qualifiers. These qualifiers suppress the copying of the logicals and the symbols, respectively. This feature can save a certain amount of time if you know that the symbols and logicals aren't needed.

Keypad definition propagation can also be controlled from the SPAWN command. Ordinarily, the key definitions established with DEFINE/KEY are copied from the parent process to the new subprocess. Using the /NOKEYPAD qualifier to the SPAWN command will cause the key definitions to be suppressed in the child subprocess. As with the /NOSYMBOLS and /NOLOGICAL_NAMES qualifiers, the rationale here is to speed up the spawning process by eliminating unnecessary copying of context information.

USES OF THE ATTACH COMMAND

When you exit a subprocess via the LOGOUT command, the subprocess is completely destroyed together with any subprocesses that the terminating subprocess created itself. The next time you wish to spawn a subprocess, a completely new copy of the subprocess must be created, with all its attendant overhead.

If you frequently need to create subprocesses or wish to leapfrog around between several subprocesses, the ATTACH command is very useful. ATTACH lets you avoid having to create a new subprocess whenever you want to change contexts. It does that by permitting you to leave a subprocess without logging out. The process or subprocess from which you just departed goes into hibernation (state HIB in the SHOW SYSTEM display), and the subprocess to which you ATTACH becomes active and gains control of the terminal.

You specify the process to which you want to ATTACH either by using the process name as the parameter to the command or by using its PID with the /IDENTIFIER= qualifier. The sequence of events for attaching to multiple subprocesses might look like this:

```
$ SPAWN /PROCESS=RSIM1
  (you now have a DCL shell named RSIM1)
$ ATTACH COOK
  (back at the top process, but RSIM1 still exists)
$ SPAWN /PROCESS=RSIM2
  (creates another DCL shell named RSIM2)
$ ATTACH RSIM1
  (terminal is now connected to RSIM1)
$ LOGOUT
  (RSIM1 is gone, COOK and RSIM2 remain)
$ ATTACH RSIM2
```

Note that you cannot ATTACH to a subprocess that was spawned with the /NOWAIT qualifier or to one that was created with a different input stream than your current process. You also cannot ATTACH to a process outside your current job, that is, you can't (even with lots of privileges) attach to another user's process.

KILLING A PROCESS WITH STOP PROCESS

On occasion, such as if you created a subprocess with a RUN command and it does not appear to be working correctly, you may need to abort a running process. The manner of killing a process is via the STOP command, as in

```
$ STOP [proc_name]
```

This only works for a process in your current group; that is, the UIC of your current process must have the same group number as the UIC of the process being stopped. If, for example, a subprocess named COOK_1 had been created with a SPAWN command, it could be aborted prior to its normal termination by typing

```
$ STOP COOK_1
```

When this DCL command is executed, whatever image (executable program) that COOK_1 is executing is aborted, just as if you had typed a CTRL/C from the console, and the subprocess COOK_1 is deleted.

The STOP command can also be used by a system administrator to terminate a process outside the current group. This method, however, can only be done using the /IDENTIFICATION= qualifier, as in

```
$ STOP /IDENTIFICATION=427
```

Here it is assumed that the PID of the process to be aborted is 427. The /IDENTIFICATION= qualifier and the process-name parameter are mutually incompatible.

PRIVILEGES REQUIRED

You are always entitled to stop any process that was created by your own process. This includes an executing image, command procedure, subprocess, or detached process.

The GROUP privilege is needed to stop a process other than your own that is in the same group. WORLD privilege entitles you to stop any process. Stopping system processes should be done with great caution since many processes will effectively halt the VMS system if they are abruptly terminated.

SUMMARY

This chapter has introduced the concept of a process, and methods for controlling the behavior of VMS in the control of individual user and group processes. A summary of the commands introduced and their options follows:

Process Control Commands

ATTACH   [process_name]
/IDENTIFICATION=pid

CONTINUE

RUN   image_filespec
/[NO]DEBUG

RUN   filespec

/[NO]ACCOUNTING   (ACNT required)
/AST_LIMIT=ast_quota
/[NO]AUTHORIZE   (DETACH required)
/BUFFER_LIMIT=buff_IO_quota
/DELAY=time_delta
/[NO]DETACHED
/[NO]DUMP
/ENQUEUE_LIMIT=lock_quota
/EXTENT=max_extent_size
/FILE_LIMIT=max_open_files
/INPUT=filespec
/INTERVAL=time_delta
/IO_BUFFERED=bio_quota
/IO_DIRECT=dio_quota
/JOB_TABLE_QUOTA=quota
/MAILBOX=unit_number
/MAXIMUM_WORKING_SET=ws_quota

/OUTPUT=filespec
/PAGE_FILE=paging_quota
/PRIORITY=number
            (ALTPRI required)
/PRIVILEGES=(priv[,...])
            (SETPRV required)
/PROCESS_NAME=name
/QUEUE_LIMIT=timer_quota
/[NO]RESOURCE_WAIT
/SCHEDULE=wakeup_time
/[NO]SERVICE_FAILURE
/SUBPROCESS_LIMIT=max_subproc
/[NO]SWAPPING
(PSWAPM required)
/TIME_LIMIT=cpu_limit
/UIC=uic_code
/WORKING_SET=ws_default

SET   PROCESS   [process_name]

/[NO]DUMP	/RESUME
/IDENTIFICATION=pid	/[NO]SUSPEND
/NAME=process_name	/SUSPEND=SUPERVISOR
/PRIORITY=number	/SUSPEND=KERNEL
/PRIVILEGES=(priv[,...])	/[NO]SWAPPING
/[NO]RESOURCE_WAIT	

SHOW   PROCESS   [process_name]

/ACCOUNTING	/[NO]OUTPUT[=filespec]
/ALL	/PRIVILEGES
/CONTINUOUS	/QUOTAS
/IDENTIFICATION=pid	/SUBPROCESSES
/MEMORY	

SHOW   STATUS

SHOW   SYSTEM

/BATCH	/[NO]OUTPUT[=filespec]
/FULL	/PROCESS
/NETWORK	/SUBPROCESS

SPAWN

/[NO]CARRIAGE_CONTROL	/OUTPUT=filespec
/CLI=filespec	/PROCESS=name
/INPUT=filespec	/PROMPT[=string]
/[NO]KEYPAD	/[NO]SYMBOLS
/[NO]LOG	/TABLE=cmd_table
/[NO]LOGICAL_NAMES	/[NO]WAIT
/[NO]NOTIFY	

STOP   [name]

/IDENTIFICATION=process_id

15

Network Access

In a networked environment, you'll need to be familiar with some basic networking concepts and special features of various DCL commands that support remote node operations. This chapter outlines the kinds of network situations in which you may be working and explains some of the essential commands you will need for multi-VAX operations.

CLUSTERED VERSUS NETWORK ENVIRONMENTS

If your site has multiple VAX systems (as many do) that can interact with each other, you will find them organized in either a VAXCluster or a networked environment. It's important to understand the difference between these environments, especially because they look significantly different to you, the user.

Networked computers have been the norm for the last decade or so. In this scheme, each computer is attached to a backbone cable that carries very high-speed data signals. A set of software in each participating CPU implements a communications protocol that DEC calls DECnet. DECnet is capable of operating over a variety of media, ranging from slow asynchronous lines to extremely high-speed fiber optic links.

The most frequent form of VAX network media is called Ethernet, which supports a raw speed of 10 megabits per second (Mbps). Often in a large network several different media are used for making various connections. A critical distinction must be made between the term DECnet, which refers to a method of intermachine communications and the network media itself. DECnet is not the same thing as Ethernet.

A sample networked environment containing two nodes, MOZART:: and CHOPIN::, is shown in Figure 15-1. The two machines are connected by a segment of Ethernet. Notice that the two VAXes do not have to be of the same hardware model.

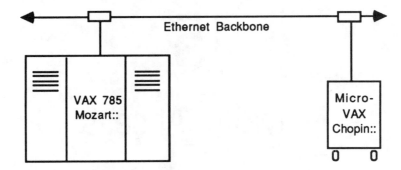

FIGURE 15-1.   Networked VAX Environment.

For the purposes of this chapter, the key idea about networked systems is that you must remember what data are stored on which node. DCL commands, by default, apply to your current logged-in node. If you need to refer to data on another node, you are responsible for supplying the correct nodename and device name in the DCL commands which support networking.

VMS does not remember that you stored your project programs on BORIS::$DISK3: while those huge data files are all kept on IGOR::$DISK1:.

Clustering is a fairly recent development in VAX systems. Because of its cost, you will not always find it used even when many CPU nodes are present. The concept of clustering entails a very close connection between the various CPU nodes making up the cluster. A clustered environment will appear to be a single, large computer with a single set of physical disks on which you can store data.

Figure 15-2 shows a typical clustered environment with an HSC at the center.

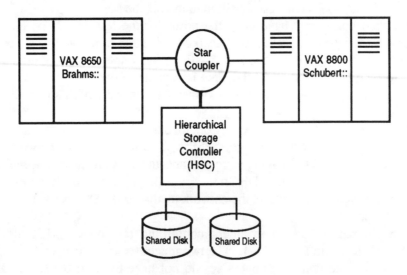

FIGURE 15-2.   Clustered VAX Environment.

With a VMS cluster, no matter which processor you log in on, you'll always see the same disk directory. The only discernible differences among the various nodes are that VMS will report distinct node names and the more powerful or lightly loaded nodes will seem to run faster.

Physically, the members of a cluster really do share the same disk drives. There are two forms of clusters that you may hear about: tightly coupled clusters and local area VAX clusters (LAVC). The tightly coupled variety has all the processors connected through a fast bus to a hierarchical storage controller (HSC), which is in turn attached to all of the cluster's disks. This method provides scorching performance and is used with the large BI-bus VAX CPUs (e.g., 8650, 8800 series).

The LAVC cluster arrangement is more a sort of poor person's emulation of the HSC – the clustered computers are actually connected via ordinary Ethernet. This provides much lower performance but is the only form of clustering available for MicroVAX machines. Fortunately, unless you are a system manager, no special DCL commands are required to deal with clustering.

THE SET HOST COMMAND

The simplest way to access a different node (computer) on a DECnet network is to simply log in to that node. Suppose that your department has three MicroVAX machines named BACH, MOZART, and CHOPIN that are connected via normal DECnet (not LAVC) and that your terminal is connected to CHOPIN. In this scenario you might have separate accounts for different purposes on all three nodes. You need not move to a different terminal in order to log into MOZART; VMS can take care of that for you.

Logging in to a different node is done with the SET HOST command. SET HOST takes one parameter, which is the DECnet nodename of the machine to which you want to log in. In the present example, to access MOZART from a terminal attached to CHOPIN, the following would happen:

- You log in on BACH as you normally would.

- You issue the command

```
$SET HOST MOZART
```

- This will produce the normal VMS Username: and Password: prompts, which are now coming from MOZART.

- You log in on MOZART using your username and password for that account. (Not from your BACH account.)

- You may now work on MOZART as if your terminal was directly connected.

- You log out from MOZART. Instead of stopping with the usual logout messages, your terminal will return to BACH's system prompt ($ unless you have changed it).

- You can resume work on BACH.

During a SET HOST session, the original process on BACH remains alive but is dormant. All terminal I/O services are redirected to the secondary session on MOZART. If the secondary process gets hung, you can abort the link by typing CTRL/Y several times. VMS will respond with a message asking if you really want to abort the remote session. If you reply Y, the remote process will be stopped and the link broken, whereupon you'll find yourself back on BACH.

You will find that your terminal response may be a bit slower (effects range from imperceptible to noticeable depending upon network link speed and loading), but otherwise you cannot tell that you are connected to a remote computer. It's even possible, though not often useful, to use several SET HOST commands to chain your way through a long string of computers. As you LOGOUT your way back through the series of links, the chain unwinds in the expected reverse order, that is, the first LOGOUT affects the most recent SET HOST link, and so on.

SET HOST can also be used to start up a new session on your own currently connected node. For example, in the example you could have typed SET HOST BACH with no ill effects even though you were already logged in on BACH. You would simply receive a new user log-in prompt and your existing job would be suspended until the new one logs out. This process is actually useful in connection with the /LOG qualifier to SET HOST. By doing a SET HOST/LOG=<filespec> to your own node, you can perform some operations and obtain a file containing everything that appeared on your screen during the session.

ACCESSING FILES ON A REMOTE NODE

Another convenient DCL network feature is the ability to perform various file operations transparently across a network of VAX computers. Most normal file and directory manipulation commands like DIRECTORY, COPY, and DELETE will accept a node specifier in front of the device name. If proxy accounts have been properly set up on your system (see below), you need only use the nodename followed by the conventional two colons. These commands do exactly what you would expect – they permit you to access files on another computer as though you were actually present on the other system.

Continuing with the example, suppose you wanted to get a copy of a file in another project directory on MOZART while you were logged in to BACH. The simplest syntax for doing this is the following:

```
$COPY MOZART::$DISK1:[PROJECT]MYFILE.TXT *
```

This command will attempt to access the [PROJECT] directory on MOZART (which is not guaranteed to succeed) and copy the file across to your current default directory on BACH.

Unfortunately, such commands will not always work properly because the correct proxy accounts are not always set up on VAX networks. If the simple, straightforward method given above doesn't work, you probably need to specify a username and password known to MOZART that have access privileges to the file you want to copy. The username and password must be placed within double quotation marks (" ") after the nodename and before the two colons separating the nodename from the device name. If your username is RALPH and your password is MAYHEM, the example becomes

```
$COPY MOZART "RALPH MAYHEM"::$DISK1:[PROJECT]MYFILE.TXT *
```

There are a couple of reasons why you normally should not use this form of the command: First, as you type the command, the system does not know that a password is being typed and will echo the account name with its password on the screen. That's the kind of thing that system managers of secure computers have bad dreams about. The second reason is that a correlated username and password end up being broadcast over the network in an easily identifiable form. (In all that Ethernet traffic, any instance of a double quoted string followed by two colons has nearly a 100 percent chance of being an account access string.)

RUNNING BATCH FILES ON REMOTE NODES

The SUBMIT/REMOTE command can be used to cause a batch file to be executed from (and on) a remote node. When the /REMOTE qualifier is used, the batch .COM file is assumed to reside on the node specified in the filespec. In this form of the SUBMIT command, a nodename is required. The following would run a remote batch job on CHOPIN:

```
$ SUBMIT/REMOTE CHOPIN::[COOK]FLUSH.COM
```

But the following command would produce a DCL error message:

```
$ SUBMIT /REMOTE [COOK]FLUSH.COM ! nodename missing
```

One limitation of this method of running remote batch jobs is that the /REMOTE qualifier precludes the use of any other qualifiers to the SUBMIT command except those that affect selection of the .COM file to be run; that is, you lose the ability to use /PARAMETERS, /HOLD, and so forth.

The only legal qualifiers that can be used in conjunction with /REMOTE are

/[NO]BACKUP

/[NO]BEFORE[=time]

/[NO]BY_OWNER[=uic-code]

/[NO]CONFIRM

/[NO]CREATED

/[NO]EXCLUDE=(filespec[,...])

/[NO]EXPIRED

/[NO]MODIFIED

/[NO]SINCE[=time]

If you should need to use other qualifiers with SUBMIT for a remote batch file, you can work around the above restriction by remotely submitting a batch file that in turn does a regular SUBMIT with the other parameters that you want to use (perhaps /QUEUE=queue_name).

HOW PROXY ACCOUNTS SAFEGUARD YOUR PASSWORDS

The designers of VMS have provided a solution to the problem of broadcasting account access information in the "USERNAME PASSWORD":: construct. The solution involves a concept called a proxy account. Your system manager can create a proxy account for remote network users that grants them certain kinds of access to a node without requiring the transmittal of a password. This comes in very handy when a system resource (such as a printer) is attached to one node and it is desired to make it generally available to the network.

The means for creating proxy accounts is beyond the scope of this book, but if you find yourself frequently typing name/password combinations, ask your system manager about creating a proxy account. It is done via the ADD/PROXY command in the AUTHORIZE utility.

If proxy accounts are correctly set up, you can issue commands like

```
$ COPY CHOPIN::[COOK]JUNK.DAT BACH::[COOK]JUNK.DAT
```

without having to log in on the remote node BACH::.

You can access a proxy account with a name other than that of your local account (assuming you have been authorized to do so) by specifying only the account name within the double quotation marks, as in

```
$ COPY CHOPIN"PROXY1"::[ROCKETSIM]NOZZLE.C *
```

FINDING OUT NETWORK STATUS

A useful command for finding out some of the available nodenames is SHOW NETWORK. This command will produce a listing of all the nodes known to your current local log-in node, with some statistics about how many DECnet hops are required to access each remote machine. The only qualifier available with this command is /OUTPUT=filespec, which is used in the normal manner to send the SHOW NETWORK output to a file. For example,

```
$ SHOW NETWORK /OUTPUT=NETWORK_STATUS.TXT
```

will send the network status summary to a file called NETWORK_STATUS.TXT.

SHOW NETWORK only produces meaningful results when your local node is a full DECnet node or router. If your local node is a nonrouter or a DECnet end node (typical of MicroVAX systems), a message will be displayed stating that your node has no network database.

THE VAX NETWORK MAIL PROGRAM

One of the most useful of all network software facilities is the VAX MAIL program. MAIL allows you to send a text message to any other user or group of users anywhere on your network (and even on other networks if you have the correct gateways available).

VMS will look for a recipient on whatever node you specify and will return the mail as undeliverable if it cannot locate the intended destination. Surveys have shown that E-mail is frequently the single most often used network facility.

The simplest usage of VMS MAIL utility is to type something like

```
$ MAIL MY_MESSAGE.TXT LEISNER
```

The MAIL program will send the file MY_MESSAGE.TXT to the user LEISNER. Both the filename and the username are optional parameters in this command. If omitted, MAIL will go into interactive mode; for example,

```
$ MAIL
MAIL>
```

MAIL is actually a utility program, not a built-in DCL command, and has numerous options and features that are not discussed here.

It's important to remember that running MAIL (or any other utility program) will destroy the context of a process interrupted with CTRL/Y. That means you *cannot* interrupt a long program run, MAIL a quick message to someone, and then CONTINUE the interrupted program – you would need to SPAWN a subprocess instead.

SUMMARY

This chapter described network access using a variety of VMS tools. The commands and options covered are listed below:

MAIL   [filespec]   [username]

`/EDIT[=(keyword[=options],...)`	`/SELF`
`]`	`/SUBJECT`
`/[NO]PERSONAL_NAME=name_string`	

SET   HOST   nodename

`/BUFFER_SIZE=number`	`/[NO]RESTORE`
`/[NO]LOG[=filespec]`	

SHOW   NETWORK

`/[NO]OUTPUT[=filespec]`

SUBMIT   filespec[,...]

`/AFTER=time`	`/[NO]EXPIRED`
`/[NO]BACKUP`	`/[NO]HOLD`
`/[NO]BEFORE[=time]`	`/[NO]IDENTIFY`
`/[NO]BY_OWNER[=uic]`	`/[NO]KEEP`
`/CHARACTERISTICS=(char[,…])`	`/[NO]LOG_FILE[=filespec]`
`/CLI=filespec`	`/[NO]MODIFIED`
`/[NO]CONFIRM`	`/NAME=job-name`
`/CPUTIME=option`	`/[NO]NOTIFY`
`/[NO]CREATED`	`/PARAMETERS=(parameter[,…])`
`/[NO]DELETE`	`/[NO]PRINTER[=queue-name]`

```
/[NO]EXCLUDE=(filespec[,…])        /PRIORITY=n
/QUEUE=queue-name[:]               /USER=username
/REMOTE                            /WSDEFAULT=n
/[NO]RESTART                       /WSEXTENT=n
/[NO]SINCE[=time]                  /WSQUOTA=n
```

16

VMS 5 Changes

NEW DCL FEATURES

This chapter outlines the changes Digital Equipment Corporation made in moving from VMS Version 4 to VMS Version 5.0. For the most part, the VMS 5.0 revisions have not been very apparent to nonprivileged users.

There are only three totally new commands – SET ENTRY, SHOW ENTRY, and SET HOST/DUP – and one major enhancement to the DCL syntax – the new IF-THEN-ELSE construct.

There is also one new lexical function – F$GETQUI, admittedly a major one – a handful of new command qualifiers, and a couple of new lexical function item codes.

New features have also been added to the MAIL utility and the EVE editor interface to the TPU editor utility. These changes provide some long-awaited functions.

In addition to the enhancements to the DCL and utilities seen by users, there are some significant additions to the commands and utilities primarily used by system managers. In many ways these are more extensive than the user-visible changes. For example, a complete new system management utility has been constructed (SYSMAN).

It's important to observe that *no commands have been deleted.*

The DEC practice of retaining basic functionality from one release to the next is deliberate – it greatly enhances the upward compatibility of VMS 4 command procedures since the underlying DCL syntax that worked previously will still work under VMS 5.0 and later versions. This does not quite guarantee that all existing command procedures will continue to function in the same manner, however.

Since the output generated by some commands has changed, complicated command procedures that analyze the output of other DCL commands may fail when they see input that doesn't match what they expect. Therefore, if you write or maintain .COM files that perform any such DCL output parsing, thoroughly retest them for each new version release to make sure they work properly.

GENERAL USER FEATURES

This section outlines the VMS 5.0 new features that are of general interest, including DCL syntax enhancements, improved commands, and new qualifiers.

IF

The DCL IF syntax has been significantly extended to permit multiple statements following the THEN clause and an optional ELSE statement. You can now write something of the form

```
$!
$! example of extended IF
$!
$ IF A .EQ. 3
$     THEN
$         WRITE SYS$OUTPUT "ATTENTION!"
$         WRITE SYS$OUTPUT "A IS 3..."
$     ELSE
$         WRITE SYS$OUTPUT "RATS -"
$         WRITE SYS$OUTPUT "A IS NOT 3..."
$ ENDIF
```

Some special conditions apply to the new IF-THEN-ELSE syntax. See Chapter 6 for detailed information.

SET ENTRY

A new command has been added, SET ENTRY, that lets you set parameters pertaining to a particular batch or print queue job. SET ENTRY can only be used on jobs that have not yet begun execution in the queue.

SHOW ENTRY

SHOW ENTRY is the counterpart of SET ENTRY. It enables you to examine the parameters that can be modified with SET ENTRY.

SET HOST/DUP

The SET HOST/DUP command lets you connect your terminal directly to a class of Hierarchical Storage Controllers. This is primarily of interest to operators, system managers, and very advanced users.

SET PROCESS/SUSPEND

Two keywords have been added to the SET PROCESS/SUSPEND command: SUPERVISOR and KERNEL. These let a suspended process continue to receive ASTs in EXEC or KERNEL mode. Formerly, no suspended process could receive any ASTs. GROUP or WORLD privileges are needed to suspend any process except your own.

SET TERMINAL

SET TERMINAL has been enhanced to support the DEC VT300 family terminals via the /[NO]DEC_CRT3 qualifier. When this qualifier is set, the terminal is flagged as having VT300 series characteristics.

SHOW TERMINAL

The output of SHOW TERMINAL is substantially altered from previous versions of VMS. The following changes have been made:

- The [NO]HOLDSCREEN field was removed.

- A new field [NO]SYSPASSWORD has been added.

- A new field [NO]DEC_CRT2 has been added (VT200 family terminal characteristics).

- A new field [NO]DEC_CRT3 has been added (VT300 family terminal characteristics).

SHOW CPU

The SHOW CPU command is new to VMS 5. It gives the status of the CPUs involved in a VAX symmetric multiprocessing system (also a new feature of VMS 5). This is an advanced feature; see the DEC *DCL Dictionary* for more information.

START/CPU

START/CPU is another new command related to symmetric multiprocessing. CMKRNL privilege is required. START/CPU initiates one or more secondary processors in a multiprocessing system.

STOP/CPU

STOP/CPU is the inverse of START/CPU; it causes the specified multiprocessing CPU to go into the STOPPED state. CMKRNL privilege is required. You may not be able to stop some critical CPUs even with CMKRNL privilege.

RECALL Qualifier: /ERASE

A new qualifier has been added to the command history RECALL command: /ERASE. This qualifier causes the entire history buffer to be wiped out. Use of this command enhances system security by permitting convenient erasure of passwords from the history buffer.

SEARCH Qualifiers

Several qualifiers have been added to the DCL SEARCH command. Among the more interesting things you can now do is cause the system to prompt you before searching each specific file (/CONFIRM), and highlight the matched strings (/HIGHLIGHT=BOLD, etc.)

SET AUDIT Qualifier: /FAILURE_MODE

A /FAILURE_MODE qualifier has been added to SET AUDIT to help define system response when security audits fail due to lack of resources.

SET FILE Qualifier: /STATISTICS

The new /STATISTICS qualifier controls whether RMS statistics gathering is enabled or disabled for a given file.

SET HOST Qualifiers

Two qualifiers have been added to the SET HOST command: /BUFFER_SIZE and /[NO]RESTORE. /RESTORE is probably more useful; it enables and disables the restoration of the remote terminal's characteristics following the SET HOST session. /BUFFER_SIZE controls the packet size of the remote messages.

SHOW QUEUE Qualifiers

Four qualifiers have been added to the SHOW QUEUE command:

/ALL_JOBS

/BY_JOB_STATUS

/SUMMARY

/GENERIC.

In addition to the new qualifiers, the /DEVICE qualifier has been enhanced.

New Lexical Function

The F$GETQUI lexical function is new in VMS 5. It produces information on the specified system queue. See Appendix C for details on using F$GETQUI.

Lexical Function Item Codes

Several item codes have been added to the F$GETDVI and F$GETSYI lexical functions. For F$GETDVI, the new items are DISPLAY_DEVNAM and TT_ACCPORNAM. The added items for F$GETSYI are ACTIVECPU_CNT, AVAILCPU_CNT, CONTIG_GBLPAGES, ERRORLOGBUFFERS, FREE_GBLPAGES, FREE_GBLSECTS, HW_MODEL, HW_NAME, and NODE_HWVERS. These items are covered in Appendix C.

NEW MAIL UTILITY FEATURES

A significant number of new commands, enhanced commands, and new qualifiers have been added to the VMS MAIL utility program. You can now mark messages, control your default print form and queue, change the default mail editor, delete arbitrary messages (not just the currently selected message), and so on. For complete information on all these features, see the *VMS Mail Utility Manual*.

IMPROVEMENTS TO THE EVE EDITOR

The EVE editor interface to VAXTPU has gotten some serious grooming in VMS 5. The most major change is that the former TPU EDT Keypad Emulator file EDTSECINI is gone; you get the EDT interface now by setting the keypad to EDT under EVE. Another significant upgrade involves the EVE HELP utility. It can now draw a keypad diagram showing the current key definitions; you then hit the desired key to get help.

Several qualifiers have been altered and added to the DCL command EDIT/TPU (the means of running EVE):

/[NO]DEBUG[=filespec] – Controls whether you run the debugger TPU$DEBUG, another TPU debugger, or none (default).

/[NO]INITIALIZATION[=filespec] – Controls whether you run an initialization file or not (default). If a file is specified, the default type is .EVE.

/[NO]MODIFY – Says whether the main buffer can be modified. Using /NOMODIFY effectively makes the file read only. The default is /MODIFY.

/START_POSITION=(row[,col]) – Sets the starting cursor location in the main buffer. Defaults to the upper-left-hand corner (1,1).

/[NO]WRITE – Controls whether the main buffer is writeable. Similar in effect to /[NO]MODIFY. Defaults to /WRITE.

/READ_ONLY – Changed so that using this does not automatically cause /NOJOURNAL.

NEW FEATURES FOR SYSTEM MANAGERS

System management topics are generally beyond the scope of this book but here are the highlights of the changes since some will be of interest to general users.

Security Features

A significant change that will be seen by users is that expired passwords now are required to be changed before the user can log in. Formerly you had a last log-in opportunity to change your password, after which you were locked out of the system if you didn't make the change before logging out. The VMS 5.0 behavior is to prompt continually for a new password at login time until a new password is set; you can't log in at all until the password is changed.

The SET AUDIT/FAILURE_MODE qualifier has been added to permit a defined response to conditions under which security alarms can't be written to the audit file (e.g, if the disk is full). This provides a means to avert having critical processes hang on resource waits.

The name of the permanent proxy database has been changed from NETUAF.DAT to NETPROXY.DAT. In general, the proxy system has been greatly improved. See the specific DEC manuals for details.

License Management Facility (LMF)

The VMS License Management Facility (LMF) is a totally new facility intended to support controls on access to licensed products on various cluster nodes and generally to facilitate per-seat or per-unit licensing arrangements. Either VMSLICENSE.COM or the LICENSE utility will be frequently used to manage license installations.

System Management Utility (SYSMAN)

DEC has developed a new, comprehensive System Mangement Utility (SYSMAN) to centralize the management of large networks and clusters. What SYSMAN does is provide an environment in which many of the normal DCL management commands (DEFINE, MOUNT, etc.) can be issued once from inside SYSMAN and applied to several nodes automatically.

Using SYSMAN is a two-step process: (1) define a working environment using the SET ENVIRONMENT command; (2) carry out the system management steps that need to be applied to that entire environment.

Miscellaneous Utility Improvements

- BACKUP now does an automatic MOUNT/FOREIGN on magtapes, eliminating the need to MOUNT the tape manually .

- BACKUP performs much more robust tape label processing, providing more protection against writing or initializing tapes to which you don't have the required access.

- BACKUP now emits an error message and does no operation if the command qualifiers are incorrect. Previously, it was possible to erase the source disk inadvertently in an image restore operation.

- INSTALL is now a DCL command, equivalent to the former RUN SYS$SYSTEM:INSTALL.

OF INTEREST TO PROGRAMMERS

The symbolic debugger DEBUG and the native VAX assembler have been upgraded to make them work as fully integrated parts of the VAX development environment. Prior to VMS 5, MACRO programs could only be debugged in the instruction display mode.

DEBUG

Many minor improvements have been made to VMS DEBUG. The most important is the addition of full source code displays, rather than just the INST mode display, for MACRO programs. Another is the addition of a /CALLS parameter to SET MODULE, which will load symbol tables for all modules currently on the CALLS stack. SET MODULE/CALLS is useful when you need to inspect local variables from several levels down in a nested calling sequence.

MACRO Assembler

MACRO is now a completely supported language in the VMS development tool set. The assembler has been enhanced to output the source-code symbols needed by DEBUG and is now compatible with the VAX Source Code Analyzer and the Language Sensitive Editor.

VMS SYMMETRIC MULTIPROCESSING (SMP)

Symmetric Multiprocessing (SMP) is undeniably the most important improvement in VMS 5.0, although it is little seen by the average user. The magnitude of development effort required to accomplish this revision and still support virtually 100% of existing VAX software is extraordinary. The innermost portions of the VMS kernel have been revamped to allow a migration from the previous asymmetric multiprocessing model to a fully symmetric scheme in which all CPUs are equivalent.

Inside the SMP system, all processors have identical hardware and execute a single copy of VMS. Because they share system memory and other resources, special synchronization mechanisms are required before memory can be modified by a processor. In order to start the system, one processor (the primary CPU) brings up the others (secondary CPUs) into the RUNning state. If any CPU crashes, failures are deliberately caused on all other CPUs so that the entire system is either up or down.

In a symmetric multiprocessing environment, any process that is ready to run can be sent to any CPU with available time to run it. This lets the system handle several processes very efficiently. Unless a program is specially coded to execute in multiple processes, however, the extra CPUs do not help a single large compute-bound job.

Symmetric multiprocessing is most important, not for its existing capabilities but for what will be accomplished by application software that has yet to be written — software that will fully exploit the parallelism which SMP provides.

SUMMARY

Several commands were altered in VMS Version 5.0, but no commands have been deleted. The major changes are in the form of additional switches, a simplification of BACKUP, and some new features in various utilities. Other changes will have a lesser effect on the average user.

A list of the affected commands follows:

IF	START/CPU
SET ENTRY	STOP/CPU
SHOW ENTRY	RECALL/ERASE
SET HOST/DUP	SEARCH
SET PROCESS/SUSPEND	SET AUDIT/FAILURE_MODE
SET TERMINAL	SET FILE/STATISTICS
SHOW TERMINAL	SET HOST
SHOW CPU	SHOW QUEUE

The lexical functions affected are:
* Item codes

Improvements in the utilities:

BACKUP	MAIL (added features)
DEBUG	EVE (improvements)
MACRO Assembler	

New features for system managers
* Security features

* License Management Facility (LMF)

* System Management Utility (SYSMAN)

* VMS Symmetric Multiprocessing (SMP)

Appendix A
DEC Manual Roadmap

DEC has extensively reorganized and successfully improved the documentation set for VMS Version 5. Its intent has been to provide users at any level with all the information they need to perform common user and system manager tasks. To this end, DEC has developed extensive documentation and subdivided it into several sets so users can order only those volumes they expect to need. Since complete sets are quite expensive, use Appendix A as a roadmap to help you select which DEC documentation you need.

BASE DOCUMENTATION SET

The base documentation set is DEC's desktop set, suitable for general users of large or small VAX systems and system managers of small systems and low-end VAXclusters. It contains enough information to perform all of the programming and system management tasks likely to be encountered by lower level users and is a great place to start if you're new at using the VAX.

The base documentation set consists of six manuals. They are high-quality paperbacks that are extremely well written and organized. This book contains a fraction of the information you will find in those manuals. Between this book and the base documentation set, you will have an excellent foundation for VMS programming.

The two manuals you will use most often are the *VMS General User's Manual* and the *VMS System Manager's Manual.*

VMS General User's Manual

The *VMS General User's Manual* contains an introduction to the basic DCL concepts, such as symbols, logical names, filespecs, and command files, as well as a large DCL command reference section. It also includes detailed information on utilities such as the EVE editor, MAIL, and the RUNOFF text processor.

VMS System Manager's Manual

The *VMS System Manager's Manual* contains information specifically of interest to system managers. It includes details of various system management utilities such as AUTHORIZE.

Overview of VMS Documentation

The *Overview of VMS Documentation* is a slim volume which includes a guide to the various DEC VMS publications and a description of how they are organized. It does not give DEC order numbers or prices and will probably not be very useful after you gain some familiarity with the VMS manuals.

Mini-Reference

The *VMS Mini Reference* is a summary of all DCL commands and common utilities, including MAIL, PHONE, and TPU. This book is essentially a command reference and does not provide a great deal of descriptive material.

Version 5.0 New Features Manual

As its title suggests, *Version 5.0 New Features Manual* is devoted entirely to the new features of VMS version 5. In content it is mainly an extraction from the *General User's* and *System Manager's Manuals*. This book is very useful if you are already familiar with VMS 4.X.

License Management Utility Manual

The *License Management Utility Manual* is the documentation for DEC's new License Management Utility, which is designed to facilitate per-seat software licensing arrangements. The License Management Utility will find increasing use as new and existing applications are reworked to take advantage of it.

THE EXTENDED DOCUMENTATION SET

The extended documentation set is full documentation for those who wish additional detail on any VMS feature. This set will meet the needs of users interested in being a hot-dog VMS programmer or of system managers of the largest systems. This extended documentation set is not necessary for most programmers and system managers. One full set is probably adequate for each large VAX or VAX network.

Information and Organization

The VMS extended documentation set is at the everything-but-the-kitchen-sink level of completeness. It is functionally divided into several kits, the most important of which are aimed at the general user, programmers, and system managers. There are also several volumes of optional documentation for special-purpose projects or development of commercial applications.

Note that programming language manuals are not included in these kits; all DEC VAX languages except DCL and MACRO-11 are sold as separate products.

The following lists the various documents in the extended documentation set. Most of the titles are self-explanatory.

General User Subkit

Volume 1: General Information

Volume 2: Using VMS

Volume 3: Using DCL

Volume 4: DCL Dictionary

Volume 5: Processing Text

System Messages

Sytem Management Subkit

Volume 1: Setup

Volume 2: Maintenance

Volume 3: Security

Volume 4: Performance

Volume 5: Networking

Programming Subkit

Volume 1: Introduction

Volume 2: Utilities

Volume 3: System Routines

Volume 4: System Services

Volume 5: Run-time Library

Volume 6: File System

Volume 7: System Programming

Volume 8: Device Support

Volume 9: VAX MACRO

Obsolete Features Kit

Obsolete Features Manual

Release Notes Kit

VMS Installation and Operations Guides

VMS Optional Documentation

VAX Volume Shadowing Manual

VAX RMS Journaling Manual

Guide to Parallel Programming on VMS

VMS Developer's Guide to VMSINSTALL

PDP-11 TECO User's Guide

Appendix B
DCL Command Summary

= (Assignment Statement)
```
symbol-name =[=] expression
symbol-name[bit-position,size] =[=] replacement-
expression
```

:= (Assignment Statement)
```
symbol-name :=[=] string
symbol-name[offset,size] :=[=] replacement-
string
```

@ (Execute Procedure)
```
@filespec[p1 [p2 [...p8]]]
```
Command qualifier	Default
/OUTPUT=filespec	--

ACCOUNTING filespec[,...]

ALLOCATE device-name[:][,...] [logical-name[:]]

Command Qualifiers	Defaults
/[NO]LOG	/LOG
/[NO]GENERIC	/NOGENERIC

ANALYZE/CRASH_DUMP filespec

ANALYZE/DISK_STRUCTURE device-name

ANALYZE/ERROR_LOG [/qualifier(s)] [filespec[,...]]

ANALYZE/IMAGE filespec[,...]

Command Qualifiers	Defaults
/[NO]INTERACTIVE	/NOINTERACTIVE
/OUTPUT=filespec	/OUTPUT=SYS$OUTPUT
Positional Qualifiers	Defaults
/FIXUUP_SECTION	--
/GST	--
/HEADER	/HEADER
/PATCH_TEXT	--

ANALYZE/MEDIA device

ANALYZE/OBJECT filespec[,...]

Command Qualifiers	Defaults
/[NO]INTERACTIVE	/NOINTERACTIVE
/OUTPUT[=filespec]	/OUTPUT=SYS$OUTPUT
Positional Qualifiers	Defaults
/DBG	--
/EOM	--
/GSD	--
/INCLUDE[=(module[,...])]	--
/LNK	--
/MHD	--
/TBT	--
/TIR	--

ANALYZE/PROCESS_DUMP dump-file

Command Qualifiers	Defaults
/FULL	--
/[NO]IMAGE[=image-name}	/IMAGE=image-running-at-dump-time
/[NO]INTERACTIVE	/NOINTERACTIVE
/MISCELLANEOUS	--
/OUTPUT=filespec	/OUTPUT=SYS$OUTPUT
/RELOCATION	--

ANALYZE/RMS_FILE filespec[,...]

ANALYZE/SYSTEM

APPEND input-filespec[,...] output-filespec

Command Qualifiers	Defaults
/BACKUP	/CREATED
/BEFORE[=time]	/BEFORE=TODAY
/BY_OWNER[=uic]	--

```
/[NO]CONFIRM                                          /NOCONFIRM
/CREATED                                                /CREATED
/EXCLUDE=(filespec[,...])                                    --
/EXPIRED                                                /CREATED
/[NO]LOG                                                  /NOLOG
/MODIFIED                                               /CREATED
/SINCE[=time]                                       /SINCE=TODAY
Positional  Qualifiers                             Defaults
/ALLOCATION=n
/[NO]CONTIGUOUS
/EXTENSION=n                                                  --
/[NO]NEW_VERSION                                  /NONEW_VERSION
/PROTECTION=(code)
/[NO]READ_CHECK                                    /NOREAD_CHECK
/[NO]WRITE_CHECK                                  /NOWRITE_CHECK
```

ASSIGN equivalence-name[,...] logical-name[:]

```
Command Qualifiers                                 Defaults
/EXECUTIVE_MODE                                 /SUPERVISOR_MODE
/GROUP                                                 /PROCESS
/JOB                                                   /PROCESS
/[NO]LOG                                                   /LOG
/NAME_ATTRIBUTES[=(keyword[,...])]                          --
/PROCESS                                               /PROCESS
/SUPERVISOR_MODE                                /SUPERVISOR_MODE
/SYSTEM                                                /PROCESS
/TABLE=name                                    /TABLE=LNM$PROCESS
/USER_MODE                                      /SUPERVISOR_MODE
Positional  Qualifiers                              Default
/TRANSLATION_ATTRIBUTES[=(keyword[,...])]                   --
```

ASSIGN/MERGE target-queue[:] source-queue[:]

ASSIGN/QUEUE queue-name[:] logical-queue-name[:]

ATTACH [process-name]

```
Command Qualifier                                   Default
/IDENTIFICATION=pid                                         --
```

BACKUP input-specifier output-specifier

CALL label [p1 [p2 [... p8]]]

```
     Command Qualifier                                    Default
     /OUTPUT=filespec                            /OUTPUT=SYS$OUTPUT
```

CANCEL [process-name]
```
     Command Qualifier                                    Default
     /IDENTIFICATION=pid                                     --
```

CLOSE logical-name[:]
```
     Command Qualifiers                                  Defaults
     /ERROR=label
     /[NO]LOG                                                /LOG
```

CONNECT virtual-terminal-name
```
     Command Qualifiers                                  Defaults
     /[NO]CONTINUE                                     /NOCONTINUE
     /[NO]LOGOUT                                        /NOLOGOUT
```

CONTINUE

CONVERT input-filespec[,...] output-filespec

CONVERT/RECLAIM filespec

COPY input-filespec[,...] output-filespec
```
     Command qualifiers                                  Defaults
     /BACKUP                                             /CREATED
     /BEFORE[=time]                                /BEFORE=TODAY
     /BY_OWNER[=uic]                                         --
     /[NO]CONCATENATE                               /CONCATENATE
     /[NO]CONFIRM                                     /NOCONFIRM
     /CREATED                                            /CREATED
     /EXCLUDE=(filespec[,...])                              --
     /EXPIRED                                            /CREATED
     /[NO]LOG                                              /NOLOG
     /MODIFIED                                           /CREATED
     /SINCE[=time]                                  /SINCE=TODAY
     Positional Qualifiers                               Defaults
     /ALLOCATION=n
     /[NO]CONTIGUOUS
     /EXTENSION=n
     /[NO]OVERLAY                                      /NOOVERLAY
     /PROTECTION=(code)
```

```
      /[NO]READ_CHECK                                      /NOREAD_CHECK
      /[NO]REPLACE                                         /NOREPLACE
      /[NO]TRUNCATE                                        /NOTRUNCATE
      /VOLUME=n
      /[NO]WRITE_CHECK                                     /NOWRITE_CHECK
```

CREATE filespec[,...]
```
      Command Qualifiers                            Defaults
      /[NO]LOG                                              /NOLOG
      /OWNER_UIC=uic                                        --
      /PROTECTION=(code)
      /VOLUME=n
```

CREATE/DIRECTORY directory-spec[,...]
```
      Command Qualifiers                            Defaults
      /[NO]LOG                                              /NOLOG
      /OWNER_UIC[=option]
      /PROTECTION=(code)
      /VERSION_LIMIT=n
      /VOLUME=n
```

CREATE/FDL =fdl-filespec [filespec]

CREATE/NAME_TABLE table-name
```
      Command Qualifiers                            Defaults
      /ATTRIBUTES[=(keyword[,...])]                         --
      /EXECUTIVE_MODE                               /SUPERVISOR_MODE
      /[NO]LOG                                              /LOG
      /PARENT_TABLE=table         /PARENT_TABLE=LNM$PROCESS_DIRECTORY
      /PROTECTION[=code]          /PROTECTION=(S:RWED,O:RWED,G:,W:)
      /QUOTA=bytes
      /SUPERVISOR_MODE                              /SUPERVISOR_MODE
      /USER_MODE                                    /SUPERVISOR_MODE
```

DEALLOCATE device-name[:]
```
      Command Qualifier                             Default
      /ALL                                                 --
```

DEASSIGN [logical-name[:]]
```
      Command Qualifiers                            Defaults
      /ALL                                                 --
      /EXECUTIVE_MODE                               /SUPERVISOR_MODE
      /GROUP                                               /PROCESS
      /JOB                                                 /PROCESS
      /PROCESS                                             /PROCESS
      /SUPERVISOR_MODE                              /SUPERVISOR_MODE
```

/SYSTEM	/PROCESS
/TABLE=name	/TABLE=LNM$PROCESS
/USER_MODE	/SUPERVISOR_MODE

DEASSIGN/QUEUE logical-queue-name[:]

DEBUG

DECK

Command Qualifier	Default
/DOLLARS[=string]	/DOLLARS=$EOD

DEFINE logical-name equivalence-name[,...]

Command Qualifiers	Default
/EXECUTIVE_MODE	/SUPERVISOR_MODE
/GROUP	/PROCESS
/JOB	/PROCESS
/[NO]LOG	/LOG
/NAME_ATTRIBUTES[=(option[,...])]	--
/PROCESS	/PROCESS
/SUPERVISOR_MODE	/SUPERVISOR_MODE
/SYSTEM	/PROCESS
/TABLE=name	/TABLE=LNM$PROCESS
/USER_MODE	/SUPERVISOR_MODE
Positional Qualifier	**Default**
/TRANSLATION_ATTRIBUTES[=(option[,...])]	--

DEFINE/CHARACTERISTIC characteristic_name characteristic-number

DEFINE/FORM form-name form-number

Command Qualifiers	Defaults
/DESCRIPTION=string	/DESCRIPTION=form-name
/LENGTH=n	/LENGTH=66
/MARGIN=(option[,...])	
/[NO]PAGE_SETUP[=(module[,...])]	/NOPAGE_SETUP
/[NO]SETUP[=(module[,...])]	/NOSETUP
/[NO]SHEET_FEED	/NOSHEET_FEED
/STOCK=string	/STOCK=form-name
/[NO]TRUNCATE	/TRUNCATE
/WIDTH=n	/WIDTH=132
/[NO]WRAP	/NOWRAP

DEFINE/KEY key-name equivalence-string

Command Qualifiers	Defaults
/[NO]ECHO	/ECHO
/[NO]ERASE	/NOERASE
/[NO]IF_STATE[=(state-name,...)]	
/[NO]LOCK_STATE	/NOLOCK_STATE
/[NO]SET_STATE[=state-name]	/NOSET_STATE
/[NO]TERMINATE	/NOTERMINATE

DELETE filespec[,...]

Command Qualifiers	Defaults
/BACKUP	/CREATED
/BEFORE[=time]	/BEFORE=TODAY
/BY_OWNER[=uic]	--
/[NO]CONFIRM	/NOCONFIRM
/CREATED	/CREATED
/[NO]ERASE	/NOERASE
/EXCLUDE=(filespec[,...])	--
/EXPIRED	/CREATED
/[NO]LOG	/NOLOG
/MODIFIED	/CREATED
/SINCE[=time]	/SINCE=TODAY

DELETE/CHARACTERISTIC characteristic-name

DELETE/ENTRY=(job-number[,...]) [queue-name:]

DELETE/FORM form-name

DELETE/QUEUE queue-name[:]

DELETE/SYMBOL [symbol-name]

Command Qualifiers	Defaults
/ALL	--
/GLOBAL	/LOCAL
/LOCAL	/LOCAL
/LOG	/NOLOG

DELETE/INTRUSION_RECORD source

DELETE/KEY [key-name]

Command Qualifiers	Defaults
/ALL	--

```
/[NO]LOG                                                /LOG
/[NO]STATE[=state-anem[,...]]                           /NOSTATE
```

DEPOSIT location=data[,...]

Command qualifiers	Defaults
/ASCII	
/BYTE	
/DECIMAL	
/HEXADECIMAL	
/LONGWORD	
/OCTAL	
/WORD	

DIFFERENCES input1-filespec [input2-filespec]

Command Qualifiers	Defaults
/CHANGE_BAR[=(format[,...])]	
/COMMENT_DELIMETER[=(delimeter[,...])]	--
/IGNORE=(option[,...]))]	--
/MATCH=size	/MATCH=3
/MAXIMUM_DIFFERENCES=n	--
/MERGED[=n]	/MERGED=1
/MODE=(radix[,...])	/MODE=(ASCII)
/[NO]NUMBER	/NUMBER
/OUTPUT[=filespec]	
/PARALLEL[=n]	--
/SEPARATED[=(input-file[,...])]	
/SLP	--
/WIDTH=n	
/WINDOW=size	

DIRECTORY [filespec[,...]]

Command Qualifiers	Defaults
/ACL	--
/BACKUP	/CREATED
/BEFORE[=time]	/BEFORE=TODAY
/BRIEF	/BRIEF
/BY_OWNER[=uic]	--
/COLUMNS=n	/COLUMNS=4
/CREATED	/CREATED
/[NO]DATE[=option]	/NODATE
/EXCLUDE=(filespec[,...])	--
/EXPIRED	/CREATED
/FILE_ID	--
/FULL	--
/GRAND_TOTAL	--
/[NO]HEADING	/HEADING
/MODIFIED	/CREATED

```
/[NO]OUTPUT=filespec                        /OUTPUT=SYS$OUTPUT
/[NO]OWNER                                           /NOOWNER
/PRINTER
/[NO]PROTECTION                                 /NOPROTECTION
/SECURITY                                                 --
/SELECT=(keyword[,...])
/SINCE[=time]                                     /SINCE=TODAY
/[NO]SIZE[=option]                                     /NOSIZE
/TOTAL                                                 /BRIEF
/[NO]TRAILING                                       /TRAILING
/VERSIONS=n                                               --
/WIDTH=(keyword[,...]
```

DISCONNECT

```
   Command Qualifier                                   Default
   /[NO]CONTINUE                                    /NOCONTINUE
```

DISMOUNT device-name[:]

```
   Command Qualifiers                                 Defaults
   /ABORT                                                   --
   /CLUSTER                                                 --
   /UNIT
   /[NO]UNLOAD                                          /UNLOAD
```

DUMP filespec[,...]

```
   Command Qualifiers                                 Defaults
   /ALLOCATED                                               --
   /BLOCKS[=(option[,...])]
   /BYTE                                               /LONGWORD
   /DECIMAL                                         /HEXADECIMAL
   /FILE_HEADER                                             --
   /[NO]FORMATTED                                     /FORMATTED
   /HEADER                                                  --
   /HEXADECIMAL                                     /HEXADECIMAL
   /LONGWORD                                           /LONGWORD
   /NUMBER[=n]
   /OCTAL                                           /HEXADECIMAL
   /OUTPUT[=filespec]                          /OUTPUT=SYS$OUTPUT
   /PRINTER                                                 --
   /RECORDS[=(option[,...])]
   /WORD                                               /LONGWORD
```

EDIT/ACL object-spec

EDIT filespec

```
   Command Qualifiers                                 Defaults
   /[NO]COMMAND[=command-file]   /COMMAND=SYS$LIBRARY:EDTSYS.EDT
   /[NO]CREATE                                          /CREATE
```

```
/[NO]JOURNAL[=journal-file]          /JOURNAL=input-filename.JOU
/[NO]OUTPUT[=output-file]         /OUTPUT=input-filename.type;n+1
/[NO]READ_ONLY                                    /NOREAD_ONLY
/[NO]RECOVER                                        /NORECOVER
```

EDIT/FDL filespec

EDIT/SUM input-file

```
Command  Qualifiers                            Defaults
/HEADER                                              --
/LISTING[=filespec]
/OUTPUT[=filespec]
Positional  Qualifier                          Default
/UPDATE[=(update-filespec[,...])]
```

EDIT/TECO [filespec]

EDIT/TECO/EXECUTE=command-file
[argument]

```
Command Qualifiers                            Defaults
/[NO]COMMAND[=command-file]           /COMMAND=TEC$INIT
/[NO]CREATE                                      /CREATE
/EXECUTE=command-file [argument]                      --
/[NO]OUTPUT[=output-file                         /NOOUTPUT
/[NO]READ_ONLY                                 /NOREAD_ONLY
```

EDIT/TPU [filespec]

$ EOD

$ EOJ

EXAMINE location[:location]

```
Command  Qualifiers                            Defaults
/ASCII
/BYTE
/DECIMAL
/HEXADECIMAL
/LONGWORD
/OCTAL
/WORD
```

EXCHANGE [subcommand] [filespec]
[filespec]

EXIT [status-code]

GOSUB label

GOTO label

HELP [keyword ...]
   Command Qualifiers   Defaults
```
   /[NO]INSTRUCTIONS                         /INSTRUCTIONS
   /[NO]LIBLIST                              /LIBLIST
   /[NO]LIBRARY[=filespec]                   /LIBRARY=HELPLIB
   /[NO]OUTPUT[=filespec]                    /OUTPUT=SYS$OUTPUT
   /[NO]PAGE                                 /PAGE
   /[NO]PROMPT                               /PROMPT
   /[NO]USERLIBRARY[=(table[,...])]          /USERLIBRARY=ALL
```

$ IF expression THEN [$] command
or

$ IF expression THEN

$ THEN [command]

$ command
    •
    •
    •

$ [ELSE [command]]

$ command
    •
    •
    •

$ ENDIF

INITIALIZE device-name[:] volume-label
   Command Qualifiers   Defaults
```
   /[NO]ERASE                                /NOERASE
```

```
/OWNER_UIC=uic                                          --
/PROTECTION=code
```

Qualifiers for Magnetic Tapes   Defaults
```
/DENSITY=density-value                                  --
/LABEL=option
/OVERRIDE=(option[,...])                                --
```

Qualifiers for Disks   Defaults
```
/ACCESSED=n                                     /ACCESSED=3
/BADBLOCKS=(area[,...])                                 --
/CLUSTER_SIZE=n
/DATA_CHECK[=(option[,...])]
/DIRECTORIES=n                                /DIRECTORIES=16
/EXTENSION=n                                    EXTENSION=5
/FILE_PROTECTION=code
/GROUP                                                  --
/HEADERS=n                                      /HEADERS=16
/[NO]HIGHWATER
/INDEX=position                               /INDEX=MIDDLE
/MAXIMUM_FILES=n
/[NO]SHARE                                         /SHARE
/STRUCTURE=level                              /STRUCTURE=2
/SYSTEM
/USER_NAME=string               /USER_NAME=current-user-name
/[NO]VERIFIED
/WINDOWS=n                                      /WINDOWS=7
```

INITIALIZE/QUEUE queue-name

Command Qualifiers   Defaults
```
/BASE_PRIORITY=n
/[NO]BATCH                                        /NOBATCH
/[NO]BLOCK_LIMIT=([lowlim,]uplim)             /NOBLOCK_LIMIT
/[NO]CHARACTERISTICS[=(characteristic[,...])]/NOCHARACTERISTICS
/CLOSE                                             /CLOSE
/CPUDEFAULT=time                             /CPUDEFAULT=NONE
/CPUMAXIMUM=time                             /CPUMAXIMUM=NONE
/[NO]DEFAULT[=(option[,...])]                     /NODEFAULT
/[NO]DESCRIPTION=string                        /NODESCRIPTION
/DEVICE[=option]                                        --
/[NO]DISABLE_SWAPPING                      /NODISABLE_SWAPPING
/[NO]ENABLE_GENERIC                          /ENABLE_GENERIC
/FORM_MOUNTED=type                        /FORM_MOUNTED=DEFAULT
/[NO]GENERIC[=(queue-name[,...])]              /NOGENERIC
/JOB_LIMIT=n                                    /JOB_LIMIT=1
/[NO]LIBRARY[=file-name]                     /LIBRARY=SYSDEVCTL
/ON=[node::][device[:]]
/OPEN                                              /CLOSE
/OWNER_UIC=uic                               /OWNER_UIC=[1,4]
/[NO]PROCESSOR[=filename]                    /PROCESSOR=PRTSMB
/PROTECTION=(code)            /PROTECTION=(S:E,O:D,G:R,W:W)
/[NO]RECORD_BLOCKING                        /RECORD_BLOCKING
```

```
/[NO]RETAIN[=option]                              /NORETAIN
/SCHEDULE=[NO]SIZE                             /SCEDULE=SIZE
/[NO]SEPARATE[=(option[,...])]                 /NOSEPARATE
/[NO]START                                       /NOSTART
/[NO]TERMINAL                                 /NOTERMINAL
/WSDEFAULT=n                               /WSDEFAULT=NONE
/WSEXTENT=n                                 /WSEXTENT=NONE
/WSQUOTA=n                                   /WSQUOTA=NONE
```

INQUIRE symbol-name [prompt-string]

```
   Command Qualifiers                           Defaults
/GLOBAL                                            /LOCAL
/LOCAL                                             /LOCAL
/[NO]PUNCTUATION                             /PUNCTUATION
```

INSTALL [subcommand][filespec]
$ JOB user-name

```
   Command Qualifiers                           Defaults
/AFTER=time                                           --
/CHARACTERISTICS=(characteristic[,...])
/CLI=file-name
/CPUTIME=n                                   /CPUTIME=NOME
/[NO]DELETE                                       /DELETE
/[NO]HOLD                                         /NOHOLD
/[NO]KEEP                                         /NOKEEP
/[NO]LOG_FILE[=filespec]
/NAME=job-name                              /NAME=INPBATCH
/[NO]NOTIFY                                     /NONOTIFY
/PARAMETERS=(parameter[,...])                         --
/[NO]PRINTER[=queue-name]                 /PRINTER=SYS$PRINT
/PRIORITY=n
/QUEUE=queue-name[:]                        /QUEUE=SYS$BATCH
/[NO]RESTART                                    /NORESTART
/[NO]TRAILING_BLANKS                       /TRAILING_BLANKS
/WSDEFAULT=n
/WSEXTENT=n
/WSQUOTA=n
```

LIBRARY library-filespec [input-filespec[,...]]

LINK filespec[,...]

LOGIN Procedure

CTRL/C

CTRL/Y

RETURN

Command Qualifiers	Defaults
/CLI=command-language-interpreter	/CLI=DCL
/[NO]COMMAND[=filespec]	/COMMAND
/DISK=device-name[:]	
/TABLES=(command-table[,...])	/TABLES=DCLTABLES

LOGOUT

MACRO filespec-list

Positional Qualifiers	Defaults
/[NO]ANALYSIS_DATE[=filespec]	/NOANALYSIS_DATA
/[NO]CROSS_REFERENCE[=(function[,...])]	/NOCROSS_REFERENCE
/[NO]DEBUG[=option]	/NODEBUG
/[NO]DIAGNOSTICS[=filespec]	/NODIAGNOSTICS
/[NO]DISABLE=(function[,...])	/DISABLE=(ABSOLUTE,DEBUG,TRUNCATION)
/[NO]ENABLE=(function[,...])	/ENABLE=(GLOBAL,TRACEBACK,SUPPRESSION)
/[NO]LIBRARY	
/[NO]LIST[=filespec]	
/[NO]OBJECT[=filespec]	
/[NO]SHOW[=(function[,...])]	/SHOW=(CONDITIONAL,CALLS,DEFINITIONS)
/[NO]UPDATE[=(update-filespec[,...])]	

MAIL [filespec] [recipient-name]

MERGE input-filespec1, input-filespec2[,...] output-filespec

MESSAGE filespec[,...]

MONITOR [class-name[,...]]

MOUNT device-name[:][,...] [volume-label[,...]] [logical-name[:]]

NCS [filespec,...]

ON condition THEN [$] command

OPEN logical-name[:] filespec

Command Qualifiers	Defaults
/APPEND	--
/ERROR=label	
/READ	/READ
/SHARE[=option]	/SHARE=WRITE
/WRITE	/READ

$PASSWORD [password]

PATCH filespec

PHONE [phone-command]

PRINT filespec[,...]

Command Qualifiers	Defaults
/AFTER=time	/NOAFTER
/[NO]BACKUP	/CREATED
/[NO]BEFORE	/BEFORE=TODAY
/[NO]BY_OWNER	--
/CHARACTERISTICS=(characteristic[,...])	
/[NO]CONFIRM	/NOCONFIRM
/[NO]CREATED	/CREATED
/DEVICE=queue-name[:]	/DEVICE=SYS$PRINT
/[NO]EXCLUDE=(filespec[,...])	--
/[NO]EXPIRED	/CREATED
/FORM=type	FORM=0
/[NO]HOLD	/NOHOLD
/[NO]IDENTIFY	/IDENTIFY
/JOB_COUNT=n	/JOB_COUNT=1
/[NO]LOWERCASE	/NOLOWERCASE
/NAME=job-name	
/NOTE=string	--
/[NO]NOTIFY	/NONOTIFY
/OPERATOR=string	--
/PARAMETERS=(parameter[,...])	--
/PRIORITY=n	
/QUEUE=queue-name[:]	/QUEUE=SYS$PRINT
/REMOTE	--
/[NO]RESTART	/RESTART
/[NO]SINCE[=time]	/SINCE=TODAY
/USER=username	
Positional Qualifiers	**Defaults**
/[NO]BURST[=keyword]	
/COPIES=n	/COPIES=1
/[NO]DELETE	/NODELETE
/[NO]FEED	/FEED

```
/[NO]FLAG[=keyword]
/[NO]HEADER                                         /NOHEADER
/PAGES=([lowlim,]uplim)
/[NO]PASSALL                                        /NOPASSALL
/SETUP=module[,...]
/[NO]SPACE                                          /NOSPACE
/[NO]TRAILER[=keyword]
```

PURGE [filespec[,...]]

```
    Command Qualifiers                              Defaults
    /BACKUP                                         /CREATED
    /BEFORE[=time]                                  /BEFORE=TODAY
    /BY_OWNER[=uic]
    /[NO]CONFIRM                                    /NOCONFIRM
    /CREATED                                        /CREATED
    /[NO]ERASE                                      /NOERASE
    /EXCLUDE=(filespec[,...])                       --
    /EXPIRED                                        /CREATED
    /KEEP=n                                         /KEEP=1
    /[NO]LOG                                        /NOLOG
    /MODIFIED                                       /CREATED
    /SINCE[=time]                                   /SINCE=TODAY
```

READ logical-name[:] symbol-name

```
    Command Qualifiers                              Defaults
    /DELETE                                         --
    /END_OF_FILE=label
    /ERROR=label
    /INDEX=n                                        /INDEX=0
    /KEY=string                                     --
    /MATCH=option                                   /MATCH=EQ
    /NOLOCK
    /PROMPT=string
    /[NO]TIME_OUT=n                                 /NOTIME_OUT
```

RECALL [command-specifier]

```
    Command Qualifiers                              Defaults
    /ALL                                            --
    /ERASE                                          --
```

RENAME input-filespec[,...] output-filespec

```
    Command Qualifiers                              Defaults
    /BACKUP                                         /CREATED
    /BEFORE[=time]                                  /BEFORE=TODAY
    /BY_OWNER[=uic]                                 --
    /[NO]CONFIRM                                    /NOCONFIRM
```

```
/CREATED                                            /CREATED
/EXCLUDE=(filespec[,...])                                  --
/EXPIRED                                             /CREATED
/[NO]LOG                                               /NOLOG
/MODIFIED                                            /CREATED
/[NO]NEW_VERSION                                 /NEW_VERSION
/SINCE[=time]                                   /SINCE=TODAY
```

REPLY ["message-text"]
```
    Command Qualifiers                               Defaults
    /ABORT=identification-number                           --
    /ALL                                                   --
    /BELL                                                  --
    /BLANK_TAPE=identification-number                      --
    /DISABLE[=(keyword[,...])]                             --
    /ENABLE[=(keyword[,...])]                              --
    /INITIALIZE_TAPE=identification-number                 --
    /[NO]LOG                                               --
    /NODE[=(VAXcluster-node[,...])]                        --
    /[NO]NOTIFY                                        /NOTIFY
    /PENDING=identification-number                         --
    /SHUTDOWN                                              --
    /STATUS                                               --
    /TEMPORARY                                             --
    /TERMINAL=(terminal-name[,...])                        --
    /TO=identification-number                              --
    /URGENT                                                --
    /USERNAME[=(username[,...])]                           --
```

REQUEST "message-text"
```
    Command Qualifiers                               Defaults
    /REPLY                                                 --
    /TO=(operator[,...])
```

RETURN [status-code]

RUN filespec
```
    Command Qualifier                                 Default
    /[NO]DEBUG                                             --
```

RUN filespec
```
    Command Qualifiers                               Defaults
    /[NO]ACCOUNTING                                /ACCOUNTING
    /AST_LIMIT=quota
    [NO]AUTHORIZE                                 /NOAUTHORIZE
    /BUFFER_LIMIT=quota
    /DELAY=delta-time                                     --
```

```
/[NO]DETACHED                                            --
/[NO]DUMP                                            /NODUMP
/ENQUEUE_LIMIT=quota
/DELAY=delta-time                                        --
/ERROR=filespec                                          --
/EXTENT=quota
/FILE_LIMIT=quota
/INPUT=filespec                                          --
/INTERVAL=delta-time                                     --
/IO_BUFFERED=quota
/IO_DIRECT=quota
/JOB_TABLE_QUOTA=quota
/MAILBOX=unit                                            --
/MAXIMUM_WORKING_SET=quota
/OUTPUT=filespec                                         --
/PAGE_FILE=quota
/PRIORITY=n
/PRIVILEGES=(privilege[,...])               /PRIVILEGES=SAME
/PROCESS_NAME=process-name                               --
/QUEUE_LIMIT=quota
/[NO]RESOURCE_WAIT                          /RESOURCE_WAIL
/SCHEDULE=absolute-time                                  --
/[NO]SERVICE_FAILURE                     /NOSERVICE_FAILURE
/SUBPROCESS_LIMIT=quota
/[NO]SWAPPING                                    /SWAPPING
/TIME_LIMIT=limit
/UIC=uic                                                 --
/WORKING_SET=default
```

RUNOFF filespec[,...]

RUNOFF/CONTENTS filespec[,...] or filespec[+...]

RUNOFF/INDEX filespec[,...] or filespec[+...]

SEARCH filespec[,...] search-string[,...]

```
Command Qualifiers                             Defaults
/BACKUP                                        /CREATED
/BEFORE[=time]                            /BEFORE=TODAY
/BY_OWNER[=uic]                                      --
/[NO]CONFIRM                                  /NOCONFIRM
/CREATED                                       /CREATED
/[NO]EXACT                                      /NOEXACT
```

```
/EXCLUDE=(filespec[,...])                                    --
/EXPIRED                                               /CREATED
/FORMAT=option                                    /FORMAT=TEXT
/[NO]HEADING                                           /HEADING
/[NO]LOG                                                /NOLOG
/MATCH=option                                        /MATCH=OR
/MODIFIED                                              /CREATED
/[NO]NUMBERS                                         /NONUMBERS
/[NO]OUTPUT[=filespec]                       /OUTPUT=SYS$OUTPUT
/[NO]REMAINING                                     /NOREMAINING
/SINCE[=time]                                      /SINCE=TODAY
/[NO]WINDOW[=(n1,n2)]                                 /NOWINDOW
```

SET option

SET ACCOUNTING

```
   Command Qualifiers                              Defaults
   /DISABLE[=(keyword[,...])]                            --
   /ENABLE[=(keyword[,...])]                             --
   /NEW_FILE                                             --
```

SET ACL object-name

```
   Command Qualifiers                              Defaults
   /ACL[=(ace[,...])]                                    --
   /AFTER=ace
   /BEFORE[=time]                                 /BEFORE=TODAY
   /BY_OWNER[=uic]
   /[NO]CONFIRM                                      /NOCONFIRM
   /CREATED                                              --
   /DEFAULT                                              --
   /DELETE                                               --
   /EDIT                                                 --
   /EXCLUDE=(filespec[,...])                             --
   /[NO]JOURNAL=[filespec]
   /LIKE=(OBJECT_TYPE=type,OBJECT_NAME=name)
   /[NO]LOG                                             /NOLOG
   /MODE=[NO]PROMPT                               /MODE=PROMPT
   /NEW                                                  --
   /OBJECT_TYPE=type                        /OBJECT_TYPE=file
   /[NO]RECOVER[=filespec]                          /NORECOVER
   /REPLACE=(ace[,...])                                  --
   /SINCE[=time]                                  /SINCE=TODAY
```

SET AUDIT

```
   Command Qualifiers                              Defaults
   /ALARM                                                --
   /DISABLE=(keyword[,...])
   /ENABLE=(keyword[,...])
   /FAILURE_MODE=option                     /FAILURE_MODE=WAIT
```

SET BROADCAST=(class-name[,...])

SET CARD_READER device-name[:]

Command Qualifiers	Defaults
/026	
/029	
/[NO]LOG	/NOLOG

SET CLUSTER/EXPECTED_VOTES [=value]

SET COMMAND [filespec[,...]]

SET [NO]CONTROL[=(T,Y)]

SET CLUSTER/QUORUM [=quorum-value]

SET DAY

Command Qualifiers	Defaults
/DEFAULT	--
/[NO]LOG	/NOLOG
/PRIMARY	--
/SECONDARY	--

SET DEFAULT [device-name[:]][directory-spec]

SET DEVICE device-name[:]

Command Qualifiers	Defaults
/[NO]AVAILABLE	--
/[NO]DUAL_PORT	--
/[NO]ERROR_LOGGING	--
/[NO]LOG	/NOLOG
/[NO]SPOOLED[=(queue-name[:],intermediate-disk-name[:])]	

SET DEVICE/ACL[=(ace[,...])] device-name

SET DEVICE/SERVED node-name$DDcu:

SET DIRECTORY [device-name[:]]directory-spec[,...]

SET DIRECTORY/ACL[=(ace[,...])]
  directory-spec[,...]

SET ENTRY entry-number
Command Qualifiers	Defaults
/[NO]AFTER=time	--
/[NO]BURST	--
/[NO]CHARACTERISTICS[=(characteristic[,...])]	--
/CLI=filespec	--
/COPIES=n	--
/CPUTIME=option	--
/[NO]FEED	--
/[NO]FLAG	--
/FORM=type	--
/[NO]HEADER	--
/[NO]HOLD	--
/JOB_COUNT=n	--
/[NO]KEEP	--
/[NO]LOG_FILE[=filespec]	--
/[NO]LOWERCASE	
/NAME=job-name	--
/NOCHECKPOINT	--
/NODELETE	--
/NOTE=string	--
/[NO]NOTIFY	--
/OPERATOR=string	--
/PAGES=([l],u)	--
/[NO]PARAMETERS	--
/[NO]PASSALL	--
/[NO]PRINTER	--
/PRIORITY	--
/RELEASE	--
/REQUEUE=[queue-name]	--
/[NO]RESTART	--
/SETUP=module[,...]	--
/[NO]SPACE	--
/[NO]TRAILER	--
/WSDEFAULT=n	--
/WSEXTENT=n	--
/WSQUOTA	--

SET FILE filespec[,...]
Command Qualifiers	Defaults
/ACL	
/[NO]BACKUP	/NOBACKUP
/BEFORE[=time	/BEFORE=TODAY
/BY_OWNER[=uic]	--
/[NO]CONFIRM	/NOCONFIRM

```
/CREATED                                              --
/DATA_CHECK[=([NO]READ,[NO]WRITE)]      /DATA_CHECK=WRITE
/END_OF_FILE                                          --
/ENTER=new-filespec                                   --
/ERASE_ON_DELETE                                      --
/EXCLUDE=(filespec[,...])                             --
/[NO]EXPIRATION_DATE[=date]                           --
/EXTENSION[=n]                                        --
/GLOBAL_BUFFER=n                                      --
/MODIFIED                                             --
/[NO]LOG                                           /NOLOG
/NODIRECTORY                                          --
/OWNER_UIC[=uic]                                      --
/PROTECTION[=(code)]                                  --
/REMOVE                                               --
/SINCE[=time]                               /SINCE=TODAY
/[NO]STATISTICS                             /NOSTATISTICS
/TRUNCATE                                             --
/UNLOCK                                               --
/VERSION_LIMIT[=n]                                    --
```

SET FILE/ACL[=(ace[,...])] filespec[,...]

SET HOST node-name

Command Qualifier	Default
/[NO]LOG[=filespec]	/NOLOG

SET HOST/DTE terminal-name

Command Qualifier	Default
/DIAL=(NUMBER:number[,MODEM_TYPE:modem-type])	--

SET HOST/HSC node-name

Command Qualifier	Default
/[NO]LOG[=filespec]	/NOLOG

SET HOST/DUP /SERVER=server-name/TASK=task-name node-name

SET KEY

SET LOGINS

Command Qualifier	Default
/INTERACTIVE[=n]	--

SET MAGTAPE device-name[:]

Command Qualifiers	Defaults
/DENSITY=density	--
/END_OF_FILE	--
/[NO]LOG	--
/[NO]LOGSOFT	--
/REWIND	--
/SKIP=option	--
/UNLOAD	--

SET MESSAGE [filespec]

Command Qualifiers	Defaults
/DELETE	--
/[NO]FACILITY	/FACILITY
/[NO]IDENTIFICATION	/IDENTIFICATION
/[NO]SEVERITY	/SEVERITY
/[NO]TEXT	/TEXT

SET   [NO]ON

SET OUTPUT_RATE[=delta-time]
SET PASSWORD

Command Qualifiers	Defaults
/GENERATE[=value]	--
/SECONDARY	--
/SYSTEM	--

SET PRINTER printer-name[:]

Command Qualifiers	Defaults
/[NO]CR	/NOCR
/[NO]FALLBACK	/NOFALLBACK
/[NO]FF	/FF
/LA11	/LP11
/LA180	/LP11
/[NO]LOWERCASE	/NOLOWERCASE
/[NO]LOG	/NOLOG
/LP11	/LP11
/PAGE=n	/PAGE=64
/[NO]PASSALL	/NOPASSALL
/[NO]PRINTALL	/NOPRINTALL
/[NO]TAB	/NOTAB
/[NO]TRUNCATE	/TRUNCATE
/UNKNOWN	/LP11
/[NO]UPPERCASE	/UPPERCASE
/WIDTH=n	/WIDTH=132
/[NO]WRAP	/NOWRAP

SET PROCESS [process-name]

Command Qualifiers	Defaults

```
/[NO]DUMP                                              /NODUMP
/IDENTIFICATION=pid
/NAME=string                            /NAME=current-process-name
/PRIORITY=n
/PRIVILEGES=(privilege[,...])
/[NO]RESOURCE_WAIT                                         --
/RESUME                                                    --
/[NO]SUSPEND=(keyword)                                     --
/[NO]SWAPPING                                          /SWAPPING
```

SET PROMPT[=string]

SET PROTECTION[=(code)] filespec[,...]

SET PROTECTION [=(code)]/DEFAULT

SET PROTECTION
=(ownership[:access],...)/DEVICE
device-name[:]

Command Qualifier	Default
/OWNER_UIC=uic	/OWNER_UIC=current uic

SET QUEUE queue-name[:]

Command Qualifiers	Defaults
/BASE_PRIORITY=n	--
/[NO]BLOCK_LIMIT=([lowlim,]uplim)	--
/[NO]CHARACTERISTICS[=(characteristic[,...])]	--
/CLOSE	--
/CPUDEFAULT=time	--
/CPUMAXIMUM=time	--
/[NO]DEFAULT[=(option[,...])]	--
/[NO]DESCRIPTION=string	/NODESCRIPTION
/[NO]DISABLE_SWAPPING	--
/[NO]ENABLE_GENERIC	--
/FORM_MOUNTED=type	--
/JOB_LIMIT=n	--
/OPEN	--
/OWNER_UIC=uic	--
/PROTECTION=code	--
/[NO]RECORD_BLOCKING	--
/[NO]RETAIN[=option]	--
/SCHEDULE=[NO]SIZE	--
/[NO]SEPARATE[=(option[,...])]	--
/WSDEFAULT=n	--
/WSEXTENT=n	--
/WSQUOTA=n	--

SET QUEUE/ENTRY=entry-number queue-name[:]

SET RESTART_VALUE=string

SET RIGHTS_LIST id-name[,...]

Command Qualifiers	Defaults
/ATTRIBUTES=keyword	--
/DISABLE	--
/ENABLE	--
/PROCESS=process-name	/PROCESS
/SYSTEM	--

SET RMS_DEFAULT

Command Qualifiers	Defaults
/BLOCK_COUNT=count	--
/BUFFER_COUNT=count	--
/DISK	--
/EXTEND_QUANTITY=n	--
/INDEXED	/SEQUENTIAL
/MAGTAPE	--
/NETWORK_BLOCK_COUNT=count	--
/PROLOG=n	/PROLOG=0
/RELATIVE	/SEQUENTIAL
/SEQUENTIAL	/SEQUENTIAL
/SYSTEM	--
/UNIT_RECORD	--

SET SYMBOL

SET TERMINAL [device-name[:]]

Command Qualifiers	Defaults
/[NO]ADVANCED_VIDEO	
/ALTYPEAHD	--
/[NO]ANSI_CRT	
/APPLICATION_KEYPAD	/NUMERIC_KEYPAD
/[NO]AUTOBAUD	
/[NO]BLOCK_MODE	
/[NO]BRDCSTMBX	
/[NO]BROADCAST	/BROADCAST
/CRFILL[=formula]	/CRFILL=0
/[NO]DEC_CRT[=value1,value2,value3)]	
/DEVICE_TYPE=terminal-type	--
/[NO]DIALUP	/NODIALUP
/[NO]DISCONNECT	/NODISCONNECT
/[NO]DISMISS	/NODISMISS

```
/[NO]DMA
/[NO]ECHO                                                    /ECHO
/[NO]EDIT_MODE
/[NO]EIGHT_BIT
/[NO]ESCAPE                                                  /NOESCAPE
/[NO]FALLBACK
/FRAME=n
/[NO]FORM
/[NO]FULLDUP                                                 /HALFDUP
/[NO]HALFDUP                                                 /HALFDUP
/[NO]HANGUP                                                  /NOHANGUP
/[NO]HARDCOPY
/[NO]HOSTSYNC                                                /NOHOSTSYNC
/INQUIRE                                                     --
/INSERT                                                      /OVERSTRIKE
/LFFILL=formula
/[NO]LINE_EDITING
/[NO]LOCAL_ECHO                                              /NOLOCAL_ECHO
/[NO]LOWERCASE
/MANUAL
/NUMERIC_KEYPAD                                              /NUMERIC_KEYPAD
/OVERSTRIKE                                                  /OVERSTRIKE
/PAGE[=n]
/[NO]PARITY[=option]                                         /NOPARITY
/[NO]PASTHRU                                                 /NOPASTHRU
/PERMANENT                                                   --
/[NO]PRINTER_PORT
/PROTOCOL=DDCMP                                              /PROTOCOL=NONE
/[NO]READSYNC                                                /NOREADSYNC
/[NO]REGIS
/[NO]SCOPE
/[NO]SECURE_SERVER                                           /NOSECURE_SERVER
/[NO]SET_SPEED
/[NO]SIXEL_GRAPHICS
/[NO]SOFT_CHARACTERS
/SPEED=rate                                                  --
/SWITCH=DECNET                                               --
/[NO]SYSPASSWORD                                             /NOSYSPASSWORD
/[NO]TAB
/[NO]TTSYNC                                                  /TTSYNC
/[NO]TYPE_AHEAD                                              /TYPE_AHEAD
/UNKNOWN
/[NO]UPPERCASE
/WIDTH=n
/[NO]WRAP                                                    /WRAP
```

SET TIME[=time]

SET UIC uic

SET [NO]VERIFY[=([NO]PROCEDURE, [NO]IMAGE)]

SET VOLUME device-spec[:][,...]

Command Qualifiers	Defaults
/ACCESSED[=n]	
/DATA_CHECK[=option[,...])]	
/[NO]ERASE_ON_DELETE	/NOERASE_ON_DELETE
/[NO]EXTENSION[=n]	
/FILE_PROTECTION=(code)	--
/[NO]HIGHWATER_MARKING	--
/LABEL=volume-label	--
/[NO]LOG	/NOLOG
/[NO]MOUNT_VERIFICATION	--
/OWNER_UIC[=uic]	
/PROTECTION=(code)	--
/[NO]REBUILD	--
/RETENTION=(min[,max])	
/[NO]UNLOAD	--
/USER_NAME[=username]	
/WINDOWS[=n]	

SET WORKING_SET

Command Qualifiers	Defaults
/[NO]ADJUST	/ADJUST
/EXTENT=n	--
/LIMIT=n	--
/[NO]LOG	/NOLOG
/QUOTA=n	--

SHOW option

SHOW ACCOUNTING

Command Qualifier	Defaults
/OUTPUT=filespec	/OUTPUT=SYS$OUTPUT

SHOW ACL object-name

Command Qualifier	Defaults
/OBJECT_TYPE=type	/OBJECT_TYPE=file

SHOW AUDIT

Command Qualifier	Defaults
/ALL	/ALL
/FAILURE_MODE	/FAILURE_MODE
/[NO]OUTPUT[=filespec]	/OUTPUT=SYS$OUTPUT

SHOW BROADCAST

Command Qualifier	Defaults
/[NO]OUTPUT[=filespec]	/OUTPUT=SYS$OUTPUT

SHOW CLUSTER

SHOW CPU [cpu_id[,...]]

SHOW DEFAULT

SHOW DEVICES [device-name[:]]

Command Qualifiers	Defaults
/ALLOCATED	--
/BRIEF	/BRIEF
/FILES	--
/FULL	/BRIEF
/MOUNTED	--
/[NO]OUTPUT[=filespec]	/OUTPUT=SYS$OUTPUT
/[NO]SYSTEM	--
/WINDOWS	--

SHOW DEVICES/SERVED

Command Qualifiers	Defaults
/ALL	--
/COUNT	--
/OUTPUT=[filespec]	/OUTPUT=SYS$OUTPUT
/RESOURCE	--
/HOST	--

SHOW ENTRY [entry-number,...]

Command Qualifiers	Defaults
/BATCH	--
/BRIEF	/BRIEF
/BY_JOB_STATUS[=(keyword,...)]	--
/DEVICE[=(keyword,...)]	--
/FILES	--
/FULL	/BRIEF
/GENERIC	--
/OUTPUT[=filespec]	--
/USER_NAME=username	--

SHOW ERROR

Command Qualifiers	Defaults
/FULL	--
/[NO]OUTPUT[=filespec]	/OUTPUT=SYS$OUTPUT

SHOW INTRUSION

Command Qualifiers	Defaults
/OUTPUT[=filespec]	/OUTPUT=SYS$OUTPUT
/TYPE=keyword	/TYPE=ALL

SHOW KEY [key-name]

Command Qualifiers	Defaults
/ALL	--
/[NO]BRIEF	/BRIEF
/DIRECTORY	--
/[NO]FULL	/NOFULL
/[NO]STATE[=(state-name[,...])]	

SHOW LOGICAL [logical-name[:][,...]]

SHOW MAGTAPE device-name[:]

Command Qualifier	Default
/[NO]OUTPUT[=filespec]	/OUTPUT=SYS$OUTPUT

SHOW MEMORY

Command Qualifiers	Defaults
/ALL	/ALL
/FILES	/ALL
/FULL	
/[NO]OUTPUT[=filespec]	/OUTPUT=SYS$OUTPUT
/PHYSICAL_PAGES	/ALL
/POOL	/ALL
/SLOTS	/ALL

SHOW NETWORK

Command Qualifier	Default
/[NO]OUTPUT[=filespec]	/OUTPUT=SYS$OUTPUT

SHOW PRINTER device-name[:]

SHOW PROCESS [process-name]

SHOW PROTECTION

SHOW QUEUE [queue-name]

SHOW QUEUE/CHARACTERISTIC [characteristic-name]

SHOW QUEUE/FORM [form-name]

SHOW QUOTA

SHOW RMS_DEFAULT

Command Qualifier	Default
/[NO]OUTPUT[=filespec]	/OUTPUT=SYS$OUTPUT

SHOW STATUS

SHOW SYMBOL [symbol-name]

Command Qualifiers	Defaults
/ALL	--
/GLOBAL	--
/LOCAL	--
/[NO]LOG	/LOG

SHOW SYSTEM

SHOW TERMINAL [device-name[:]]

Command Qualifiers	Defaults
/[NO]OUTPUT[=filespec]	/OUTPUT=SYS$OUTPUT
/PERMANENT	--

SHOW [DAY]TIME

SHOW TRANSLATION logical-name

SHOW USERS [username]

SHOW WORKING_SET

Command Qualifier	Default
/[NO]OUTPUT[=filespec]	/OUTPUT=SYS$OUTPUT

SORT input-filespec[,...] output-filespec

SPAWN [command-string]

Command Qualifiers	Defaults
/[NO]CARRIAGE_CONTROL	
/[NO]CLI[=cli]	
/INPUT=filespec	

```
/[NO]KEYPAD                                        /KEYPAD
/[NO]LOG                                              /LOG
/[NO]LOGICAL_NAMES                        /LOGICAL_NAMES
/[NO]NOTIFY                                      /NONOTIFY
/OUTPUT=filespec
/PROCESS=subprocess-name
/[NO]PROMPT[=string]
/[NO]SYMBOLS                                      /SYMBOLS
/[NO]TABLE[=command-table]
/[NO]WAIT                                            /WAIT
```

START/CPU [cpu-id, ...]

START/QUEUE queue-name[:]

```
Command  Qualifiers                              Defaults
/ALIGN[=(option[,...])]                               --
/BACKWARD=n                                           --
/BASE_PRIORITY=n
/[NO]BATCH                                       /NOBATCH
/[NO]BLOCK_LIMIT=([lowlim,]uplim)         /NOBLOCK_LIMIT
/[NO]CHARACTERISTICS[=(characteristic[,...])]/NOCHARACTERISTICS
/CLOSE                                             /CLOSE
/CPUDEFAULT=time                          /CPUDEFAULT=NONE
/CPUMAXIMUM=time                          /CPUMAXIMUM=NONE
/[NO]DEFAULT[=(option[,...])]                  /NODEFAULT
/[NO]DESCRIPTION=string                    /NODESCRIPTION
/[NO]DISABLE_SWAPPING                  /NODISABLE_SWAPPING
/[NO]ENABLE_GENERIC                       /ENABLE_GENERIC
/FORM_MOUNTED=type                   /FORM_MOUNTED=default
/FORWARD=n                                            --
/[NO]GENERIC[=(queue-name[,...])]             /NOGENERIC
/JOB_LIMIT=n                                  /JOB_LIMIT=1
/[NO]LIBRARY[=filename]                 /LIBRARY=SYSDEVCTL
/NEXT
/ON=[node::][device[:]]
/OPEN                                              /CLOSE
/OWNER_UIC=uic                          /OWNER_UIC=[1,4]
/[NO]PROCESSOR[=filename]               /PROCESSOR=PRTSMB
/PROTECTION=(code)            /PROTECTION=(S:E,O:D,G:R,W:W)
/[NO]RECORD_BLOCKING                     /RECORD_BLOCKING
/[NO]RETAIN[=option]                           /NORETAIN
/SCHEDULE=[NO]SIZE                         /SEHCDULE=SIZE
/SEARCH="search-string"                               --
/[NO]SEPARATE[=(option[,...])]                /NOSEPARATE
/[NO]TERMINAL                               /NOTERMINAL
/TOP_OF_FILE                                          --
/WSDEFAULT=n                              /WSDEFAULT=NONE
/WSEXTENT=n                                /WSEXTENT=NONE
/WSQUOTA=n                                  /WSQUOTA=NONE
```

START/QUEUE/MANAGER [filespec]
   Command Qualifiers   Defaults
   /BUFFER_COUNT=n   /BUFFER_COUNT=50
   /EXTEND_QUANTITY=n   /EXTEND_QUANTITY=100
   /[NO]NEW_VERSION   /NONEW_VERSION
   /[NO]RESTART   /NORESTART

STOP/CPU [cpu-id,...]

STOP [process-name]
   Command Qualifier   Default
   /IDENTIFICATION=pid   --

STOP/QUEUE queue-name[:]

STOP/QUEUE/ABORT queue-name[:]

STOQ/QUEUE/ENTRY=entry-number queue-name[:]

STOP/QUEUE/ENTRY=entry-number/REQUEUE [=queue-name]queue-name[:]
   Command Qualifiers   Defaults
   /ENTRY=entry-number
   /HOLD
   /PRIORITY=n

STOP/QUEUE/MANAGER

STOP/QUEUE/NEXT queue-name[:]

STOP/QUEUE/REQUEUE[=queue-name] queue-name[:]

STOP/QUEUE/RESET queue-name[:]

SUBMIT filespec[,...]
   Command Qualifiers   Defaults
   /AFTER=time   --
   /[NO]BACKUP   /CREATED

```
/[NO]BEFORE[=time]                                      /BEFORE=TODAY
/[NO]BY_OWNER[=uic]                                         --
/CHARACTERISTICS=(characteristic[,…])                       --
/CLI=filespec
/[NO]CONFIRM                                             /NOCONFIRM
/CPUTIME=option                                         /CPUTIME=NONE
/[NO]CREATED                                             /CREATED
/[NO]EXCLUDE=(filespec[,…])                                 --
/[NO]EXPIRED                                             /CREATED
/[NO]HOLD                                                /NOHOLD
/[NO]IDENTIFY                                            /IDENTIFY
/[NO]KEEP
/[NO]LOG_FILE[=filespec]
/[NO]MODIFIED                                            /CREATED
/NAME=job-name
/[NO]NOTIFY                                              /NONOTIFY
/PARAMETERS=(parameter[,…])                                 --
/[NO]PRINTER[=queue-name]                               /PRINTER=SYS$PRINT
/PRIORITY=n
/QUEUE=queue-name[:]                                    /QUEUE=SYS$BATCH
/REMOTE                                                     --
/[NO]RESTART                                             /NORESTART
/[NO]SINCE[=time]                                        /SINCE=TODAY
/USER=username                                              --
/WSDEFAULT=n
/WSEXTENT=n
/WSQUOTA=n
Positional  Qualifier                                   Default
/[NO]DELETE                                              /NODELETE
```

SYNCHRONIZE [job-name]

```
Command Qualifiers                                      Defaults
/ENTRY=entry-number                                        --
/QUEUE=queue-name[:]                                    /QUEUE=SYS$BATCH
```

TYPE filespec[,…]

```
Command Qualifiers                                      Defaults
/BACKUP                                                 /CREATED
/BEFORE[=time]                                          /BEFORE=TODAY
/BY_OWNER[=uic]                                            --
/[NO]CONFIRM                                            /NOCONFIRM
/CREATED                                                /CREATED
/EXCLUDE=(filespec[,…])                                    --
/EXPIRED                                                /CREATED
/MODIFIED                                               /CREATED
/[NO]OUTPUT[=filespec]                                  /OUTPUT=SYS$OUTPUT
/[NO]PAGE                                               /NOPAGE
/SINCE=time                                             /SINCE=TODAY
```

UNLOCK filespec[,...]

Command Qualifiers	Defaults
/[NO]CONFIRM	/NOCONFIRM
/[NO]LOG	/NOLOG

WAIT delta-time

WRITE logical-name expression[,...]

Command Qualifiers	Defaults
/ERROR=label	
/SYMBOL	
/UPDATE	

Appendix C
Lexical Function Reference

STRING MANIPULATION

F$EXTRACT(startPos, nChars, string)

Extracts nChars characters from string, beginning at offset startPos. startPos must be greater than or equal to zero; nChars must be less than or equal to the length of the string.

F$LENGTH(string)

Returns the length of string, in characters. The string may be any valid DCL character-string expression.

F$EDIT(string, edit_list)

Performs special editing on the specified string according to edit_list. The edit_list is a character string expression containing a comma-separated list of one or more of the following keywords:

COLLAPSE	string	Deletes all spaces and/or tabs.
COMPRESS	string	Multiple spaces/tabs converted to one space.
LOWERCASE	string	Convert all chars to lowercase.
TRIM	string	Deletes leading and trailing spaces/tabs.
UNCOMMENT	string	Deletes all comments.
UPCASE	string	Convert all chars to uppercase.

These keywords may not be abbreviated. To preserve sections of the input string, enclose them in quotes.

F$ELEMENT(el_number, delim, string)

Selects one element (word) from a string containing a concatenated list of elements. The delim argument specifies the character used to separate the elements in the string. An example usage follows:

```
$ COLORS = "RED|BLUE|ORANGE|PURPLE"
$ MYCOLOR = F$ELEMENT(3,"|",COLORS)
$ SHOW SYMBOL MYCOLOR
  MYCOLOR = "ORANGE"
```

F$LOCATE(subString, string)

Finds the position of the given substring within the string argument and returns the offset of the first character of subString as an integer. The first character of string is offset zero. If subString is not found, the returned value is the offset of the last character of string, plus one.

F$PARSE(filespec[,default][,related][,field][,type])

Uses the RMS $PARSE system call to parse a filespec. Returns either (a) the fully expanded filespec of the selected file or (b) the requested filespec field. Filespec is the input filespec to be parsed, whereas default and related give two levels of default substitution for items omitted in filespec. Field names a specific field of the filespec to be returned, and can be one of the following:

NODE	Node name.
DEVICE	Device specifier.
DIRECTORY	Directory name in [].
NAME	File name (only).
TYPE	File type (only).
VERSION	Version number.

The optional type argument modifies the default behavior of $PARSE, and may be one of the following:
- NO_CONCEAL – Causes the CONCEAL attribute in a logical name to be ignored; parsing will not end when a concealed name is found.

- SYNTAX_ONLY – Inhibits $PARSE from verifying that a specified directory actually exists. A simple example of F$PARSE follows, showing how a complete filespec can be recovered from a partial one:

```
$ SET DEFAULT $DISK1:[LEISNER]
$ FILESPEC = F$PARSE("PROJECT.COM")
$ SHOW SYMBOL FILESPEC
  FILESPEC = "$DISK1:[LEISNER]PROJECT.COM;4"
```

F$SEARCH(filespec [,stream])

F$SEARCH Runs the RMS $SEARCH facility to hunt for a specified file or files. A string containing the full filespec is returned if the file exists. If the file does not exist, a null string ("") is returned. Wildcards may be used in the filespec. Consecutive calls to F$SEARCH return succeeding files that match the input filespec. The optional stream argument is an integer that specifies what context the F$SEARCH is executing in. If you are running more than one series of F$SEARCH calls in parallel, the stream ID is necessary so that each search will start from the appropriate point in the directory.

F$STRING(expression)

Evaluates the given expression and returns the equivalent string. Either an integer or string expression may be given. Integer expressions are evaluated first and then converted to a decimal format string with leading zeros suppressed. String expressions are simply evaluated. F$STRING is mainly useful as a simple way of converting integer-valued symbols to string-valued symbols.

ENVIRONMENT INFORMATION

F$ENVIRONMENT(envitem)

F$ENVIRONMENT Returns a piece of data (usually string-valued) about the currently active DCL environment. The envtem argument is a keyword that identifies the data to be returned:

CAPTIVE	string	TRUE or FALSE depending on whether the current login is a captive account.
CONTROL	string	Gives a comma-separated list of control characters currently enabled via SET CONTROL or the null string if no control characters are enabled.

DEFAULT	string	Returns the same information as obtained by SHOW DEFAULT (device/directory).
DEPTH	integer	Returns the current command procedure nesting depth.
INTERACTIVE	string	TRUE or FALSE depending upon whether the current DCL command interpreter is executing interactively or not.
KEY_STATE		Returns the current terminal keypad state, either APPLICATION_KEYPAD or NUMERIC_KEYPAD.
MAX_DEPTH	integer	Returns the maximum permissible command procedure nesting depth.
MESSAGE	string	Gives all current SET MESSAGE qualifiers. Output format is compatible with the SET MESSAGE command to enable save-and-restore operations on the message state.
NOCONTROL	string	Gives a comma-separated list of the control characters currently disabled via SET NOCONTROL or the null string ("") if no control characters are now disabled.
ON_CONTROL_Y	string	TRUE if ON_CONTROL_Y is set and a command procedure is currently executing. Always gives FALSE otherwise.
ON_SEVERITY	string	Gives a string containing the severity level associated with the current ON command in a command procedure. If SET NOON is active or you are at DCL command level, NONE is always returned.
OUTPUT_RATE	string	(applies only to batch jobs) Gives a VMS delta time string specifying the interval at which the batch log file is updated. Always returns a null string ("") if used in interactive mode.

PROCEDURE	string	(applies only to command procedures) Gives a filespec for the current command procedure. Returns "" if used in interactive mode.
PROMPT	string	Returns the current DCL prompt.
PROMPT_CONTROL	string	TRUE if the DCL prompt is preceded by a CR/LF combination.
PROTECTION	string	Returns the current default file protection.
SYMBOL_SCOPE	string	Returns the active symbol scope state, one of [NO]GLOBAL or [NO]LOCAL.
VERIFY_IMAGE	string	TRUE if SET VERIFY=IMAGE is active.
VERIFY_PROCEDURE	string	TRUE if SET VERIFY=PROCEDURE is active.

F$GETDVI(deviceName, devItem)

F$GETDVI gives a specific piece of data about a VMS device. The deviceName argument is a string expression that specifies the device. As in F$ENVIRONMENT, devItem is a character expression that must evaluate to one of the keywords in the following (long) list. Note that essentially anything that can be set for a terminal with SET TERMINAL can be read back using F$GETDVI via the TT_xxxxx items.

ACPPID	string	Gives the ACP process PID value.
ACPTYPE	string	Returns the ACP type as one of the following: F11CV1, F11V2, JNL, MTA, NET, REM.
ALL	string	TRUE or FALSE; TRUE means the device is currently allocated.
ALLDEVNAM	string	Gives the allocation class device name.
ALLOCLASS	integer	(integer longword in range 0-255) Returns the allocation class of the host.
ALT_HOST_AVAIL	string	TRUE or FALSE; TRUE indicates the host for the alternate path is available.
ALT_HOST_NAME	string	Returns nodename of the alternate path host.
ALT_HOST_TYPE	string	Gives the type of the alternate path host.

AVL	string	TRUE or FALSE; TRUE indicates the device is available.
CCL	string	TRUE or FALSE; TRUE indicates that the device has carriage control.
CLUSTER	integer	Storage volume cluster size.
CONCEALED	string	TRUE or FALSE; TRUE indicates that the device logical name translates to a name having the CONCEALED attribute.
CYLINDERS	integer	Gives number of cylinders on a disk volume.
DEVBUFSIZ	integer	Gives the buffer size for the device.
DEVCHAR	integer	Returns the device characteristics word.
DEVCHAR2	integer	Returns the secondary device characteristics word.
DEVCLASS	integer	Returns a code specifying the class of device.
DEVDEPEND	integer	Returns a word of device-specific data.
DEVDEPEND2	integer	Returns another word of device-dependent data.
DEVLOCKNAM	string	Gives the unique lock name.
DEVNAM	string	Returns the device name.
DEVSTS	integer	Returns the device-specific status word.
DEVTYPE	integer	Returns a code specifying the device type.
DIR	string	TRUE or FALSE; TRUE indicates the device is directory structured.
DMT	string	TRUE or FALSE; TRUE indicates the device has been marked for DISMOUNT.
DUA	string	TRUE or FALSE; TRUE indicates a generic device.
ELG	string	TRUE or FALSE; TRUE indicates error logging is enabled.
ERRCNT	integer	Returns the error count for the device.

EXISTS	string	TRUE or FALSE; TRUE indicates the device actually exists in the logged-in system.
FOD	string	TRUE or FALSE; TRUE indicates a file-oriented device (disk or tape).
FOR	string	TRUE or FALSE; TRUE indicates a device mounted with /FOREIGN.
FREEBLOCKS	integer	Returns the quantity of free blocks on a disk volume.
FULLDEVNAM	string	Gives the full device name.
GEN	string	TRUE or FALSE; TRUE indicates a generic device.
HOST_AVAIL	string	TRUE or FALSE; TRUE indicates the primary path host is available.
HOST_COUNT	integer	How many hosts are making the given device available to other cluster nodes.
HOST_NAME	string	Name of the primary path host.
HOST_TYPE	string	Type of the primary path host.
IDV	string	TRUE or FALSE; TRUE indicates the device can generate input.
LOCKID	integer	Cluster lock ID.
LOGVOLNAM	string	Name of the logical volume associated with the device.
MAXBLOCK	integer	How many logical blocks are on the volume.
MAXFILES	integer	Limiting number of files on a disk volume.
MBX	string	TRUE or FALSE; TRUE indicates the device is a mailbox.
MEDIA_ID	string	Returns the media ID in non-decoded form.
MEDIA_NAME	string	Gives name of disk for disk volumes or a tape type for tape volumes.
MEDIA_TYPE	string	Returns the device name two-character prefix.

MNT	string	TRUE or FALSE; TRUE indicates the device is currently mounted.
MOUNTCNT	integer	Returns the device mount count.
NET	string	TRUE or FALSE; TRUE indicates a network device.
NEXTDEVNAM	string	Name of the next device in a disk volume set.
ODV	string	TRUE or FALSE; TRUE indicates the device can generate output.
OPCNT	integer	Returns the operation count for the device.
OPR	string	TRUE or FALSE; TRUE indicates an operator device (OP prefix).
OWNUIC	string	Gives the UIC of the device owner.
PID	string	Returns the PID of the owner.
RCK	string	TRUE or FALSE; TRUE indicates read checking is currently enabled.
RCT	string	TRUE or FALSE; TRUE indicates a disk device contains RCT.
REC	string	TRUE or FALSE; TRUE indicates a record-oriented device.
RECSIZ	integer	Gives the record size on a record-oriented device.
REFCNT	integer	Count of processes accessing the device.
REMOTE_DEVICE	string	TRUE or FALSE; TRUE indicates a remote device.
RND	string	TRUE or FALSE; TRUE indicates a random access device (usually disk).
ROOTDEVNAM	string	Gives the name of the root (first) volume in a disk volume set.
RTM	string	TRUE or FALSE; TRUE indicates a real-time device.
SDI	string	TRUE or FALSE; TRUE indicates a single directory structured device.
SECTORS	integer	Gives number of disk sectors per track.

SERIALNUM	integer	Gives the disk volume serial number.
SERVED_DEVICE	string	TRUE or FALSE; TRUE indicates a served device.
SHR	string	TRUE or FALSE; TRUE indicates a shared or shareable device.
SPL	string	TRUE or FALSE; TRUE indicates a spooled device.
SPLDEVNAM	string	Returns the name of the spooled device.
SQD	string	TRUE or FALSE; TRUE indicates a sequential block (tape) device.
STS	integer	Returns a status word.
SWL	string	TRUE or FALSE; TRUE indicates software write lock is active.
TRACKS	integer	Gives tracks per cylinder for disk devices.
TRANSCNT	integer	Returns the transaction count for a volume.
TRM	string	TRUE or FALSE; TRUE indicates the device is a terminal.
TT_ACCPORNAM	string	Gives terminal server and port names for a terminal on a server.
TT_ALTYPEAHD	string	TRUE or FALSE; TRUE indicates a terminal having an alternate typeahead buffer.
TT_ANSICRT	string	TRUE or FALSE; TRUE indicates an ANSI-compliant terminal.
TT_APP_KEYPAD	string	TRUE or FALSE; TRUE indicates the terminal keypad is in APPLICATION_KEYPAD.
TT_AUTOBAUD	string	TRUE or FALSE; TRUE indicates terminal /AUTOBAUD is in effect.
TT_AVO	string	TRUE or FALSE; TRUE indicates a VT100 AVO-style terminal.
TT_BLOCK	string	TRUE or FALSE; TRUE indicates block mode capability.

TT_BRDCSTMBX	string	TRUE or FALSE; TRUE indicates the terminal receives broadcast mailbox traffic.
TT_CRFILL	string	TRUE or FALSE; TRUE indicates the terminal needs null fillers after CR.
TT_DECCRT	string	TRUE or FALSE; TRUE indicates a DEC terminal.
TT_DIALUP	string	TRUE or FALSE; TRUE indicates a dialup line terminal.
TT_DISCONNECT	string	TRUE or FALSE; TRUE indicates the terminal is capable of being disconnected.
TT_DMA	string	TRUE or FALSE; TRUE indicates a DMA-mode terminal.
TT_DRCS	string	TRUE or FALSE; TRUE indicates the terminal accepts downloadable character sets.
TT_EDIT	string	TRUE or FALSE; TRUE indicates /EDIT is enabled for the terminal.
TT_EDITING	string	TRUE or FALSE; TRUE indicates advanced editing is available.
TT_EIGHTBIT	string	TRUE or FALSE; TRUE indicates the use of 8-bit ASCII.
TT_ESCAPE	string	TRUE or FALSE; TRUE indicates the terminal can generate escape sequences as input.
TT_FALLBACK	string	TRUE or FALSE; TRUE indicates multinational fallback is available on the terminal.
TT_HALFDUP	string	TRUE or FALSE; TRUE indicates a half-duplex terminal.
TT_HANGUP	string	TRUE or FALSE; TRUE indicates the /HANGUP attribute is set.
TT_HOSTSYNC	string	TRUE or FALSE; TRUE indicates /HOSTSYNC is in effect.
TT_INSERT	string	TRUE or FALSE; TRUE indicates insert-mode line editing (vs overstrike).

TT_LFFILL	string	TRUE or FALSE; TRUE indicates null fillers are needed after LF.
TT_LOCALECHO	string	TRUE or FALSE; TRUE indicates /LOCALECHO is set.
TT_LOWER	string	TRUE or FALSE; TRUE indicates the terminal handles lowercase characters.
TT_MBXDSABL	string	TRUE or FALSE; TRUE indicates terminal mailboxes are disabled from getting unsolicited input.
TT_MECHFORM	string	TRUE or FALSE; TRUE indicates mechanical formfeed terminals (hardcopy devices).
TT_MECHTAB	string	TRUE or FALSE; TRUE indicates the terminal can do automatic tab expansion.
TT_MODEM	string	TRUE or FALSE; TRUE indicates a modem-connected terminal.
TT_MODHANGUP	string	TRUE or FALSE; TRUE indicates the modify hangup attribute is enabled.
TT_NOBRDCST	string	TRUE or FALSE; TRUE indicates the terminal refuses broadcast messages.
TT_NOECHO	string	TRUE or FALSE; TRUE indicates that /NOECHO is set.
TT_NOTYPEAHD	string	TRUE or FALSE; TRUE indicates that the /NOTYPEAHD attribute is enabled.
TT_OPER	string	TRUE or FALSE; TRUE indicates an operator terminal (OP).
TT_PAGE	integer	Returns the setting of /PAGE=.
TT_PASTHRU	string	TRUE or FALSE; TRUE indicates the /PASTHRU attribute is set to pass binary and control characters.
TT_PHYDEVNAM	string	Returns the physical device name associated with a specified virtual terminal.
TT_PRINTER	string	TRUE or FALSE; TRUE indicates a printer port exists on the terminal.

TT_READSYNC	string	TRUE or FALSE; TRUE indicates read synchronization is supported by the terminal.
TT_REGIS	string	TRUE or FALSE; TRUE indicates that REGIS graphics commands are understood.
TT_REMOTE	string	TRUE or FALSE; TRUE indicates a remote terminal.
TT_SCOPE	string	TRUE or FALSE; TRUE indicates a CRT-type terminal (not hardcopy).
TT_SECURE	string	TRUE or FALSE; TRUE indicates the /SECURE_SERVER attribute is set.
TT_SETSPEED	string	TRUE or FALSE; TRUE indicates rate setting is enabled.
TT_SIXEL	string	TRUE or FALSE; TRUE indicates SIXEL graphics are supported.
TT_TTSYNC	string	TRUE or FALSE; TRUE indicates /TTSYNC is enabled.
TT_SYSPWD	string	TRUE or FALSE; TRUE indicates a system password is required for the terminal.
TT_WRAP	string	TRUE or FALSE; TRUE indicates the /WRAP attribute is set
UNIT	integer	Returns the unit number for the device.
VOLCOUNT	integer	Returns the number of volumes in a disk volume set.
VOLNAM	string	Returns the name of a volume.
VOLNUMBER	integer	Gives the index of the specified volume in a disk volume set.
VOLSETMEM	string	TRUE or FALSE; TRUE indicates the specified volume is a member of a disk volume set.
VPRO	string	Gives the volume protection mask in standard SOGW:RWED format.

WCK	string	TRUE or FALSE; TRUE indicates write checking is enabled for the specified device.

F$GETJPI(PID, JPIitem)

Returns information on the specified process using the $GETJPI service. WORLD or GROUP privileges are required to access processes other than your own. The PID is given as a character string; a null string is interpreted as your current process PID. The type of the returned value varies according to the item. JPIitem is a character expression keyword from the following list:

ACCOUNT	string	Gives the current account name string, padded with trailing blanks. Length is always eight characters.
APTCNT	integer	Gives the active page table count.
ASTACT	integer	Returns active AST access modes.
ASTCNT	integer	Gives the number of ASTs left in your quota.
ASTEN	integer	Returns access modes having ASTs enabled.
ASTLM	integer	Returns the AST limit.
AUTHPR	integer	Gives the highest priority you can set without invoking ALTPRI privilege.
AUTHPRIV	string	Gives a list of all privileges that your process can enable.
BIOCNT	integer	Returns unused portion of the buffered I/O quota.
BIOLM	integer	Gives total buffered I/O quota.
BUFIO	integer	Tells how many buffered I/O operations the process has performed.
BYTCNT	integer	Gives unused portion of byte count quota for buffered I/O.
BYTLM	integer	Gives total byte count quota.
CLINAME	string	Always gives DCL.
CPULIM	integer	Process CPU time limit in centiseconds. Zero means unlimited CPU.

CPUTIM	intesger	Returns CPU time already used, in centiseconds.
CURPRIV	string	Gives a list of privileges currently enabled by your process.
DFPFC	integer	Gives the current page fault cluster default.
DFWSCNT	integer	Gives the current default working set count.
DIOCNT	integer	Gives the unused portion of the DIO quota.
DIOLM	integer	Gives the total DIO quota.
DIRIO	integer	Gives the actual count of DIO operations performed by your task.
EFCS	integer	Returns the first 32 local event flags.
EFCU	integer	Returns the second 32 local event flags.
EFWM	integer	Returns the current event flag wait mask.
ENQCNT	integer	Gives unused portion of the process lock request quota.
ENQLM	integer	Gives the total lock request quota.
EXCVEC	integer	Returns the address of the process exception vector table.
FILCNT	integer	Returns the unused portion of the open file quota.
FILLM	integer	Returns the total open file quota.
FINALEXC	integer	Gives the address of the process final exception vector table.
FREP0VA	integer	Returns virtual address of the first free page at the end of P0 program memory space.
FREP1VA	integer	Returns virtual address of the first free page at the end of P1 control memory space.
FREPTECNT	integer	Gives count of available pages for expansion of virtual memory.

GPGCNT	integer	Gives Global Page Count in current working set.
GRP	integer	Returns the Group field of the current process UIC.
IMAGECOUNT	integer	Gives how many image run-downs the process has had.
IMAGNAME	string	Returns filespec of the current image.
IMAGPRIV	string	Gives a list of privileges installed with the current image.
JOBPRCCNT	integer	Returns number of existing subprocesses currently owned by the given process.
LOGINTIM	string	Gives absolute time at which the current process logged in or was created.
MASTER_PID	string	Gives the PID of the topmost process in the current process's tree of creators.
MEM	integer	Gives the member field of the current process UIC.
MODE	string	Returns one of BATCH, INTERACTIVE, NETWORK, OTHER.
MSGMASK	integer	Gives the default message mask.
OWNER	string	Returns the PID of the owner of the current process.
PAGEFLTS	integer	Returns number of page faults generated by the current process.
PAGFILCNT	integer	Returns unused portion of page file quota.
PAGFILLOC	integer	Returns the location of the current page file.
PGFLQUOTA	integer	Gives the total virtual page count limit.
PHDFLAGS	integer	Gives the PHD flagword.
PID	string	Returns the PID of the current process.
PPGCNT	integer	Returns the current page count for the process.

PRCCNT	integer	Returns the number of subprocesses under the current process.
PRCLM	integer	Returns the limiting number of subprocesses (subprocess quota).
PRCNAM	string	Returns the name of the current process.
PRIB	integer	Gives the base priority of the current process.
PROCPRIV	string	Returns the default privilege list for the current process.
SITESPEC	integer	Gives the site-specific longword.
STATE	string	Returns the current process state (same states as in SHOW SYSTEM).
STS	integer	Gives the current process status flagword.
SWPFILLOC	integer	Returns the virtual memory location of the swap file.
TERMINAL	string	Gives the terminal name for interactive processes.
TMBU	integer	Gives the unit number of the process termination mailbox that is notified when the process is deleted.
TQCNT	integer	Gives the unused portion of the timer queue quota.
TQLM	integer	Gives the total timer queue quota for the process.
UIC	string	Returns the whole UIC of the process owner.
USERNAME	string	Gives a trailing-blank padded username string for the process.
VIRTPEAK	integer	Returns the largest virtual address size for the process.
VOLUMES	integer	Returns number of volumes currently mounted.
WSAUTH	integer	Gives the authorized maximum working set size, in pages.

WSAUTHEXT	integer	Gives the authorized maximum working set extent, in pages.
WSEXTENT	integer	Gives the current extent of the working set, in pages.
WSPEAK	integer	Gives the maximum working set size used so far, in pages.
WSQUOTA	integer	Returns the WS size quota, in pages.
WSSIZE	integer	Returns the instantaneous working set size.

F$GETQUI(functKwd,[QUIitem],[QObjID],[QUIflags])

F$GETQUI Returns information about batch and print queues, jobs pending in those queues, and form/characteristic definitions for those queues. F$GETQUI is a very complex lexical function, with about 150 items and various constraints on combinations of functions and the other arguments. Internally, F$GETQUI uses the $GETQUI system service and supports all features of $GETQUI.

Function codes are specified as character string expressions; the possibilities are described below:

CANCEL_OPERATION	Kills all wildcard operations started by previous F$GETQUI calls.
DISPLAY_CHARACTERISTIC	Causes information to be returned describing a characteristic definition (or the next characteristic in a wildcard operation sequence).
DISPLAY_ENTRY	Gives information about the next job entry. Works like DISPLAY_JOB but doesn't demand that you first establish a context.
DISPLAY_FILE	Gives data about the next file in the current job context. Requires that calls first be made to DISPLAY_QUEUE and DISPLAY_JOB (or DISPLAY_ENTRY) to establish a context for the DISPLAY_FILE.
DISPLAY_FORM	Gives data about a form definition.
DISPLAY_JOB	Gives data about the next job, using the current queue context established by a DISPLAY_QUEUE call.

DISPLAY_QUEUE	Gives data about the next queue.
TRANSLATE_QUEUE	Returns the equivalence name for a queue by translating the queue logical name.

QUitem

The QUitem argument is a character expression that must evaluate to one of the keywords listed at the end of the F$GETQUI section. This list is extremely long so we don't present it immediately.

The QUjbID argment specifies the name and/or number of the item for which you want to search. This is also a character expression, which may include wildcards for functions DISPLAY_CHARACTERISTIC, DISPLAY_ENTRY, DISPLAY_FORM and DISPLAY_QUEUE. Anytime you use a wildcard object ID, successive calls to F$GETQUI will return information about the next object in sequence, as long as you don't change the queue context. When a wildcard sequence terminates, a null string is returned by F$GETQUI.

The QUIflags argument is a character expression consisting of a comma-separated list of search flags for the $GETQUI system service. These flags are generally valid only for one or two function codes and are listed below:

ALL_JOBS	(DISPLAY_JOB) – Causes all jobs matching the username of the caller in the current queue context to be searched.
BATCH	(DISPLAY_QUEUE, DISPLAY_ENTRY) – Searches batch queues.
EXECUTING_JOBS	(DISPLAY_ENTRY, DISPLAY_JOB) – Searches all executing jobs (not pending ones).
FREEZE_CONTEXT	(DISPLAY_xxxx) – Inhibits advance of a wildcard to the next item that would otherwise be selected.
GENERIC	(DISPLAY_QUEUE) – Searches generic queues only.
HOLDING_JOBS	(DISPLAY_ENTRY, DISPLAY_JOB) – Searches only jobs held unconditionally.
PENDING_JOBS	(DISPLAY_ENTRY, DISPLAY_JOB) – Searches only pending jobs (opposite effect of EXECUTING_JOBS).
PRINTER	(DISPLAY_QUEUE, DISPLAY_ENTRY) – Searches print queues only.

RETAINED_JOBS	(DISPLAY_ENTRY, DISPLAY_JOB) – Searches only retained jobs.
SERVER	(DISPLAY_QUEUE, DISPLAY_ENTRY) – Searches only server queues.
SYMBIONT	(DISPLAY_QUEUE, DISPLAY_ENTRY) – Same as specifying TERMI-NAL,SERVER,PRINTER; that is, searches all output queues.
TERMINAL	(DISPLAY_QUEUE, DISPLAY_ENTRY) – Searches terminal queues only.
THIS_JOB	(DISPLAY_FILE, DISPLAY_JOB, DISPLAY_QUEUE) – Searches jobs associated with the calling batch context or command file.
TIMED_RELEASE_JOBS	(DISPLAY_ENTRY, DISPLAY_JOB, DISPLAY_CHARACTERISTIC) – Searches only jobs held pending a certain time.
WILDCARD	(DISPLAY_CHARACTERISTIC, DISPLAY_ENTRY, DISPLAY_FORM, DISPLAY_QUEUE) – Sets up a context for use in wildcard operations.

F$GETQUI

The F$GETQUI item keywords are now described in all their glory. Types of return value are enclosed in parentheses.

ACCOUNT_NAME	string	Gives the account name string for the job's owner.
AFTER_TIME	string	Gives the absolute time after which the specified job will execute.
ASSIGNED_QUEUE_NAME	string	Gives the name of the actual queue assigned to the specified logical queue name.
BASE_PRIORITY	integer	Gives priority at which batch jobs are run in a batch queue or the priority of the symbiont managing an output queue.

CHARACTERISTICS	string	Returns the characteristic(s) belonging to the given job or queue.
CHARACTERISTIC_NAME	string	Returns a characteristic name.
CHARACTERISTIC_NUMBER	integer	Gives the characteristic number.
CHECKPOINT_DATA	string	For batch jobs, returns the value of BATCH$RESTART.
CLI	string	For batch jobs, the filespec of the CLI being used.
COMPLETED_BLOCKS	integer	For print jobs, gives the total number of blocks completed by the symbiont for that job.
CONDITION_VECTOR	integer	Returns the job's completion status vector.
CPU_DEFAULT	string	For batch queues, gives the default CPU time limit in centiseconds.
CPU_LIMIT	string	For batch queues and jobs, the maximum CPU time limit in centiseconds.
DEFAULT_FORM_NAME	string	For output queues, gives the name of the default form.
DEFAULT_FORM_STOCK	string	For output queues, the name of the default form stock.
DEVICE_NAME	string	For batch queues, gives the node name on which the queue runs. For output queues, gives the device name.
ENTRY_NUMBER	integer	Gives the queue entry number for the given job.
EXECUTING_JOB_COUNT	integer	Returns the count of currently executing jobs in the specified queue.
FILE_BURST	string	TRUE or FALSE; TRUE indicates flag/burst pages are being printed.
FILE_CHECKPOINTED	string	TRUE or FALSE; TRUE indicates a checkpointed file.
FILE_COPIES	integer	For output queues, gives the file copy repetition count.

FILE_COPIES_DONE	integer	For output queues, counts how many copies of the current file have been completed so far.
FILE_DELETE	string	TRUE or FALSE; TRUE indicates a request for deletion of the current file upon completion.
FILE_DOUBLE_SPACE	string	TRUE or FALSE; TRUE indicates output files are to be double-spaced.
FILE_EXECUTING	string	TRUE or FALSE; TRUE indicates the file is currently being processed by the given queue.
FILE_FLAG	string	TRUE or FALSE; TRUE indicates a flag page is to be printed before the file.
FILE_FLAGS	integer	Gives the options invoked for the specified file.
FILE_IDENTIFICATION	string	Returns the unique file ID value for the specified file.
FILE_PAGE_HEADER	string	TRUE or FALSE; TRUE indicates a header is printed on each output page.
FILE_PAGINATE	string	TRUE or FALSE; TRUE indicates formfeeds (FF) characters are inserted when the output symbiont reaches the bottom of the page.
FILE_PASSALL	string	TRUE or FALSE; TRUE indicates a file is being printed in PASSALL.
FILE_SETUP_MODULES	string	For output queues, gives names of device control library modules to be used with the given job.
FILE_SPECIFICATION	string	Gives the full filespec of the specified job/file.
FILE_STATUS	integer	Returns the file status word.
FILE_TRAILER	string	TRUE or FALSE; TRUE indicates a trailer page is to be printed following the file.
FIRST_PAGE	integer	For output queues, returns the first page number to be output.

FORM_DESCRIPTION	string	Returns the forms description string in effect for the given job.
FORM_FLAGS	integer	Gives the options word for the indicated form.
FORM_LENGTH	integer	For output queues, gives the number of lines comprising a page of the current form.
FORM_MARGIN_BOTTOM	integer	Returns the lower margin of the current form, in lines.
FORM_MARGIN_LEFT	integer	Returns the left margin of the current form, in characters.
FORM_MARGIN_RIGHT	integer	Returns the right margin of the current form, in characters.
FORM_MARGIN_TOP	integer	Returns the upper margin of the current form, in lines.
FORM_NAME	string	Gives the name of the indicated or currently mounted form.
FORM_NUMBER	integer	Returns the form number of the indicated or currently mounted form.
FORM_SETUP_MODULES	string	For output queues, gives a list of the device control library modules used in the SETUP phase of the indicated form.
FORM_SHEET_FEED	string	TRUE or FALSE; TRUE indicates a pause at the end of each page for manual sheet feeding.
FORM_STOCK	string	Gives the name of the STOCK for the specified form.
FORM_TRUNCATE	string	TRUE or FALSE; TRUE indicates that characters off the right margin are thrown away.
FORM_WIDTH	integer	Returns the indicated form's width, in characters.
FORM_WRAP	string	TRUE or FALSE; TRUE indicates that characters off the right margin are wrapped to the next output line.

GENERIC_TARGET	string	For generic output queues, lists the names of specific execution queues that get jobs from the indicated generic queue.
HOLDING_JOB_COUNT	integer	Returns the number of jobs currently on hold in the indicated queue.
INTERVENING_BLOCKS	integer	For output queues, gives the number of blocks that have to be handled before the indicated job starts.
INTERVENING_JOBS	integer	For output queues, gives the number of entire jobs that must complete before the indicated job will start.
JOB_ABORTING	string	TRUE or FALSE; TRUE indicates that the indicated job is in the process of being aborted.
JOB_COPIES	integer	Returns the number of times that the indicated output job will be repeated.
JOB_COPIES_DONE	integer	Gives the number of completed copies of the indicated output job.
JOB_CPU_LIMIT	string	TRUE or FALSE; TRUE indicates a job CPU time limit is in effect.
JOB_ECECUTING	string	TRUE or FALSE; TRUE indicates the given job is currently printing or executing.
JOB_FILE_BURST	string	TRUE or FALSE; TRUE indicates a a burst page has been specified for the indicated job.
JOB_FILE_BURST_ONE	string	TRUE or FALSE; TRUE indicates the file burst page has been specified only for the first copy.
JOB_FILE_FLAG	string	TRUE or FALSE; TRUE indicates the flag page has been enabled for the indicated job.
JOB_FILE_FLAG_ONE	string	TRUE or FALSE; TRUE indicates the flag page occurs only before the first file in the indicated job.
JOB_FILE_PAGINATE	string	TRUE or FALSE; TRUE indicates the pagination option has been explicitly given for the job.

JOB_FILE_TRAILER	string	TRUE or FALSE; TRUE indicates the trailer page is enabled for the indicated job.
JOB_FILE_TRAILER_ONE	string	TRUE or FALSE; TRUE indicates the trailer only occurs after the last copy of the last file.
JOB_FLAGS	integer	Gives the option flagword for the job.
JOB_HOLDING	string	TRUE or FALSE; TRUE indicates the job is in an explicit HOLD state.
JOB_INACCESSIBLE	string	TRUE or FALSE; TRUE indicates the caller lacks READ access to the indicated job. This limits the available information to the following items:

AFTER_TIME

COMPLETED_BLOCKS

ENTRY_NUMBER

INTERVENING_BLOCKS

INTERVENING_JOBS

JOB_SIZE

JOB_STATUS

JOB_LIMIT	integer	For batch queues, gives the maximum number of jobs that can execute simultaneously.
JOB_LOG_DELETE	string	TRUE or FALSE; TRUE indicates the job log file will be deleted after printing.
JOB_LOG_NULL	string	TRUE or FALSE; TRUE indicates that no job log file will be created.
JOB_LOG_SPOOL	string	TRUE or FALSE; TRUE indicates the job log file is to be queued to a printer upon completion.
JOB_LOWERCASE	string	TRUE or FALSE; TRUE indicates the job log file will be sent to a printer having the LOWERCASE attribute.
JOB_NAME	string	Returns the name of the indicated job.

JOB_NOTIFY	string	TRUE or FALSE; TRUE indicates a broadcast message goes to a terminal when the indicated job completes.
JOB_PENDING	string	TRUE or FALSE; TRUE indicates the indicated job is pending in the specified queue.
JOB_PID	string	For batch jobs, returns a string containing the process ID of the job.
JOB_REFUSED	string	TRUE or FALSE; TRUE indicates job was refused by the output symbiont and is awaiting acceptance.
JOB_RESET_MODULES	string	Returns a comma-separated list of device control library modules to be sent to the output device upon job completion.
JOB_RESTART	string	TRUE or FALSE; TRUE indicates the indicated job can be restarted.
JOB_RETAINED	string	TRUE or FALSE; TRUE indicates a completed job is being retained in the queue.
JOB_SIZE	integer	For output queues, gives the total number of blocks in the indicated job.
JOB_SIZE_MAXIMUM	integer	For output queues, gives the maximum number of blocks that will be accepted for service in one job.
JOB_SIZE_MINIMUM	integer	For output queues, gives the minimum number of blocks that comprise an acceptable job.
JOB_STARTING	string	TRUE or FALSE; TRUE indicates the job controller has begun processing the job. Gives FALSE if the job has progressed to begin execution.
JOB_STATUS	integer	Returns the job status word.
JOB_SUSPENDED	string	TRUE or FALSE; TRUE indicates the job is currently suspended in the queue.
JOB_TIMED_RELEASE	string	TRUE or FALSE; TRUE indicates the job is being held for release at a specific time.

JOB_WSDEFAULT	string	TRUE or FALSE; TRUE indicates a default WS size has been specified for the given job.
JOB_WSEXTENT	string	TRUE or FALSE; TRUE indicates a default WS extent has been specified for the given job.
JOB_WSQUOTA	string	TRUE or FALSE; TRUE indicates a WS quota has been attached to the given job.
LAST_PAGE	integer	For output queues, returns the page number at which the job is expected to end.
LIBRARY_SPECIFICATION	string	For output queues, returns the name of the queue's associated device control library.
LOG_QUEUE	string	For batch jobs, returns the name of the output queue into which the printed copy of the logfile will be deposited.
LOG_SPECIFICATION	string	For batch queues, returns the name of the log file to be generated for the indicated job.
NOTE	string	For output queue jobs, returns the value of the note string that will be printed on the flag pages.
OPERATOR_REQUEST	string	Returns the message that will be sent to the operator when the indicated job is ready to start.
OWNER_UIC	string	Gives the UIC of the owner of the indicated queue.
PAGE_SETUP_MODULES	string	Returns a comma-separated list of the device control library module(s) used to initialize each page of output in an output execution queue.
PARAMETER_n [n in range 1-8]	string	These items return the values of the user-defined parameters (from the /PARAMETER qualifier) which become symbols P1 to P8 in a batch job.

PENDING_JOB_BLOCK_COUNT	integer	Gives the grand total of all pending blocks in the entire output queue.
PENDING_JOB_COUNT	integer	Gives the total number of pending jobs in an entire output queue.
PENDING_JOB_REASON	integer	Returns a reason code explaining why the indicated job is pending.
PEND_CHAR_MISMATCH	string	TRUE or FALSE; TRUE indicates a job needs characteristics currently unavailable on its queue.
PEND_JOB_SIZE_MAX	string	TRUE or FALSE; TRUE indicates a job is pending because its size exceeds the value of JOB_SIZE_MAXIMUM.
PEND_JOB_SIZE_MIN	string	TRUE or FALSE; TRUE indicates a job is pending because its size is less than the value of JOB_SIZE_MINIMUM.
PEND_LOWERCASE_MISMATCH	string	TRUE or FALSE; TRUE indicates a job is pending because it wants a printer with the LOWERCASE attribute.
PEND_NO_ACCESS	string	TRUE or FALSE; TRUE indicates a job is pending because the job's owner has no access to the queue.
PEND_QUEUE_BUSY	string	TRUE or FALSE; TRUE indicates a job is pending because the number of executing jobs already equal JOB_LIMIT.
PEND_QUEUE_STATE	string	TRUE or FALSE; TRUE indicates a job is pending because of an inactive queue state.
PEND_STOCK_MISMATCH	string	TRUE or FALSE; TRUE indicates a job is pending because its form request does not match the currently mounted form.
PRIORITY	integer	Returns the queue scheduling priority of the indicated job.
PROCESSOR	string	Returns the name of the symbiont associated with the job.

PROTECTION	string	Returns the queue protection code, in SOGW/RWED format.
QUEUE_ACL_SPECIFIED	string	TRUE or FALSE; TRUE indicates an ACL has been attached to a queue.
QUEUE_ALIGNING	string	TRUE or FALSE; TRUE indicates that alignment pages are in effect for the queue.
QUEUE_BATCH	string	TRUE or FALSE; TRUE indicates a batch queue.
QUEUE_CLOSED	string	TRUE or FALSE; TRUE indicates the indicated queue is not currently open to execute jobs.
QUEUE_CPU_DEFAULT	string	TRUE or FALSE; TRUE indicates a default time limit is attached to the queue.
QUEUE_CPU_LIMIT	string	TRUE or FALSE; TRUE indicates a maximum CPU time limit has been attached to the queue.
QUEUE_FILE_BURST	string	TRUE or FALSE; TRUE indicates flag/burst pages are enabled for each file in all jobs in the queue.
QUEUE_FILE_BURST_ONE	string	TRUE or FALSE; TRUE indicates the flag/burst pages are only enabled for the first file in each job.
QUEUE_FILE_FLAG	string	TRUE or FALSE; TRUE indicates a flag page is emitted before each file in each job.
QUEUE_FILE_FLAG_ONE	string	TRUE or FALSE; TRUE indicates the flag page occurs only before the first file in each job.
QUEUE_FILE_PAGINATE	string	TRUE or FALSE; TRUE indicates whether pagination with formfeeds is enabled for the queue.
QUEUE_FILE_TRAILER	string	TRUE or FALSE; TRUE indicates trailer pages are attached to each file of each job in the queue.
QUEUE_FILE_TRAILER_ONE	string	TRUE or FALSE; TRUE indicates the trailer page is only emitted for the last file in each job.

QUEUE_FLAGS	integer	Returns the queue options flagword.
QUEUE_GENERIC	string	TRUE or FALSE; TRUE indicates a generic queue (as opposed to an execution queue).
QUEUE_GENERIC_SELECTION		string TRUE or FALSE; TRUE indicates the indicated queue is an execution queue being fed by a generic queue.
QUEUE_IDLE	string	TRUE or FALSE; TRUE indicates the queue is currently idle.
QUEUE_JOB_BURST	string	TRUE or FALSE; TRUE indicates that burst pages are enabled at the start of every job.
QUEUE_JOB_FLAG	string	TRUE or FALSE; TRUE indicates a flag page is emitted at the top of every job.
QUEUE_JOB_SIZE_SCHED	string	TRUE or FALSE; TRUE indicates the given output queue will process smaller jobs first.
QUEUE_JOB_TRAILER	string	TRUE or FALSE; TRUE indicates a trailer page is emitted after every job.
QUEUE_LOWERCASE	string	TRUE or FALSE; TRUE indicates the queue's printer can print lowercase characters.
QUEUE_NAME	string	Returns the name of the indicated queue.
QUEUE_PAUSED	string	TRUE or FALSE; TRUE indicates the queue is in the PAUSED state.
QUEUE_PAUSING	string	TRUE or FALSE; TRUE indicates the queue will be PAUSEd after the current job completes.
QUEUE_PRINTER	string	TRUE or FALSE; TRUE indicates an output print queue.
QUEUE_RECORD_BLOCKING	string	TRUE or FALSE; TRUE indicates that the output records may be blocked together.
QUEUE_REMOTE	string	TRUE or FALSE; TRUE indicates an output queue is attached to a remote device.

QUEUE_RESETTING	string	TRUE or FALSE; TRUE indicates the queue is currently resetting.
QUEUE_RESUMING	string	TRUE or FALSE; TRUE indicates the queue coming out of the PAUSE state.
QUEUE_RETAIN_ALL	string	TRUE or FALSE; TRUE indicates all jobs are RETAINed after completion.
QUEUE_RETAIN_ERROR	string	TRUE or FALSE; TRUE indicates that unsuccessful jobs will be retained in the queue.
QUEUE_SERVER	string	TRUE or FALSE; TRUE indicates that a server symbiont is attached to the queue.
QUEUE_STALLED	string	TRUE or FALSE; TRUE indicates the output queue's device is stalled.
QUEUE_STARTING	string	TRUE or FALSE; TRUE indicates the queue is being started.
QUEUE_STATUS	integer	Returns the indicated queue's status flag-word.
QUEUE_STOPPED	string	TRUE or FALSE; TRUE indicates the queue is in the STOPPED state and is not executing any jobs.
QUEUE_STOPPING	string	TRUE or FALSE; TRUE indicates the queue is being halted.
QUEUE_SWAP	string	TRUE or FALSE; TRUE indicates jobs in the queue can be swapped.
QUEUE_TERMINAL	string	TRUE or FALSE; TRUE indicates the queue is generic and can deposit jobs only in terminal execution queues.
QUEUE_UNAVAILABLE	string	TRUE or FALSE; TRUE indicates the device attached to a queue is not available.
QUEUE_WSDEFAULT	string	TRUE or FALSE; TRUE indicates a WS default is attached to each job.
QUEUE_WSEXTENT	string	TRUE or FALSE; TRUE indicates a WS extent is attached to each job.
QUEUE_WSQUOTA	string	TRUE or FALSE; TRUE indicates a WS quota limit is attached to each job.

REQUEUE_QUEUE_NAME	string	Returns name of the queue on which the indicated job will be requeued. (A confusing keyword.)
RESTART_QUEUE_NAME	string	Gives the name of the queue in which the job is placed if it must be restarted.
RETAINED_JOB_COUNT	integer	Gives the count of retained jobs in the queue.
SCSNODE_NAME	string	Gives the node name of the CPU on which the queue's jobs will run.
SUBMISSION_TIME	string	Gives the absolute time at which a job was enqueued.
TIMED_RELEASE_JOB_COUNT	integer	Returns the total number of timed release jobs pending in the queue.
UIC	string	Gives the owner UIC of the indicated job.
USERNAME	string	Returns the username (up to 12 characters, trailing blank padded) of the job owner.
WSDEFAULT	integer	Returns the default WS size associated with a job or queue.
WSEXTENT	integer	Returns the default WS extent size associated with a job or a queue.
WSQUOTA	integer	Returns the WS quota limit associated with a job or a queue.

F$GETSYI(sys_item[,nodename])

F$GETSYI returns a value obtained from the $GETSYI system service pertaining to the specified nodename and item. The nodename argument is a string containing the SCSNODE_NAME of a cluster member and can only be used when your logged-in node is a cluster member. The sys_item is a character string keyword specifying what information is to be returned. sys_item comes from the following list:

Items for Your Local Node Only

ARCHFLAG	string	Returns architecture flags for the local system.

BOOTTIME	string	Returns absolute time the local system was last booted.
CHARACTER_EMULATED	string	TRUE or FALSE; TRUE indicates that the CPU implements character instructions by emulation.
CPU	integer	Returns the SID register value giving the processor type.
DECIMAL_EMULATED	string	TRUE or FALSE; TRUE indicates that the decimal string instructions are implemented by emulation.
D_FLOAT_EMULATED	string	TRUE or FALSE; TRUE indicates that the D-floating instructions are implemented by emulation.
ERRORLOGBUFFERS	integer	Returns number of pages used as error log buffers.
F_FLOAT_EMULATED	string	TRUE or FALSE; TRUE indicates that the F-floating instructions are emulated.
G_FLOAT_EMULATED	string	TRUE or FALSE; TRUE indicates that the G-floating instructions are implemented by emulation.
PAGEFILE_FREE	integer	Returns number of unused pages in the current paging files.
PAGEFILE_PAGE	integer	Returns total number of pages in the current paging files.
SID	integer	Returns the contents of the system ID register.
SWAPFILE_FREE	integer	Returns the number of unused memory pages in the current swap files.
SWAPFILE_PAGE	integer	Returns the total number of memory pages in the current swap files.
VERSION	string	Returns an 8-character string giving the version number of VMS.

Items Applying to Either the Local Node or Other Cluster Members

ACTIVECPU_CNT	integer	Returns number of CPUs participating in the current SMP boot.

AVAILCPU_CNT	integer	Returns number of recognized CPUs in the cluster.
CLUSTER_FSYSID	string	Returns the SID for the original (founding) node in the cluster.
CLUSTER_FTIME	string	Returns absolute time when the founding member of the cluster was booted.
CLUSTER_MEMBER	string	TRUE or FALSE; TRUE indicates the given node is a member of the local cluster.
CLUSTER_NODES	integer	Returns the number of nodes in the cluster.
CLUSTER_QUORUM	integer	Returns the quorum for the cluster.
CLUSTER_VOTES	integer	Returns the aggregate number of votes in cluster.
CONTIG_GBLPAGES	integer	Returns the total count of available contiguous global pages.
FREE_GBLPAGES	integer	Returns the total count of available global pages.
FREE_GBLSECTS	integer	Returns the total count of available global sections.
HW_MODEL	integer	Returns the VAX model number of the system.
HW_NAME	string	Returns the VAX model name of the system.
NODENAME	string	Returns the system nodename.
NODE_AREA	integer	Returns the DECnet area number of the system.
NODE_CSID	string	Returns a hex number giving the CSID of the system.
NODE_HWTYPE	string	Returns the hardware type of the system.
NODE_HWVERS	string	Returns the hardware version of the system.
NODE_NUMBER	integer	Returns the DECnet number of the system.
NODE_QUORUM	integer	Returns the quorum count of the system.

NODE_SWINCARN	integer	Returns the software incarnation number of the system.
NODE_SWTYPE	string	Gives the type of VMS software running on the specified system.
NODE_SWVERS	string	Gives the VMS version running on the specified system.
NODE_SYSTEMID	string	Returns the hex SID of the specified system.
NODE_VOTES	integer	Gives the number of votes that the specified node is entitled to.
SCS_EXISTS	string	TRUE or FALSE; TRUE indicates that SCS is currently loaded on the specified system.

F$LOGICAL(logical name)

F$LOGICAL returns the equivalence name for a specified logical name by translating the logical name. This routine is obsolescent; use F$TRNLNM instead.

F$MODE()

F$MODE returns INTERACTIVE, BATCH, NETWORK, or OTHER, depending on the current process mode. Parentheses are required (as for all lexical functions) even though there are no arguments.

F$MODE()

F$TIME returns an absolute time string giving the current system time in the following format:
dd-mmmm-yyyy hh:mm:ss.cc

F$TRNLNM(log_name[,lnm_table][,index][,mode][,case][,item_key])

F$TRNLNM returns the equivalence name associated with the input logical name. This can also return requested attributes of the logical name. The translation step is only done once; if the equivalence string is itself a logical name, you must make additional F$TRNLNM calls to translate it. F$TRNLNM searches the process, job, group, and system name tables in that order.

The *log_name* argument is a character expression that specifies the logical name to be translated. The table argument must either specify a logical name table or itself be a logical name that translates to a list of logical name tables. The default table name is LNM$DCL_LOGICAL.

Index is an integer specifying which equivalence name should be returned if there is more than one translation for log_name. Index defaults to 0.

Mode must give a string specifying the access mode: USER, SUPERVISOR, EXECUTIVE, or KERNEL.

Case is either CASE_BLIND or CASE_SENSITIVE. This controls how the translation is performed.

Item is a standard lexical function keyword identifying which piece of information should be returned. The list follows.

ACCESS_MODE	string	Returns one of the access modes listed above under the mode argument.
CONCEALED	string	TRUE or FALSE; TRUE indicates the logical name has the CONCEALED attribute.
CONFINE	string	TRUE or FALSE; TRUE indicates the logical name is confined and is not propagated automatically to subprocesses.
CRELOG	string	TRUE or FALSE; TRUE indicates the name was created with $CRELOG. FALSE indicates it was made with $CRELNM.
LENGTH	integer	Returns the length of the equivalence name.
MAX_INDEX	integer	Returns the largest index for the given logical name. Zero indicates there is one translation.
NO_ALIAS	string	TRUE or FALSE; TRUE indicates the logical name possesses the NO_ALIAS attribute.
TABLE	string	TRUE or FALSE; TRUE indicates the specified logical name is itself the name of a logical name table.
TABLE_NAME	string	Returns the name of the table in which the specified logical name was found.
TERMINAL	string	TRUE or FALSE; TRUE indicates the name has the TERMINAL attribute.

VALUE	string	Returns the equivalence name for the specified logical name and index. This is the default if the item argument is omitted.

F$USER()

F$USER returns the UIC of the current process as a string. The UIC is in alphanumeric format.

PROCESS CONTROL

F$PID(context_sym)

F$PID produces the PID of the current process (additional processes if you have WORLD or GROUP privileges) as a string. The first call to F$PID always returns the PID of the first process for which it has enough privilege to access. With privileges enabled, successive calls to F$PID give the PIDs of subsequent processes in the system's table, until the list is finally exhausted and F$PID returns the null string (""). Without either WORLD or GROUP, F$PID will return only your own PID.

The argument *context_sym* is the name of a symbol that DCL uses to store the pointer into the system process table last accessed. Upon the first F$PID call, this symbol must either have the null string value or be undefined. You can use different context_sym symbols to maintain parallel streams of F$PID calls.

F$PRIVILEGE(privilege_list)

F$PRIVILEGE returns a string TRUE or FALSE according to whether your process has all of the privileges specified in privilege_list. If you lack any of the privileges in privilege_list, F$PRIVILEGE returns FALSE. The argument privilege_list is a character expression that must evaluate to a comma-separated list of privileges. The list may not contain [NO]ALL. For example, in

```
$ HAVE_IT = F$PRIVILEGE("GROUP, WORLD")
$ SHOW SYMBOL HAVE_IT
  HAVE_IT = "FALSE"
```

you find that your process does not have both GROUP and WORLD currently enabled.

F$PROCESS()

F$PROCESS returns the current process name in the form of a string. Parentheses are required even though there aren't any arguments.

F$SETPRV(privilege_list)

Using the $SETPRV service, F$SETPRV attempts to set the privileges specified in privilege_list . The argument privilege_list is a character expression that must evaluate to a comma-separated list of privileges. F$SETPRV returns a string containing the states of the requested privileges before the F$SETPRV call. An example follows:

```
$ CURSTATE = F$SETPRV("ALTPRI,TMPMBX,NOGROUP")
$ SHOW SYM CURSTATE
  CURSTATE = "NOALTPRI,TMPMBX,GROUP"
```

The result in CURSTATE indicates that before the F$SETPRV, you had TMPMBX and GROUP enabled but not ALTPRI. To determine if the F$SETPRV operation succeeds, you must call F$PRIVILEGE with the same string as was used in the F$SETPRV call.

FILE AND DIRECTORY INFORMATION

F$DIRECTORY()

F$DIRECTORY returns the current directory name (not including the device) as a string. Parentheses are required even though there are no arguments.

F$FILE_ATTRIBUTES(file_spec, item_name)

F$FILE_ATTRIBUTES returns information about the RMS attributes of a given file. The file_spec argument is a character expression that must not include wildcards. The item argument can be any one of the keywords listed below:

ALQ	integer	Returns the allocation quantity.
BDT	string	Returns the date and time of the last backup.
BKS	integer	Returns the bucket size.
BLS	integer	Returns the block size.
CBT	string	TRUE or FALSE; TRUE indicates Contiguous Best Try method of allocation.

CDT	string	Returns date and time of file creation.
CTG	string	TRUE or FALSE; TRUE indicates file is contiguous.
DEQ	integer	Returns the default extension quantity.
DID	string	Returns the directory identification string.
DVI	string	Returns the device name on which the file is located.
EDT	string	Returns the file expiration date and time.
EOF	integer	Returns the total number of blocks used in the file.
FID	string	Returns the file identification string.
FSZ	integer	Returns the Fixed Control Area size.
GRP	integer	Returns the group field of the owner's UIC.
KNOWN	string	TRUE or FALSE; TRUE indicates file was INSTALLed.
MBM	integer	Returns the member field of the owner's UIC.
MRN	integer	Returns the Maximum Record Number of the file.
MRS	integer	Returns the Maximum Record Size of a file (especially useful for variable-length record files).
NOA	integer	Returns Number Of Areas.
NOK	integer	Returns Number Of (RMS) Keys associated with the file.
ORG	string	Returns file organization; either SEQ, REL, or IDX.
PRO	string	Returns file protection code string in SOGW/RWED format.
PVN	integer	Returns the prolog version number.
RAT	string	Returns record attributes; either CR, PRN, FTN, or a null string.

RCK	string	TRUE or FALSE; TRUE indicates read checking enabled.
RDT	string	Returns date and time of last revision to file.
RFM	string	Returns the Record Format string; either VAR, FIX, VFC, UDF, STM, STMLF, or STMCR.
RVN	integer	Returns the revision number of a file.
UIC	string	Returns the owner's UIC.
WCK	string	TRUE or FALSE; TRUE indicates write checking is enabled.

VARIABLE TYPE CONVERSIONS

F$CVSI(startbit, nbits, string)

F$CVSI converts bits extracted from a string to a signed integer. Returns an integer value. The arguments startbit and nbits are integers; the input string is a character expression. An example follows:

```
$ BITS[0,32] = "    "              ! 4 blanks
$ NIBBLE = F$CVSI(0,8,BITS)
$ SHOW SYM NIBBLE
  NIBBLE = 32
```

F$CVUI(startbit, bits, string)

F$CVUI converts bits extracted from a string to an unsigned integer. Returns an integer. Works exactly like F$CVSI except for producing an unsigned result.

F$IDENTIFIER(rights_identifier, conversion_kind)

F$IDENTIFIER returns either the integer or the alphanumeric form of a rights identifier, converted from the opposite form. Rights_identifier is a character expression evaluating to the name of a system rights identifier. Conversion_kind is a keyword string, either NAME_TO_NUMBER or NUMBER_TO_NAME. Note that identifiers are case-sensitive.

F$INTEGER(expression)

F$INTEGER evaluates the expression argument, converts it to an integer, and returns the result. If a string expression is given that does not convert successfully to an integer, F$INTEGER returns the value 1 if the first character of the string is T, t, Y, or Y (from TRUE and YES); it returns 0 otherwise.

F$TYPE(symbol)

F$TYPE returns a string describing the type of a symbol. The result is INTEGER if the symbol is an integer-valued symbol or a character symbol that can successfully be converted to an integer. Here is an example:

```
$ NSYM = "357"+"8"
$ CSYM = "XYZZY"
$ TYPE1 = F$TYPE(NSYM)
$ TYPE2 = F$TYPE(CSYM)
$ TYPE3 = F$TYPE(JUNK)
$ SHOW SYM TYPE1
  TYPE1 = "INTEGER"
$ SHOW SYM TYPE2
  TYPE2 = "STRING"
$ SHOW SYM TYPE3  ! undefined
  TYPE3 = ""
```

MISCELLANEOUS

F$FAO(control[,arg1][,arg2...arg15])

F$FAO returns a formatted output string written according to the control string. F$FAO is similar to a FORTRAN formatted write operation.

F$MESSAGE(system_status)

F$MESSAGE returns a string giving the full VMS error message corresponding to a given integer system_status. Use F$MESSAGE to convert status codes from system and library services to English messages.

F$VERIFY([proc_val][,image_val])

F$VERIFY produces an integer result showing whether SET VERIFY is active or not for the current command procedure. A return value of 1 means VERIFY is on; 0 means it's off. The procedure value and image value arguments let you specify that procedure and/or image verification should be turned on or off at the same time. Note that F$VERIFY lets you set both procedure and image verification but only returns the procedure verify state.   To obtain the image verification state, you must use F$ENVIRONMENT("VERIFY_IMAGE").

SUMMARY

```
F$CVSI (start-bit,number-of-bits,string)
F$CVTIME ([input_time][,output_time_format][,output_field]
F$CVUI (start-bit,number-of-bits,string)
F$DIRECTORY ()
F$EDIT (string,edit-list)
F$ELEMENT (element-number,delimeter,string)
F$ENVIRONMENT (item)
F$EXTRACT (start,length,string)
F$FAO (control-string [,arg1,arg2...,arg15])
F$FILE_ATTRIBUTES (filespec,item)
F$GETDVI (device-name,item)
F$GETJPI (pid,item)
F$GETQUI (function,[item],[object-id],[flags])
F$IDENTIFIER (identifier,conversion-type)
F$INTEGER (expression)
F$LENGTH (string)
F$LOCATE (substring,string)
F$LOGICAL (logical-name)
F$MESSAGE (status-code)
F$MODE ()
F$PARSE (filespec[,default-spec][,related-spec][,field][,parse-
type])
F$PID (context-symbol)
F$PRIVILEGE (priv-states)
F$PROCESS ()
F$SEARCH (filespec[,stream-id])
F$SETPRV (priv-states)
F$STRING (expression)
F$TIME ()
F$TRNLNM (logical-name[,table][,index][,mode][,case][,item])
F$TYPE (symbol-name)
F$USER ()
F$VERIFY ([procedure-value][,image-value])
```

Appendix D
ASCII Character Set

The American Standard Code for Information Interchange (ASCII) character set is nearly a universal standard for computer interaction with serial devices such as terminals. The ASCII code spans 128 integers, starting with 0 (the NULL). The DEC Multinational Character Set is a superset of the ASCII set that uses the code values above 127 (i.e., those with the highest bit on) to represent some characters with foreign diacritical marks.

The ASCII character set is presented in a chart form. Figure D-1 is a legend for the ASCII chart. Figure D-2 is the complete ASCII character set. In the figure, the two leftmost columns contain the control characters. Also note that upper and lowercase versions of the same character are separated by 32 (hexadecimal 20).

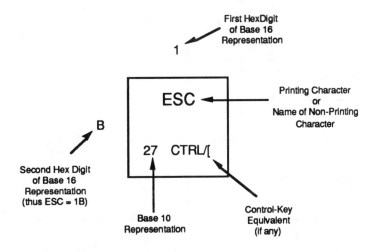

FIGURE D-2.   ASCII Chart Legend.

First Hex Digit

	0	1	2	3	4	5	6	7
0	NULL 0 CTRL/@	DC1 16 CTRL/P	SPACE 32	0 48	@ 64	P 80	` 96	p 112
1	SOH 1 CTRL/A	XON 17 CTRL/Q	! 33	1 49	A 65	Q 81	a 97	q 113
2	STX 2 CTRL/B	DC2 18 CTRL/R	" 34	2 50	B 66	R 82	b 98	r 114
3	ETX 3 CTRL/C	XOFF 19 CTRL/S	# 35	3 51	C 67	S 83	c 99	s 115
4	EOT 4 CTRL/D	DC4 20 CTRL/T	$ 36	4 52	D 68	T 84	d 100	t 116
5	ENQ 5 CTRL/E	NAK 21 CTRL/U	% 37	5 53	E 69	U 85	e 101	u 117
6	ACK 6 CTRL/F	SYN 22 CTRL/V	& 38	6 54	F 70	V 86	f 102	v 118
7	BEL 7 CTRL/G	ETB 23 CTRL/W	' 39	7 55	G 71	W 87	g 103	w 119
8	BS 8 CTRL/H	CAN 24 CTRL/X	(40	8 56	H 72	X 88	h 104	x 120
9	TAB 9 CTRL/I	EM 25 CTRL/Y	) 41	9 57	I 73	Y 89	i 105	y 121
A	LF 10 CTRL/J	SUB 26 CTRL/Z	* 42	: 58	J 74	Z 90	j 106	z 122
B	VT 11 CTRL/K	ESC 27 CTRL/[	+ 43	; 59	K 75	[91	k 107	{ 123
C	FF 12 CTRL/L	FS 28 CTRL/\	, 44 comma	< 60	L 76	\ 92	l 108	| 124
D	CR 13 CTRL/M	GS 29 CTRL/]	- 45	= 61	M 77	] 93	m 109	} 125
E	SO 14 CTRL/N	RS 30 CTRL/^	. 46 period	> 62	N 78	^ 94	n 110	~ 126
F	SI 15 CTRL/O	US 30 CTRL/	/ 47	? 63	O 79	95	o 111	DEL 127

Second Hex Digit

FIGURE D-1.   ASCII Chart.

Index